# *Fanny Seward*

TRUDY KRISHER

# *Fanny Seward*

A LIFE

*Syracuse University Press*

First Edition 2015

15 16 17 18 19 20 6 5 4 3 2

∞ The paper used in this publication meets the minimum requirements of the American National Standard for Information Sciences—Permanence of Paper for Printed Library Materials, ANSI Z39.48-1992.

For a listing of books published and distributed by Syracuse University Press, visit www.SyracuseUniversityPress.syr.edu.

ISBN: 978-0-8156-1041-0 (cloth) 978-0-8156-5295-3 (e-book)

**Library of Congress Cataloging-in-Publication Data**

Krisher, Trudy.

Fanny Seward : a life / Trudy Krisher. — 1st ed.

pages cm

Includes bibliographical references and index.

ISBN 978-0-8156-1041-0 (cloth : alk. paper) — ISBN 978-0-8156-5295-3 (e-book)

1. Seward, Frances Adeline, 1844–1866. 2. Seward, William Henry, 1801–1872. 3. Seward family. 4. United States—History—Civil War, 1861–1865—Women—Biography. 5. Young women—Washington (D.C.)—Biography. 6. Washington (D.C.)—History—Civil War, 1861–1865—Biography. I. Title.

CT275.S43458K75 2014

975.3'02092—dc23

[B] 2014040701

*Manufactured in the United States of America*

*To the irrepressible Jennifer Haines*

"One can read a poem or a novel without coming to know its author, look at a painting and fail to get a sense of its painter, but one cannot read a diary and feel unacquainted with its writer."

—Thomas Mallon, *A Book of One's Own: People and Their Diaries*

# Contents

# Illustrations

# Fanny Seward

# I

# In the Shadow of Death

It was a day of celebration that would turn into a night of horrors. Its events would shake a nation already shaken by four years of Civil War. Its aftermath would launch months of political retribution, decades of sectional bitterness, and a century of setbacks on the road to racial equality.

It was April 14, 1865.

The elements of this tumultuous night are well known: It featured a beloved president and a famous actor. It involved a drama in a theatre. It led to death in a humble boardinghouse and shock in every corner of the land. It plunged a nation into mourning, its citizens choked on grief as black as the smoke from the funeral train that chugged its way across the American landscape.

But what is not so well known is the parallel drama that occurred on that same night. It took place at the very moment that the famous actor was lifting a pistol to the beloved president's head. Its action unfolded across town from Ford's Theatre in an elegant house on Lafayette Square. On April 14, 1865, the curtain rose on the second act of a less familiar but equally riveting drama.

That parallel tragedy featured a powerful cabinet member, his horrified family and servants, a cleverly forced entrance, a double-bladed knife, and blood. Rivers and rivers of blood.

Although this second act is not as well known as the first, much of what is known about the scene that opened on Lafayette Square is because of an unlikely eyewitness, a shy and largely unknown young woman barely out of her teens. Fortunately for history, this young woman, an aspiring writer, had the habit of keeping a diary.

Her name was Fanny Seward, and she was the twenty-year-old daughter of President Abraham Lincoln's secretary of state. Like the scores of unknowns who perished at Gettysburg, she has been little noted, nor long remembered, her brief life a candle snuffed out all too soon. But Fanny Seward had quite a tale to tell.

This is her story.

On the evening of April 14, 1865, Fanny Seward was sitting by her father's bedside. She was reading to him. Father and daughter were in the third-floor bedroom of their house on Lafayette Square, a house just across the way from the White House.

Fanny loved reading, but she loved her father even more. In fact, there was no one she loved more than William Henry Seward. She had been devoted to him all her young life. Undoubtedly, Fanny's bedridden father was soothed by the sound of his daughter's voice. Everyone in the family knew one thing: this young woman was her father's favorite child.

The bond between father and daughter was evident from the beginning. When Frances Adeline Seward was born in Auburn, New York, on December 9, 1844, she assumed a singular place in her family: she became the fourth and last child and the only girl. Sadly, the family's only other daughter had died of smallpox in infancy.[1] Moreover, the significance of Fanny's birth was heightened by the death of Fanny's grandmother, Mary Jennings Seward, only days after Fanny's arrival. Obviously, there was nothing like a birth, especially the birth of a daughter, to ease the grief of those two female deaths. Providentially, providing solace would become a lifelong role for this new baby girl.

Fanny's father was especially captivated by his delightful little daughter whose eyes were as full of laughter as those of his beloved mother, a mother who was more kindly and open-hearted than his stubborn and dogmatic father had been. In Fanny, William Henry Seward saw the rekindled spirit of his mother "blazing anew in the soft, sweet face."[2]

1. The affection between Fanny and her father was evident from an early age. Collections of the Seward House Museum, Auburn, NY.

As Fanny grew from infancy to girlhood, those early feelings intensified. In fact, father engaged daughter in a lifelong correspondence that began as soon as Fanny had learned to write. Fanny's father sometimes tucked tender remembrances into letters, sending her a tiger lily from the river banks at Mount Vernon[3] or a pink rose that required doing battle with a huge bumblebee in order for father to send daughter a loving memento.[4]

As Fanny matured, the affection between them continued to flourish. On her thirteenth birthday, Seward sent Fanny a remarkable letter that was a deeply loving testament to his devotion: " . . . [Y]ou have realized," he declared, "all that a loving father could ask, from a youngest child, and only daughter." He signed it by bestowing "[m]y blessing on you, my beloved one, now and forever."[5]

On the evening of April 14, 1865, that favored daughter, like all of the Seward family members, had been taking her turn at her ailing father's beside. Outside the window of the quiet bedroom, however, the streets below had borne noisy witness to celebrations unique in the pages of American history.

The celebrations, which had been in progress for over a week, had begun when a sixteen-year-old boy operating the telegraph wire in the War Department received the news that Union troops were marching into Richmond. In his excitement, the boy knocked over an inkwell, but soon Edwin M. Stanton, the secretary of war himself, was hoisting young W. E. Kettles to the window and shouting, "My friends, here is the young man who received the telegram which tells us of the fall of Richmond!"[6]

By April 9, less than a week later, General Robert E. Lee had surrendered the Confederate army at Appomattox Court House. In Washington, the news was greeted by a 500-gun salute, a salute so loud that it shattered windows.[7]

Despite their concern for the bedridden head of their family, Fanny Seward and her family members shared in the jubilation. On the evening of April 13, there had been a grand illumination of the city. Hundreds of candles lit the windows of the post office; thousands of them glowed at the windows of the Patent Office. Euphoric crowds, their spirits similarly aglow, cheered alongside the soaring rockets and waving banners and shimmering torches. From the upstairs window of her father's sickroom, Fanny watched the marvelous fireworks in Lafayette Square that were like bursting shells on the battlefield. Now, blessedly, the beautiful signal lights in red and yellow and green were a joyous reminder that the battlefield clashes of the Civil War were over.[8]

By all accounts, even the melancholy President Lincoln considered the next morning, Friday, April 14, 1865, to be one of the happiest days of his life. In fact, on a carriage ride in the afternoon, President Lincoln had startled his wife with his cheerfulness.[9] But the reasons for his happiness were not surprising, for his joy simply matched that of his nation. Finally, the exhausted president realized, the long and bloody turmoil of civil war was over.

Likewise, Fanny Seward shared President Lincoln's happiness. Because her father had served at Lincoln's right hand as his secretary of state, Fanny and her family had experienced the tumultuous events of the last four years with particular intensity. As the drama of the Civil War unfolded, they watched from front row seats as the nation passed through the inauguration of President Lincoln, the firing on Fort Sumter, the humiliation at Bull Run, the bloodshed at Antietam, the anguish over emancipation, and the agitation of copperheads fighting to end the war immediately, prematurely, and at any price. With relief, the Seward family, like the nation, watched the final curtain fall.

But on the night of April 14, 1865, Fanny had her own private reason to be happy: her father was finally improving.

Only nine days earlier, on April 5, on the heels of the fall of Richmond, the vigorous and healthy secretary of state had suffered a terrible carriage accident. Four of them had been in the carriage: Fanny, her friend Mary Titus, her brother Fred, and her father. As they drove out Vermont Avenue, the carriage door refused to stay shut. When the coachman halted to fix the problem, the horses bolted, hurtling toward home. Leaping from the carriage, Fanny's brother Fred fell as he tried to arrest the team. When Seward himself attempted to jump from the carriage to rein in the horses, Fanny, in the back seat, protested. But once the secretary of state sprang from the carriage, his daughter, whirling down the avenue at the mercy of the careening steeds, could not tell whether her father had made it safely to the ground.[10]

When the horses were finally stopped, Fanny learned the worst: Seward, catching his heel on the way out of the carriage, had tumbled headlong to the ground. Fanny's sixty-four-year-old father was unconscious, and he had sustained serious injuries: a concussion, a dislocated shoulder, a broken arm, and a fractured jaw.[11] Entering the sickroom, Fanny was shocked by what she saw: her father's eyes were swollen shut, his face was disfigured by bruises, and his nose gushed suffocating amounts of blood.[12]

It must have been shocking, too, to see him flat on his back, for Fanny's father had always been an energetic dynamo. Restless, rarely still, Seward was always animated with irrepressible vigor, a kettle steaming with energy and ideas. Fanny's injured father had pursued a political career remarkable for its longevity as well as its accomplishments: He had made sweeping changes to the prison system in New York; fought to end slavery in the new territories; helped midwife the birth of the new Republican Party; resisted the severing of the Union until resistance proved impossible; prevented foreign countries from taking up the Southern cause; urged the declaration of the Emancipation Proclamation; and, in a final triumph yet in the future, persuaded a reluctant Congress to purchase Alaska.[13] Fanny's father lived by the adage "rest [is] rust."[14]

Even though it seemed impossible to imagine this vital man immobilized by such severe injuries, the presence of his daughter Fanny by his side was entirely predictable. Fanny's watchful vigils between April 5 and April 14 were entirely in keeping with her character: after all, from birth her destiny was to provide solace. Seated by her father's bedside on April 14, Fanny was overjoyed to see that the indefatigable secretary of state had been improving for the last several days: he had regained consciousness, and the swelling had gone down in his face. The doctors had stabilized his fractured jaw by wiring one tooth to another.[15] On the fourteenth, Fanny was heartened by her father's progress: he was sitting up in bed for short periods and he was breakfasting on solid food for the first time since the calamity.[16]

In fact, just five days earlier, Fanny had also been heartened by a special bedside visitor who had dropped by to cheer the secretary of state. He was President Abraham Lincoln, returning from his joyous victory visit to Richmond, Virginia, the heart of the now-defeated Confederacy. Fanny's diary for April 9, 1865, made note of the way Lincoln had stretched his angular frame across the foot of her father's bed and launched into his favorite pastime: storytelling.

These were stories worth sharing, for as Lincoln made the two-mile walk to Richmond's Capitol Square, he was swamped by crowds of African Americans. Finally free, they had swarmed from shanties and shacks, stumbling over the rubble of the war-ravaged capital to shout their hallelujahs to their beloved Father Abraham.[17]

Fanny listened intently as Lincoln described his visit to a hospital in Richmond: "One of his last [?] acts was going through a hospital of seven thousand men, & shaking hands with each one. He spoke of having worked as hard at it as sawing wood—& seemed in his goodness of heart, much satisfied at the labor." Later, after the terrible night of April 14 was over, Fanny reflected forlornly on that recent memory of Lincoln sprawled across her father's bed: it was the last she would ever see of her nation's president or her family's friend.[18]

But on the night of April 14, both Fanny Seward, reading a book, and Abraham Lincoln, watching a play, had every reason to be hopeful. After all, only six weeks earlier, Lincoln had been preparing his second inaugural address. It was to be a message of hope to a people who had gone through four years of despair. His plea for forgiveness and reconciliation to the South was to be delivered against the impressive and symbolic backdrop of a newly completed Capitol dome topped by a bronze statue of Freedom.

Unfortunately, the hours before the president's second inauguration seemed anything but hopeful. In spite of the waving handkerchiefs and the flying flags, in the face of crowded stoops and jostling reporters, the disappointing weather offered only a steady drip of ominous rain, draping the atmosphere in a bleak foreboding. It was an atmosphere that symbolized the accumulated suffering of four years of death, destruction, and despair. Nevertheless, when Lincoln began to speak, the sun suddenly burst through the clouds: it seemed nature's attempt to signal that hope might return to a despairing nation. The gathered hearts, exhausted by war, seized upon this sunny omen[19] as a fitting backdrop for Lincoln's message. Received in hushed silence,[20] Abraham Lincoln offered reasons to be hopeful, for the words of his second inaugural address presented to a defeated South the twin olive branches of "malice toward none" and "charity for all."

On the very morning of the inaugural, however, despite the blustery weather, photographers had been intent on setting up cameras. Photographer William Morris Smith, for example, had set his up a block away from the Capitol, imagining the perfect shot capturing an historical moment: the first presidential inauguration with the impressive new Capitol dome as background. Closer in was Alexander Gardner,[21] who worked with the famous Mathew Brady to capture riveting pictures of life and death on Civil War battlefields. Ironically, Gardner, in only a few months' time, would be training his lens on another historical event that rivaled the inauguration of a president: the hanging of four Lincoln conspirators joined in an assassination plot against him. In March, however, a chilling image was captured, one which, in hindsight, telegraphed a message of grim foreboding. Above the viewing stands near a balcony railing stood a handsome young man with a clear view of the president. That man, sporting a moustache and top hat, was John Wilkes Booth,[22] the man who, in little over a month, would forever link the families of Abraham Lincoln and Fanny Seward.

Now, on the morning of April 14, only six weeks after Lincoln's Second Inaugural, another eerie foreboding foretold disaster. A cabinet meeting had taken place at the White House. Fanny's brother Frederick had been there. Fred had served his father as assistant secretary of state throughout the war, and, with his father recovering from his carriage accident, it was only natural for him to have taken his father's place at this morning meeting. As a result, Fred heard firsthand President Lincoln's account of the strange recurring dream he had experienced only the night before. The dream had evoked a floating sensation, as if the president were drifting on an elusive expanse toward an unfamiliar shore. Frederick was aware that Lincoln's dreams were often premonitions that portended events or disasters to follow.[23]

Later, after the disaster had struck, the chilling observation from a keen eyewitness of the previous month's inaugural address proved prescient: Lincoln, "illumined by the deceptive brilliance of a March sunburst, was already standing in the shadow of death."[24]

So, too, was Fanny's father.

On the evening of April 14, Fanny was reading to her bedridden father from the *Legends of Charlemagne*.[25] As a subject for her ailing father, Charlemagne was a fitting choice. The eighth-century leader had undertaken war in order to bring peace and unity to a diverse people torn by unending conflict. Likewise, Abraham Lincoln, aided by Fanny's father, had served as a similar leader eleven centuries later.

Now, looking over at her father, Fanny noticed that he was falling asleep. She turned down the gas and then laid her book on a stand at the foot of his bed.[26] Perhaps she performed a loving bedside ritual, settling the blanket around him or kissing the top of his head. Perhaps she went to the window to adjust the curtains before she turned down the light.

In the park across the street, however, two men lurked. Associates of John Wilkes Booth, they had been carefully watching Fanny's house. They had seen one of the family doctors leave around ten p.m., having finished the nightly assessment of Secretary Seward's health.[27] They had seen the lights go down in the third floor window. Perhaps they had seen Fanny Seward's shadow as she moved to adjust the curtains at the window or turn down the light.

Now one of the men, the tall and imposing one, walked with purpose across the street. He stood outside the Seward mansion, his fingers poised to ring the bell.[28] At that same moment, in the theatre across town, the fingers of John Wilkes Booth, gripping a derringer, were similarly poised.

Earlier that morning, unaware of the tragedy that would unfold before her eyes, Fanny had penciled a curious note in her pocket diary. She had wondered whether that day would bring her "anything unusual" to record.[29]

2

# From Innocence to Experience

On a dawning Christmas Day in 1858, fourteen-year-old Fanny Seward picked up a pen.[1]

Her family was living in a rented house on F Street in Washington, DC, where her father was serving as United States senator.[2] It is likely she began this, her earliest surviving diary entry, from a tiny second-floor room at the end of a hall that her mother described as "hardly bigger than a closet."[3] This first diary entry showed an innocent young girl aglow with the excitement of Christmas morning.

> I woke very early and 'rose with the sun,' after lying awake for some time, on coming into my little room I saw on a chair beside the chimney piece . . . a large white box with a beautiful picture on the top, on opening it I found a most beautiful little Theatre, of paper . . . and was delighted with it.[4]

The diary entries that continued until 1866, the year of Fanny's death, offered a portrait of a young woman rapidly leaving that early innocence behind, witnessing events that not only challenged but transformed her country, her generation, her family, and herself.

Fanny's diaries would reveal how life was lived as the nation anticipated, then erupted into, Civil War. They would record the seminal events of the Civil War: the firing on Fort Sumter, the transformation of Washington from a fledgling capital into an armed camp, the effects of the Emancipation Proclamation, the slow turning of the tide after Gettysburg and Vicksburg that signaled a final Northern victory, and an assassination that would shatter a peace so tragically and recently won.

Fanny's diaries would capture the experience of a generation of young people struggling to mature amidst the cauldron of war. They would show young men enlisting in the war, their female counterparts waving tearful good-byes at railroad depots, supporting their efforts by stitching trousers and collecting lint for bandages. They would depict wrenching accounts of battlefield slaughter and the homecomings of the injured, the maimed, and the dead. They would also chronicle a youthful generation strengthened by war: young men who tested their courage and leadership; young women who managed farms or nursed soldiers or headed philanthropic organizations, gradually turning those new skills into post-war steps toward independence for themselves.

Fanny's diaries would portray the unique experiences of her own family during the drama of the Civil War. The family separations that resulted from William Seward's political career now included the likelihood of danger. Three of the men in Fanny's family—her father and brothers Augustus and Frederick—served the nation in Washington, DC, at the pulsing heart of the Northern war effort. Later, Will, Junior, the youngest Seward son, would enlist, serve, and fight for the Union. As a result, Fanny's diaries roiled with anxieties. There had been pre-inaugural assassination threats in Baltimore; would Abraham Lincoln and the cabinet that included the family's husband and father be safely inaugurated? When the war began, Washington, DC, was utterly defenseless, surrounded by seceded Virginia and Southern-sympathizing Maryland; how could the safety of Gus, Fred, and Secretary Seward be assured? The early battles of the war had been shocking defeats for the North; what could be done by Fanny, alone with her mother in Auburn, to support a father whose political enemies not only thwarted him at every turn but attempted to lay all Union defeats at his weary feet?

Above all, the diaries of Fanny Seward provide a record of her life as the daughter of one of the nation's most powerful and progressive Republican leaders. "I love," she confessed, "to remember all Father says and does."[5] In her diaries, those memories are set down for posterity.

The chronology of events presented in Fanny's diaries offered a calendar of her life as she moved from childish innocence to maturing experience.

In 1858, the year she began her diaries, politics surely loomed large at the Christmas table. In the fall, there had been those passionate Lincoln-Douglas debates on the issue of slavery. There had been Fanny's father's own speech in October at Rochester, New York, a speech both praised and condemned; in it, William Seward had declared that the divisions between North and South represented an "irrepressible conflict."[6]

In 1859, Fanny suffered when a family dog was poisoned because of her family's anti-slavery beliefs, and a lonely Fanny saw her father off, as the most likely future candidate for president of the United States, across the ocean to meet European leaders.

In 1860, Fanny witnessed her father's reaction to his loss of the presidential nomination to Lincoln and soon thereafter accompanied a rebounding Seward on a month-long campaign tour on his rival's behalf.

In 1861, Fanny was captivated by brother Will's eyewitness account of Lincoln's safe inauguration, and in the fall, following tragedies in Baltimore and at Bull Run, Fanny visited Washington, where she met Lincoln and his wife Mary, and other national leaders.

In 1862, a dismal year began with a winter health crisis for Fanny, which forced her to withdraw from the Philadelphia boarding school she was attending. In the spring, she waved good-bye to Auburn boys, now soldiers, embarked on a dangerous naval campaign with the ironclad *Merrimac* patrolling the waters. The fall became the most intense and challenging period of the war for her as she sent beloved brother Will off to war, attended the Auburn funeral of a young man slain on the eve of the battle of Antietam, and learned that her father's political enemies demanded his ouster from Lincoln's cabinet.

In 1863, Fanny made her January debut on the same day that her brother and father witnessed Lincoln's signing of the Emancipation Proclamation; she visited General Joseph Hooker's camp on the eve of what became the Battle of Chancellorsville; she celebrated the turning of the tide of war represented by twin victories at Gettysburg and Vicksburg; alone in Auburn, Fanny and her mother defended their home from potential draft rioters who threatened their safety; Fanny also toured the new Ford's Theatre, traversing the same ground that John Wilkes Booth would traverse on assassination night.

In 1864, Edwin Booth, the assassin's older brother, dined in the Seward home, and Fanny recorded her impressions of the man whose brother would soon target her family in his conspiracy. During these waning years of the Civil War, Fanny was seriously pursuing the disciplined and demanding work of play and novel writing.

In 1865, as the war was winding down, Fanny accompanied her father to General Grant's headquarters at City Point. Then, with victory at hand, her father suffered the tragic carriage accident, and only days later, Booth's assassins targeted the Seward home; on April 14, 1865, their plot changed Fanny's life forever. Soon thereafter, poor health, compromised by the shock of events, led to the death of Fanny's mother Frances, on the eve of the hanging of the four Lincoln conspirators.

In 1866, Fanny struggled with religious questions, hoping to achieve acceptance for the wrenching experiences of her young life and her own now-failing health. Sadly, Fanny died in October, her life a brief candle snuffed out all too soon, her grief-stricken family left to mourn another family death.

But when Fanny first took up her diary, the war had not yet begun, and the earliest entries in Fanny's diaries provided an innocent portrait of this still-peaceful time. They described the way a young girl like Fanny came of age in mid-nineteenth-century America, making molasses candy, taking dancing lessons, minding her manners, mourning lost pets, and swapping photographs available through the new art of photography[7] the way modern youth swap Facebook entries.

Above all, they offered a portrait of a still-childlike young girl.

One quality that defined Fanny's personality from a very early age was her chronic shyness. To her diary Fanny often confessed her reticence, referring on more than one occasion to herself as "bashful me."[8] Overwhelmed by the company at a dinner party, for instance, shy Fanny often sought a back room or was relieved when she had somehow "escaped" the crowd.[9]

Coupled with this shyness was an excruciating sensitivity. Fanny Seward was a tenderhearted girl. She could not bear to punish her dog Bell, even after he had chewed off a corner of her favorite Christmas present. She thought bullfights were cruel and barbaric. She couldn't understand the Southern custom of firing pistols to celebrate Christmas; after all, she wondered, wasn't Christmas supposed to be a day of peace? When her painting teacher asked her to practice on the subject of a little boy fishing, she painted over the fishing rod and put flowers in the boy's hands. Surely a fisherman understood what happened to his fish. It was "wicked," Fanny shuddered to her diary, to fish for "amusement."[10] Early on, Fanny's mother remarked on her daughter's "tenderness of feeling," worrying that such sensitivity might one day "give her much pain."[11]

In addition, this sensitive and shy young girl was also awkward. At dancing school, she was grateful to have been reminded to remove her rubbers before taking to the dance floor and making a fool of herself. At the train station, a simple country girl pointed out that the more refined Fanny had let her collar slip. Naturally, this shy teenager was often embarrassed by her awkwardness. Falling frequently as she was learning to skate, she lamented her slipping feet which managed to slide either "too far behind or before me."[12]

Not surprisingly, such a shy and awkward girl was often self-conscious about her appearance. With candor, the young Fanny assessed herself in the pages of her diary. At age fourteen, she regretted, for instance, that she was the largest girl present in her dancing class.[13] Like any teenager watching the scales and rationalizing a weight gain, she noted in 1861 that she had gained six pounds to weigh 118, but it was possible that without her shawl the weight was only 115 and, after all, the dress she was wearing was of very heavy fabric.[14]

A photograph from this awkward period showed a stoop-shouldered young woman who was tall, thin, and plain. Her dark brown

2. The teenaged Fanny Seward was shy and reserved. Collections of the Seward House Museum, Auburn, NY.

hair was parted demurely down the middle of her forehead and combed simply behind each ear. Without ribbons or flounces or any unnecessary adornment, it was a hairstyle designed to avoid attention. Her skin, however, was clear and glowing, and her eyes and mouth suggested sensitivity and intelligence. Yet the overall impression was one of a well-behaved schoolgirl, shy and retiring.

Although by training and station Fanny had learned the importance of tact, she was at heart a strikingly honest and direct young girl, prizing honesty and directness in others. When her friend Fanny Bailey came to spend the day, Fanny Seward noticed that Miss Bailey's manners could have used some polishing, but an assessment from her diary confirmed that Fanny Seward preferred an honest spirit to a proper mien:

> At dinner . . . she talked . . . while father was speaking, which reminded me that I was not always attentive myself. [When she] passed—her plate for more of the dessert, when we had nearly finished, and just as all were ready to leave the table, asked for more nuts, afterwards [when all had gone] continuing to take more, till, with my help the dish was emptied. She is a robust, hearty, goodnatured person, always speaking exactly as she feels, she informed me with equal candor at lunch when offered cranberry that she 'could not bear it, at [sic] much preferred currant jelly— . . . —So, though you are quite likely to hear disagreeable things, yet when you are complimented you may know it is with sincerity.[15]

Fanny, like her father, also possessed a tolerant, forgiving nature. Although Fanny might criticize herself, she routinely refused to criticize others. Although not herself a Catholic, Fanny could appreciate a Roman Catholic church service, which was quite novel to her; other more judgmental worshippers in her company refused to enjoy the service merely because it was Catholic. Although a playmate had been very rude to her, she conceded that if better trained, this rude boy could be an "uncommonly nice child." Admitting that Lady Napier, wife of the British ambassador, possessed a few less-than-admirable personality traits, Fanny refused to "chronicle" her defects, even in the private pages of her diary.[16]

In addition to her honesty and her tolerance, this usually shy and sometimes awkward young woman was, like her father, characteristically merry and humorous, especially within her family circle. Her diaries and letters abound with examples. In a letter to her brother, the twelve-year-old Fanny chortled over the comic appearance of young robins, newly hatched, which look "very funny without any feathers."[17] With her friend Sarah How, she poked fun at affected speakers uttering "Cawn't" and "New Yauk."[18]

Fanny loved anecdotes, and she often recorded the jokes and witticisms of both the famous and the obscure. When her father first introduced Fanny's Aunt Lazette to President Lincoln in the Seward parlor, the discussion centered on the ultra-militant "on to Richmond" partisans. When Lazette objected to being classed among them, Lincoln parried with an appropriate anecdote from the War of 1812, which Fanny paraphrased in her diary. According to Fanny, Lincoln told the group this story:

> . . . [A]ll the young women were engaged in making keep-sakes for their lovers who were joining the army. They made belts, with mottoes wrought upon them. One young girl said to her lover—'Now what shall I put on this belt—'Liberty or Death'?' 'Well' was the reply—'I guess that's rather strong—suppose you make it 'Liberty or *be crippled*.'[19]

Fanny's diary also recorded amusing stories from incidents involving children. At a Seward dinner party, Fanny overheard an anecdote about Willie Lincoln, the president's young son. Apparently some "gentlemen of distinction" were being escorted to the White House and came across the young boy playing on the grounds. The gentlemen, bowing "ceremoniously," made their introductions to the president's boy, and Willie courteously returned their greetings by "pointing to the ground" and replying "Gentlemen, I am very happy to see you—pray be seated."[20] In another anecdote, Fanny was walking with her young friend Tommy, the grandson of a family friend. They came across Lord Napier, the handsome young British minister. Fanny introduced Tommy to Lord Napier, and the young boy dropped his jaw, asking, "Was that the *Lord?*"[21]

In fact, the maturing Fanny Seward developed a charming capacity for laughing at herself. Encouraged by the Spanish minister to practice her French with him, Fanny chuckled at her lack of fluency: "When I did use a french [sic] sentence, he answered me in english [sic] and did not appear to notice that I had . . . spoken in french [sic]."[22] In addition, as the Sewards were entertaining guests for dinner one Saturday in 1862, Fanny laughed at her clumsiness. Setting her father's teacup down, she had gotten tangled up in her knitting yarn, "& pretty soon this sprawling englishman [sic] was down on the floor with me, having a general untwisting."[23]

Fanny's most important characteristic, however, was not her shyness or awkwardness or honesty or humor: it was her passion for reading and writing.

From an early age, Fanny Seward was an enthusiastic reader. As a child, she favored stories about animals, fairies, and books with rhymes. In her teen years she read poetry, history, romances, and novels. When she died, she left approximately 350 volumes behind her.[24] Her diaries abounded with the records of her reading. She read *Paradise Lost* and learned Longfellow's poems. She read Thackeray's *Vanity Fair* and Hawthorne's *The Marble Faun*. She read Dickens's *Dombey and Son* and *Bleak House* and *Great Expectations*.[25] That she was serious about her reading was confirmed by her regular diary reflections on books and authors and their ideas. With enthusiasm she declared to her diary that she never tired of "things written."[26]

Fanny was fortunate to have been growing up during a time which saw a staggering increase in the availability of printed material. So abundant were the numbers of books, magazines, and newspapers that even the Bible faced stiff competition for the eyes of the reading public.[27] In an era without television or movies or computers, reading was the kind of leisure activity that appealed to an intelligent and sensitive girl like Fanny Seward.

Reading offered a number of rewards. It was a pleasure that could be indulged alone or in groups. Books could be read out loud to amuse or to solace the ailing. Books were an item of exchange which could be borrowed, bought, or given as gifts. Above all, books were an intellectual pleasure that sparked conversation, dialogue, and debate. In Auburn, New York, where the winters were long and brutal, firesides served double duty: they kept housebound families warm, and they illuminated the pages of their books.[28]

Fanny's diary tells us that the pages of books were often the vehicle through which relations with family and friends were cemented. On Fanny's sixteenth birthday, brother Will had been sick in bed, so Fanny read to him in *Pilgrim's Progress.* In the winter of 1863, Fanny was entertained by her friend Sue Ward, reading aloud from *Les Miserables.* Fanny and her best friend, Ellen Perry, read Tennyson's "In Memoriam" together, marking the passages that "seem almost inspired." During a brief thaw between two very heavy Auburn snows, Fanny and her mother read Shakespeare together. At a large dinner party in 1863, Fanny was happy to be sitting with Judge Swayne, who talked "books" with her. As Fanny was recovering from dental extractions a few days before Christmas in 1862, she was treated to a reading from George Eliot by her Aunt Lazette, whom Fanny described as a "capital reader."[29]

Given her familiarity with books and the role they played in her life, Fanny Seward grew into an equally "capital reader," herself.

For the teenaged Fanny, reading became an activity as necessary to her well-being as breathing, and it walked hand-in-hand with reading's twin: writing. Even as a young girl, Fanny possessed a facility for words. In a letter to her mother when she was only nine, she wrote charmingly of a little bird that "sips from one of the puddles" left by a rainstorm. Barely fourteen, Fanny described the end-of-the-year transition this way: "December folds him gently in her arms and they go to rest together." A few days later, on the way to the Capitol with her family, Fanny captured the snow-covered Washington scene:

> . . . [T]he tops of the houses were covered with snow. Little faces peeped from the windows, and business men drew up there [sic] faces as the[y] braved the storm, boys were sliding down the Capitol hill, one alone on his hand sled, or even three together—.[30]

The number of pieces she wrote and sometimes sought publication for, even when very young, testified to an interest in writing bordering on a passion. In a letter to her mother, ten-year-old Fanny asked if she had liked "My Little Room," the poem she was writing for the *Young America* magazine. When Fanny was barely twelve, her story about Watch, the family dog, was published in the December 1856 issue of *Merry's Museum and Parley's Magazine*; brother Fred glowed with pride over the talent of "Our Fanny" and her "pretty little piece." Fanny's diary revealed that in February, 1861 she was writing something called "Little Face Against the Pane" and beginning a book of extracts, a collection of favorite quotations that filled nine pages.[31]

In hindsight, then, it is unsurprising that Fanny Seward would choose to keep a diary. In fact, on December 25, 1858, the day of Fanny's first diary entry, when the nation was still at peace, even her most memorable Christmas gift seems prescient. It had been a year and a half since she first wrote her father requesting a "Juvenile Theatre." This play theater came in its own box and contained about a dozen puppets with stands to support them and wires to move them about, and there was a playbook as well as a curtain and scenery.[32] Now, on Christmas morning, she had opened that longed-for gift, a present certain to please a young reader and writer with a passion for dramatic narratives.

It was therefore not surprising that on April 14, 1865, Fanny would have been jotting notes to expand upon in her diary or that she would have been reading to her bedridden father. As Fanny had moved from the innocence of childhood to the experience of young womanhood through the course of the Civil War, that abiding passion for reading and writing continued both to define and sustain her.

# 3
# Being a Seward

Fanny's most intimate family members included her father, William Henry Seward; her mother, Frances Adeline Miller; her silent and sturdy eldest brother Augustus Henry Seward, eighteen years her senior; her studious middle brother, Frederick William Seward, fourteen years old when Fanny was born; and youngest brother William Henry Seward Jr., six years older than Fanny and her spirited favorite sibling. Other members of Fanny's family circle included great-aunt Clarinda Miller and grandfather Elijah Miller, both long-time residents of the homestead in Auburn. Another active presence in the family's life was Fanny's aunt Lazette Worden, her mother's older sister and closest friend.[1]

By most accounts, the Sewards were a happy family, devoted to the best interests of its members. They read together, dined together, traveled together, entertained together, explored the garden together, took carriage rides together, played cards together, enjoyed the theater together, and discussed the issues of the day together.

Many of Fanny's diary entries underscore this family's happiness. For instance, a highlight of the family's Christmas morning was watching Fanny bring one special mitten down from the mantle. It was a stocking for Bell, her terrier, and Fanny reported on the merriment as the Sewards watched Bell capering over his stocking treats.[2] One year on Christmas Eve, spunky Aunt Lazette offered Bell another gift: some of her own dog Trippy's fur wrapped in paper. On Christmas morning, Bell returned the favor by giving some of his fur to Trip.[3]

Fanny herself contributed to the high spirits at family dinners. At the table, Fanny offered backhanded praise for the morning sermon at

St. John's, dubbing it an "excellent outburst."[4] During meals, the family often enjoyed turtle soup, her father's favorite, but Fanny seized an opportunity to offer her own horrified opinion. After all, the tenderhearted girl had watched Louisa, the cook, scalding to death "eight unfortunate terripins [sic]—poor things"; as a result, the youngest Seward vowed not to eat "turtles, terripins [sic], lobsters, eels, and frogs," forswearing "snakes and lizards," too.[5]

If the Seward family in which Fanny was maturing was often happier than most, perhaps it was because it was also especially blessed.

For one thing, the family rarely worried about money. They maintained two houses, one in Auburn and one in Washington, DC. The red brick townhouse on the east side of Lafayette Square in Washington, occupied after William Seward became Lincoln's secretary of state, was the site of frequent and lavish entertainments, entertainments which young Fanny attended. The home contained a dining table that could seat twenty-four at once and could be set by twenty-four matched place settings of imported blue and gold china. Even on a pedestrian Tuesday evening, Fanny exclaimed that there were "17 guests for dinner!"[6]

On Lafayette Square, Fanny Seward dined on delicacies prepared by Washington's most elegant caterers. Gautier's, for instance, employed French cooks and sometimes prepared Fanny's favorite dish, a wine-seasoned wild turkey boned and stuffed with boiled French chestnuts.[7] Some dinners could last four hours, and the guests might consume nearly a dozen courses. A typical menu might offer "soup, fish, roast beef; then roast turkey and vegetables; then asparagus, sweetbreads, quails, green peas, terrapins, ducks, a tenth course of ice cream, wine jelly, pies, finally apple, nuts and prunes."[8] Hers was not the lunch pail of cold sausage or stale bread familiar to ordinary Civil War youngsters.

In addition, the family was also advantaged by William Seward's immense political power. The Seward family members traveled in the highest political, diplomatic, and cultural circles, not merely meeting with but forming friendships with presidents, ambassadors, generals, politicians, and artists, and their family members. Opportunities for each of the members of the Seward family were abundant. Augustus, the oldest Seward son, who had attended West Point, secured favorable military appointments far away from the battle lines both before and during the Civil War. Frederick, the second son, was able to serve as his father's assistant at the State Department, dealing with matters of state at the highest levels of government. William Henry, Junior, the third son, developed important business connections in Auburn through networks of family connections that allowed him to flourish in the banking business.

Young Fanny was also afforded privileges, and she recorded her frequent introductions to "Officers, Princes, Counts, Barons & various Generalships, Colonelships, Majorships & Captaincies."[9] These introductions allowed Fanny, a quiet young girl with a passion for writing, abundant material for her diaries. Such connections offered Fanny up-close snapshots of famous senators and generals and diplomats who debated policies, welcomed a respite from war plans, and flirted with the ladies in the Seward home. As Fanny listened quietly from the parlor, the reception hall, or the carriage seat, she keenly scrutinized and then recorded her impressions of those who would wind up in the history books: President Lincoln and his wife Mary; Secretary of War Edwin Stanton; Senator Charles Sumner; Generals George McClellan and Benjamin Butler; Secretary of the Treasury Salmon P. Chase and his daughter Kate; humanitarian Dorothea Dix; actors Edwin Booth and Charlotte Cushman; writers Anthony Trollope and George William Curtis.

Although their wealth and power provided the family with many opportunities, the Sewards possessed characteristics as a family that helped reinforce their connections with one another. One was their love of the natural world. Both of Fanny's parents were proud of the family's grounds and garden in Auburn, passing on this love of nature to their daughter and other children. As a young woman, Fanny recognized that her father's heart was kept "younger than many a boy's" by his deep affection for nature, so at breakfast on summer mornings, Fanny was alert to her father's remarks about "what new flower was in bloom, what fruit had ripened, what birds had come." When her father was away in Washington, embroiled in the challenges of managing a war, she offered him letters blooming with references to the life of the South Street garden as a form of solace: "The rain has partly destroyed the beauty of the horsechestnut blossoms, with which the trees were loaded. We never had so many mosquitoes and caterpillars as this year they are everywhere."[10]

Another connection among the Sewards was their passion for animals. Any large home with abundant grounds could expect to become the habitat for starlings in the barn or chipmunks in the woodpile. But in Auburn, New York, the house and grounds of the Seward family on South Street encouraged all animal guests, whether invitees or intruders.

Between 1816 and 1872, Seward House was home not only to dogs and cats but also to canaries and parrots, horses and cows, and even an Alaskan bald eagle. Jenny, a pet deer given as a gift to William Seward in Albany, never made it to Auburn; Jenny did, however, make it into two paintings of the governor's residence in Albany when Seward was serving as governor of New York. An informal catalogue of family pets included from time to time two stout grey horses; canaries Dickie and Jenny; Bob the mockingbird; Snip, a stray spaniel; Neptune, a Newfoundland dog; a couple of parrots; some California ponies; and assorted goldfish, pigeons, cats, and hens. An unofficial tally of pets buried in the family garden surmised that there were five dogs, two horses, and at least one cat buried there. Simply put, the Seward estate was "quite the zoo."[11]

Fanny's own affection for animals was indulged in a household swarming with them, but her dog Bell, a terrier that was a gift from a family friend, occupied center stage in the innocent early pages of her diary. Fanny's diary provided charming pictures of Bell sleeping on her knee while she practiced piano or dozing at night in the rocker by Fanny's bed. Fanny crowed with pride when Mr. McLeod, the painting teacher, declared that Bell must be a "real scotch [sic] terrier." When Mr. Mattison, a dinner guest, offered grace, Bell climbed into his lap and licked his face. The Miller family, knowing Fanny's affection for Bell, sent her home from a visit with a cake for Bell.[12]

But Bell was not the only family dog to tug at young Fanny's heart. Fanny was also fond of Rover, who had inherited the "war spirit" of a mother who had allegedly served in the Mexican War. Rover's martial spirit asserted itself when, wrote Fanny, he tried to quiet a noisy crowd by barking.[13] Fanny even received a letter in the mail from Rover. Rover had help, of course, from Fanny's clever Aunt Lazette:

> Auburn, January 23rd
>
> My dear young Mistress,
>
> I have been very well since you left me—excepting a lame foot which your Aunty has cured with arnica . . . my voice has not been at all impaired by this sore on my foot. I can bark as shrill as ever . . . Goodbye—I must join a barking party assembled in Mr. Woodruff's door and there are none but bass voices there and mine is wanted.
>
> Your affectionate Rover[14]

In the Seward family, pets were present at holidays, on birthdays, and for special occasions. Spirited Aunt Lazette adored her own dog Trip, also known as Trippy. She involved Fanny in planning a birthday party for Trippy, and Fanny issued invitations to the "birthday fete," inviting her brother Will and the Perry sisters. Ellen and Esther Perry replied by thanking "his dogship" for the invitation.[15] Part of the fun of being a Seward involved frolicking with their pets.

But there was something that went beyond family celebrations, wealth, power, and a love of the natural world that most accurately characterized the Sewards. That was the Latin phrase "*Esse Quam Videre*" that adorned each of the blue-and-gold china place settings. It meant "to be rather than to seem." This defining family motto, in the center of each china dish, was an important indicator of the genuineness that was the central value of the Seward family's life.[16]

In fact, all the Sewards, despite their privilege and wealth, were remarkably unpretentious. If William Seward's feet were damp, he would take off his shoes and dry them before the fire—even in the presence of dignitaries.[17] Despite the important people they knew and the high circles in which they traveled, especially after Fanny's father was named Lincoln's secretary of state, visitors to the Seward family home in Auburn remarked on its "comfortable simplicity."[18]

Reflecting her own preference for the comforts of simplicity, Fanny, like the other members of her family, scorned affectation. She favored friendships with girls like Mary Adams who were "unaffected" and talk "not of beaux and dress." To her friend Sarah How, Fanny shared her dislike of "affected reading and talking." Valuing a genuineness of character that reflected the "*Esse Quam Videri*" spirit of her family, Fanny cringed, for example, before a wedding announcement in which the name-dropping of famous relations had been "piled on rather thick." She was put off by the carriage of the postmaster general, known for his extravagance, for he employed a footman and garbed his servants in livery.[19]

In fact, the Sewards' relationships with their own servants further confirmed their generous and unpretentious spirit. Kate Barrett, for instance, Frances Seward's helpmate, shared stockings and presents alongside the other family members at Christmas. Eliza Freeman, whom Fanny called "Aunt Eliza," began working for the family in 1845 as Fanny's nurse, and she was so beloved that she was treated almost like a member of the family. Nicolas Bogart, coachman to the Sewards for many years, was also special to the family. That he was treated with consideration is shown by an incident in which Fanny's mother changed her plans for Sunday church to make it easier for Nicolas to attend his own place of worship.[20]

The Sewards' steadfast fidelity to "*Esse Quam Videre*" shared much with the Civil War regiment known as the Seventh New York. Celebrated as the "silk-stocking" regiment, these soldiers were made up of New York City's blue bloods. On their way to rescue Washington, for instance, they fed on sandwiches from Delmonico's and rested their collective bottoms on "velvet-covered camp stools."[21] Fanny was able to observe this regiment first-hand when she attended the dedication of Clark Mills's equestrian statue of George Washington on the first president's birthday remembrance on February 22, 1860.[22] The Seventh New York could have confined itself to such lightweight ceremonial functions, but like the Seward family itself, and to its credit, it chose not to lounge on the cushions of privilege but to serve the nation. Ultimately, these blue bloods earned their praise as the saviors of Washington when they rose to the rescue of the beleaguered capital in the spring of 1861, becoming one of the first Northern regiments to guarantee its security by rushing to its aid, despite their fancy sandwiches and velvet stools. Likewise, the Seward family chose service to the nation over self, adhering to the family spirit of "*Esse Quam Videre*."

However, just as the nation harbored tensions between North and South, frontier and civilization, and slavery and freedom, the Seward family harbored tensions as well. Although united in their devotion to their family, the Sewards also occupied their own kind of divided house.

Those divisions, documented by Patricia Johnson Rauch's compelling research into the family dynamics, had their origin in the family's long separations. These separations began after Seward's 1830 election to the New York Senate, his first political office. By 1847 he had spent only eight Christmases in Auburn, and not a single one thereafter until the end of the Civil War.[23] The absences became so much a part of their lives that when William and Frances did at one point reunite, Frances called him "just a visitor."[24]

The separations were the result of Seward's obsession with politics. Ambitious and restless, he had caught the "political virus."[25] By 1860, when called on by Lincoln to assume the cabinet office of secretary of state, Seward wrote his wife that when his country called at such a momentous time, he " . . . could not be well or happy at home."[26]

Naïve Fanny often held out hope that they might one day reunite as a family on a more permanent basis. After Seward lost the presidential nomination in 1860, she confided to actress and friend Charlotte Cushman her longing for her father to give up politics and return to Auburn, where they might be "the happiest family imaginable." But Cushman was not naïve. Her father, Cushman told Fanny bluntly, "never would retire, such a thing would never occur in his life."[27]

Because of her father's long absences, Fanny's diaries confirmed that she was often a lonely young girl. Her father's lifelong public service required their relationship to be conducted at a distance, and Fanny felt his departures most keenly. From the time she was small, she was described as "her father's shadow."[28] When home, Seward indulged in exuberant games with Fanny and her friends, and it is easy to imagine his dark-haired daughter tagging after her famous father, begging him to extend his stay.[29]

There is pathos in this image of a young girl shadowing her father, refusing to let him out of her sight. The fact was that William Henry Seward was simply absent from the family's home in Auburn for long periods of time. Sometimes he was away on campaign trips. Sometimes he was away on business for New York as state senator and then governor. Sometimes he was away as a United States senator. Sometimes he was away stumping for national candidates. By the time he became secretary of state, immersed in the terrible business of civil war, his pattern was well established. Seward was not just away "sometimes": he was rarely home.[30] Fanny was to feel his absences all her life.

For instance, when Senator Seward left for a tour of Europe in 1859 as the likely next candidate for president of the United States, Fanny, in her early teenage years, was heartbroken at another leave-taking. As a parting gift, she had crocheted him a pair of white wool slippers to sleep in so his feet might never be cold. As his departure neared, she fetched him cheese, cut him maple sugar, and wore the locket that contained the senator's hair. On the night before her father's departure, Fanny gave up an overnight visit with a friend in order to prolong her time with "dear, dear Father," a time they spent playing the senator's favorite game of whist. At departure time, she pulled her Shaker bonnet down over her eyes to hide her tears, vowing to keep from crying "so that the last he saw her face it would be smiling." While he was away, introducing himself to the European heads of state, Fanny cross-stitched a new pair of slippers for him, carefully placing them right under his dressing gown in the closet. With pride, Fanny recalled the political hoopla surrounding her father's departure like the waving flags and the playing of "Hail to the Chief." Still, after her celebrated father departed, he left behind one lonely young girl.[31]

But Seward's addiction to politics was not the only cause of the family's separation. Frances, Fanny's mother, had made choices of her own that made it difficult for the family to live together. Devoted to Auburn, not rowdy Albany or boisterous Washington, DC, Frances refused to move from the family homestead on South Street. Admittedly, her inflexible and controlling father, Judge Miller, had driven a cruel bargain when the widowed judge had insisted in 1824 that the young couple could marry only if they would live in his house and if Frances would agree to care for him until he died. Astonishingly, Frances and her future husband agreed.[32] This arrangement, as Patricia Johnson Rauch pointed out, left Frances conveniently cared for by family and servants when her husband was away, but sadly it also kept husband and wife from establishing a separate household of their own.[33] It was to prove a fateful choice that relegated their family to endless separation and their children to unending anxiety as they attempted to negotiate the dissimilar poles of Auburn and Washington.

The Seward children, wrestling with divided loyalties, eventually made choices about where to live, and why. The family tensions likely caused stolid Augustus, the eldest son, to retreat into profound silences.[34] Gus had chosen a military career against the wishes of his pacifist mother and with the approval of his father; the controversy over that choice rankled for years.[35] Eventually, Gus chose a quiet life in the military bureaucracy while residing in the family home in Washington.

Fred, the second child, was studious, even bookish, and appeared to be following in his father's impressive footsteps. Frederick attended Union College, his father's alma mater; he studied law and was admitted to the bar. Like his father, he never felt drawn to legal work, so he served for a time as an assistant editor at the *Albany Evening Journal*, still not sure of a clear career direction. When his father offered Fred a job as his assistant secretary of state during the Lincoln administration, Fred found that the work suited him and never looked back.[36] Fred's wife Anna, gifted at putting people at ease, sustained the family's social standing in Washington, becoming a beloved member of the family whom Fanny called "sister."[37]

William Henry, Junior—the youngest son, closest in age to his little sister Fanny—was not entranced by Washington, and his preference for life in Auburn over life in Washington, where his father flourished, was always apparent. Never much of a student, Will inherited instead his father's sociability, and the good-looking boy, a bit of a hellion, was always popular. Surprisingly unaffected by his father's fame, yet still searching for his place in the world, Will eventually found it in the banking business, a career which he pursued in his beloved Auburn, where he proved a natural civic leader brimming with his father's energy.[38]

Fanny, the beloved youngest child, felt most keenly the pull between Auburn and Washington. The shy young girl evolved during the war years into a serious young woman who shared some of the anxieties of her overprotective mother, who cautiously supervised Fanny's Auburn upbringing. On the other hand, William Seward pointedly encouraged Fanny to explore the people and places of wartime Washington, an insistence that helped modulate her anxieties and mitigate her shyness until, at the end of the war, she appeared to be casting her lot with the family in Washington. Fanny's own spirit deserves credit for helping her find her way between the opposing poles of Auburn and Washington: her devotion to her writing was an important way of imagining an independent life of her own.

In addition to the tension caused by separation, another major source of tension between Frances and William Seward, the husband Frances affectionately called "Henry," was that wife and husband were essentially two different personalities. He was garrulous and sociable; she was aloof and reclusive. He loved the social whirl of parties and receptions and dinners; she hated all such activities, dismissing them as frivolous. Furthermore, Frances was a teetotaler who would pointedly refuse all alcohol, and William's wine cellar was admired by political Washington.[39]

During the holiday season of 1858, Fanny's earliest diary entries documented the tensions between her parents on the topic of alcohol, Fanny recording a tiff over the use of spirits at the family's traditional

New Year's reception. Fanny described her father reluctantly informing the servant John that he must find another use for the dozen lemons he had on hand, for Mrs. Seward had refused the serving of whiskey punch.[40] Eventually Frances left all of her official hostessing duties to her daughter-in-law Anna, Frederick's wife.[41]

Sadly, however, another point of tension between husband and wife was their differing physical constitutions. Seward, robust and hearty, was brimming with health, rarely ill, and inclined to recover rapidly from any physical debility. Frances, unfortunately, was delicate and fragile and rarely well. Fanny's father believed that ill-health was developed by days "spent on the sofa, or by the study fire,"[42] and Fanny's mother found the sofa and the fireside appealing.

There is no doubt that Frances's constant ill health had an impact on her children. Playing with her visiting friend Fanny Bailey over the Christmas holidays in 1858, Fanny recorded an incident in which merely a barking dog sent Frances to bed:

> After dinner mother was sitting in the parlor with Bell, whom Fanny [Bailey] excited so much as to make him bark, I tried . . . to quiet him and although I intimated that it would give mother a headache, she continued to excite him again and again, till mother, too ill to remain, left the room, when as she rose, the heedless Fanny [Bailey] cried 'Does he make your head ache Mrs. Seward?'[43]

Sadly, Frances was never reluctant to address the state of her health in her many letters to her children. To Augustus she wrote of being confined to home by the cold weather, which was aggravating to her neuralgia.[44] She seemed to collude in making her children worry with her. To Fred she confessed the severity of her neuralgia, even though she had recovered.[45] In an age that had yet to discover psychology, perhaps Frances was unaware that such disclosures might affect and disturb her children, particularly the daughter whose sensitivity was already such a worry. Frances's preoccupation with her ill health became an invisible family member whose ghostly presence loomed over dinner tables and family outings.

In fact, those preoccupations were felt especially keenly by Fanny. Even as a very young girl, she was profoundly aware of the fluctuating state of her mother's health and the accommodation it required. Although excited about her gifts of bonbons and books during Christmas of 1853, nine-year-old Fanny was still worried enough about her mother's health to write her father: "Will you pleas [sic] to write to me soon Mother is not verry [sic] well your affectionate daughter Fanny."[46] Between the lines of at least one letter lurked a martyrdom on the part of Fanny's mother that evoked guilt on the part of her daughter. Ten-year-old Fanny wrote to her mother, "I hope you are well again thank you for writing when you were unable."[47] No wonder Fanny Seward suffered from anxieties. She longed for the father who was absent and worried about the mother who was present.

Young people everywhere sense the tensions bubbling under the surface of even the happiest family. In Fanny's case, the struggle involved the pull between Auburn and Washington, between her reserved mother and her ebullient father, between her mother's poor health and her father's hearty robustness. To those struggles would be added even more worrisome tensions: those of a wrenching national conflict in which the Seward family occupied center stage.

# 4

# "My Affinity"

Fanny Seward was devoted to her family members from her earliest years. She adored her father, but that relationship had to be carried on from a distance. The relationship with her mother, however, was conducted close at hand. Auburn made up Fanny's mother's world, and it was in that setting that Fanny spent her formative years.

In 1844, when Fanny Seward was born, Auburn was a thriving community in the heart of the Finger Lakes region of central New York. Blessed with abundant water resources as well as the energy of its farmers, speculators, artisans, businessmen, and entrepreneurs, Auburn was marked by growth and prosperity at mid-century. In the decade after Fanny's birth, Auburn, the county seat of Cayuga County, had seen its rough frontier edges rounded off, and it was a place that could now boast of factories, churches, a hotel, a newspaper, and the New York State Prison, a model of reform.[1]

For growing girls like Fanny Seward, outdoor activities revolved around the weather. Fall brought its pumpkin festivals and spring its May queens. In the summer there were strolls by the lake, and in the winter there were skating parties where Fanny learned to ice skate on the frozen lake with a broomstick balanced in her unsteady hands.[2] Thus, Auburn offered a pleasant and active setting for Fanny's growing up.

Inside the house on South Street, Fanny could put on plays or enjoy checkers or dominoes. Outside the painted brick house, Fanny could roll hoops across the grassy lawn and romp with brother Will, who managed to get out of scrapes as easily as he got into them. The elms and evergreens provided hiding places for games of blindman's buff, made even more fun when Fanny's father joined in.[3]

Because Fanny's father was so often away, the most significant influence on this growing girl was her mother. As the only two females in a family of boys and with a husband and father pursuing a career far from home, Fanny and her mother developed a closeness born of both necessity and choice.

Such closeness between mother and daughter was common in an age that kept women and men in "separate spheres." But across the years, this mother and daughter became inseparable. They read together. They strolled the garden together. They shared news of weddings and anniversaries and new babies together. They stitched and sewed for the Ladies' Aid Society together. They learned to operate the new sewing machine together. They took tea and visited with friends and neighbors together.[4]

The bond between them was well established by Fanny's diaries and letters, which were replete with endearments to her mother. Frances, Fanny's namesake, was "dearest Mother" and "my dear considerate mother." A little drawing appended to a letter from nine-year-old Fanny shows an oval drawing in the center of the page, below which is written: "here is a kiss yours most treuley [sic] Fanny L Seward." In a charming phrase, the more mature Fanny depicted her closeness to her mother, lovingly referring to her as "my affinity."[5]

Mother and daughter also shared many common traits. Both were slim and tall for the times, with sleek black hair and dark black eyes. Both women had retiring natures; they preferred quiet pleasures like reading that permitted withdrawal from the world. Fanny was an introvert like her mother, not an extrovert like her father. She was idealistic like her mother, not pragmatic like her father. Furthermore, mother and daughter were both extraordinarily sensitive. The little girl who thought fishing for pleasure was wicked had a mother so sensitive that she could not watch a favorite tree being cut down, Frances claiming she could feel "every stroke of the axe—."[6]

The one trait that defined both daughter and mother most emphatically, however, was their poor health. Fanny's diaries were flooded with examples of her own numerous illnesses. In addition to ordinary chills, neuralgia, fever, headaches, and other ailments, there

3. Fanny's mother Frances is surrounded by her sons Fred, Will, and Gus. Collections of the Seward House Museum, Auburn, NY.

were frequent mentions of ulcerated throats that led to long bouts of "quinsy," the nineteenth-century name for tonsillitis. Sometimes an illness forced Fanny to offer only cursory notations in her diary or to abandon her entries altogether for a while. And there were records of several extended illnesses that were positively alarming. Four-year-old Fanny was acutely ill with scarlet fever,[7] and the eighteen-year-old Fanny had become so ill at boarding school that she had to be withdrawn.[8]

Parental anxieties about illness were reasonable in an age when childhood diseases like whooping cough, diphtheria, and scarlet fever could quickly be fatal. For example, Sue Ward, Fanny's friend from boarding school, visited Fanny in Washington in February of 1863; by March, Sue had suddenly died of diphtheria. Fanny herself noted her father's concern for her own well-being. He was, she wrote, "always looking out for something to improve my poor health." But the efforts were often futile. On one occasion, for instance, after her father encouraged her to exercise, she promptly caught a cold. On another occasion, an invigorating sleigh ride was followed quickly by backache and headache. She did seem unusually vulnerable and delicate. Even a short walk from church in the bitter cold led to a severe cold.[9]

But Fanny's mother was the parent close at hand who worked most diligently to improve her delicate daughter's health. Frances hovered over Fanny during scores of illnesses, caring for her around the clock. Fanny's diaries were filled with examples of her mother's unwavering care. In late December, 1860, during a Christmas season when Fanny was "not strong enough for walking or dancing," her mother was "unremitting" in her care.[10]

Complicating these health matters were the severe winters that were a fact of life in the Finger Lakes region of New York. The years of William Seward's governorship of New York included weather like this:

> The long winters of this locality were a dread . . . The season lasted eight or nine months, and four or five of these were invariably bitter. The sting and bite from the Canadian country . . . gathered strength over Lake Ontario, then seemed to settle over Western New York for long, unrelieved weeks. Then came colds, sickness, deaths. It was no wonder that the cemeteries of the time carried so many gravestones with notations of the death of infants and of young people.[11]

The risks inherent in such brutal weather were compounded by a medical science that was in its infancy in Fanny's time. Homeopathic treatments were the only remedies. Fanny's swollen throat that suggested diphtheria was treated with a warm poultice of Indian meal. A chill was to be treated immediately with brandy, and bronchitis required frequent doses of hot gin and water. In the absence of antibiotics, a pneumonia patient like Fanny's Aunt Lazette could simply wrap her torso in raw cotton and hope.[12] Furthermore, since the role of germs in the spread of disease was not understood by doctors until late in the nineteenth century, Civil War-era Americans like Fanny

Seward suffered contagious illnesses including diphtheria, typhus, scarlet fever, diarrhea, typhoid, and typhoid fever.

Unfortunately, Fanny Seward inherited the delicate constitution of her mother instead of the robust constitution of her father. Still, Fanny's ill health was present from toddlerhood; her mother's ailments began only after she married, and seemed at first to be gynecological in nature. In addition, however, Frances also complained of neuralgia, digestive problems, bothersome coughs, and eye ailments that prevented her from reading. On carriage rides, simply bumping over rough pavement made her sick. On an evening visit at the British minister's home, the gaslights made her feel as though she were in a "fiery furnace"; the piano playing upset her even further. To her sister Lazette, Frances complained of her hostess's insensitivity in failing to comprehend "the condition of a person whose nerves are unnaturally acute from disease—very few do." Unfortunately, those who failed to comprehend her condition included her doctors. Indeed, some of her maladies, like her suspicion of a "tumor in the intestines" or her belief that her vascular system was "deranged," seem downright odd, suggesting that Frances Seward may have been a hypochondriac.[13]

Fortunately for Fanny Seward, health was not her mother's only preoccupation. In fact, Mrs. Seward's commitment to education and her passion for progressive ideas were two of the most important influences on young Fanny's life.

Women of intelligence like Fanny's mother had few outlets for their talents in mid-nineteenth-century America. The needs of women in general were given little notice, as if they were no more than an "invisible parlor fixture, like an antimacassar or a lamp."[14] But Frances Seward made herself a notable exception.

Fanny Seward was blessed to have had her education supervised by her mother, a woman with intellectual interests who had been given rare educational opportunities herself. In a day when upper-class girls were provided with merely ornamental educations that introduced them to drawing, dancing, parlor French, and the needle arts, Fanny's mother had been sent by her father to the Troy Female Seminary in Troy, New York. Founded in 1821, this school was heralded as offering the most complete course of study for girls in the country, offering even mathematics and science.[15]

Like other mothers of her day from wealthy families, Frances Seward educated her young children at home. Fanny and Will took three-hour lessons from Frances most mornings, and Fanny's mother may have developed her curriculum by consulting *Mother's Reminiscences of a Course of Reading and Instruction*, a book which she gave to Fanny in 1851.[16] Fanny also intermittently attended the Auburn Young Ladies' Institute, and she was sent to the Mapes boarding school in Philadelphia for a brief time during the winter of 1862.[17]

But Fanny herself was not an exceptional student. Her diaries mentioned subjects like arithmetic and geography as well as music, history, and French. From Auburn she dutifully reported to her father in Washington that she was studying physiology, moral philosophy and rhetoric, but it was clear that the wild flowers she had gathered and the prospect of June's lilies and roses excited her more keenly. The early diaries also showed a young girl struggling with spelling. She had trouble with "aufully" and "delecatly," and although we cannot know whether she enjoyed the visits in her "parler" or resented the three "quaters" of an hour devoted to music practice, we do know that spelling the words in those remarks was a challenge.[18]

In May of 1859 she was taking grammar, Latin, and geography at the Auburn Young Ladies' Institute, but Fanny's diary comments on her school attendance there were indifferent and terse. They included a brief "went to school" and a short "nothing of consequence."[19] Although Fanny coveted a dressing case with its smart grooming implements like its tooth and nail brushes, she was only allowed to buy it if she studied her arithmetic for half an hour on Wednesdays.[20]

Still, like all good parents attempting to nurture the talents of their children, Fanny's parents were pressed to discover a talent in their daughter at which she might excel. After all, Fanny was tutored in riding and singing. She was provided with a painting master and music lessons. She attended dancing school; on one occasion, exposed to an evening practice session following an afternoon class, she grumbled that her evening performance with the quadrille and the polka was "not a whit better than in the afternoon." Innumerable French teachers and their lessons passed through Fanny's diaries, and while attending boarding school in Philadelphia, she tried to demonstrate her accomplishment by writing several letters to her father in French. Still, by her own admission, she rarely made herself understood to a native speaker.[21]

But the years would reveal that Fanny possessed not a scholar's but a writer's sensitivity. Her passion would become reading, writing, and words, and the keen eye for observation she was quietly developing on her own would become the gift to surpass the singing, painting, dancing, and French.

One of the strongest influences on Fanny Seward's life was her mother's passion for progressive ideas. Possessing great intellectual curiosity, Frances Seward was well-versed on the issues of the day. She was witness to the dramatic changes facing nineteenth-century Americans: the cotton gin and the steel plow were changing farming; steamboats and railroads were changing transportation; the telegraph was changing communication; immigrants were changing cities; manufacturing was changing the nature and quantity of material goods; and the movement west was changing the very borders of the nation. Observing the murals on the walls of the Capitol, Fanny herself summed up the changes in her era as "the reaping of old with the sicle [sic], and now with the machine—."[22]

But Frances Seward understood that the political world was rapidly changing, too. The flammable issue of slavery was seeping into every corner of American politics, and it was an issue which would eventually threaten to tear the nation in two. In fact, during the years of Fanny's growing up, questions about slavery were on every American mind: Was slavery a moral wrong or an economic right? Could slaves ever be considered citizens, or were they merely human chattel and thus the property of their owners? Did the Founding Fathers intend for the Constitution to permit slavery everywhere—even in the new and expanding western territories?

Although Fanny's mother was sympathetic to causes like peace and women's rights, she was uncompromising in her passion for emancipation of the slave, a passion that lasted a lifetime. Especially active on behalf of black children, Fanny's mother made inquiry to a school headmistress about the education of "a pretty little colored girl," and she took at least one black child, a boy named John, into her household. In addition, when a poor black child placed by her in the Auburn Orphan Asylum died, Frances paid for the funeral. Furthermore, Fanny's mother supported the efforts of a Washington, DC "School for Colored Girls," founded in 1851. In spite of the Southern abhorrence of such educational efforts on behalf of blacks, the school succeeded, and both mother and daughter frequently visited there. The family's support of the school was more than just applause from a distance, as an incident from Fanny's diary confirmed. Two of the school's teachers, Miss Howland and Miss Searing, were met by accident in the street after church on Christmas Day and were promptly invited to Christmas dinner, sharing in the family's Christmas turkey and plum pudding.[23]

Given the progressive attitudes of both her parents, it is not surprising to find many striking instances in Fanny's diaries of her own sympathy with the slave.

In 1853, when she was only nine, Fanny was reading *Uncle Tom's Cabin.* When Harriet Beecher Stowe's novel about the blight of slavery appeared in 1852, it was an immediate success. In the first week of its release, over ten thousand copies were sold. The nation was gripped by the story of the slave Eliza with babe in arms as she navigated the ice floes of the Ohio River with a pack of snarling bloodhounds snapping at her heels. Stowe's portrayal of rapacious masters, brutal overseers, and desperate slaves literally fleeing for their lives as they followed the North Star from slavery in the South into freedom in the North touched a raw nerve in an already anxious nation. In fact, Mrs. Stowe's novel incited ordinary Americans to denounce slavery, encouraged abolitionists to defy the Fugitive Slave Law with even more passion, and alarmed those in authority. Fanny's father had already created both enemies and friends when he opposed the Fugitive Slave Law and declared in 1850 that there was a "higher law" which, in league with the "noble purposes" of the Constitution, required a stewardship over the western territories consistent with freedom, not slavery.[24]

Fanny, an active young reader, took her reading of *Uncle Tom's Cabin* seriously, providing a sketch of characters Tom and Eva in a letter to her mother. Encouraging her daughter's interest, Fanny's mother presented her with a puzzle called "Uncle Tom's Cabin Dissected" at Christmas. The puzzle pieces fitted together to form a three-dimensional cardboard "cabin," still on display at Seward House in Auburn, New York.[25]

When Fanny was only fourteen, she made note of the *Wanderer* incident in her diary. The *Wanderer* was a schooner that brought a cargo of hundreds of slaves from Africa to land on the shores of Georgia. It was an example of a brazen attempt to continue illicit slave trading even in the face of an 1807 law abolishing the slave trade. "The nation is quite stirred up about it," wrote Fanny. "I hope the 'stealers of men' will be justly punished, and the poor Africans be restored to their native land."[26]

In addition, Fanny had a sharp eye for conversations, incidents, and behavior that touched on the issue of slavery. She recorded the dinner party conversation of Lord Radstock, who described an English lady who visited America and then wrote a book in favor of slavery, describing the Englishwoman as someone who was a "poor goose with an unbalanced mind."[27] In 1862, Fanny was irate about the treatment of Nicholas, one of the Sewards' African American servants; despite the official passes from his employer, the secretary of state, Nicholas was detained at the Baltimore railroad station "out of mere spite of his color."[28]

But by the mid-1840s, when Fanny was born, a creative enterprise for freeing slaves was well established. Called the Underground Railroad, it was a secret network that enabled slaves to escape into freedom. This railroad to freedom eventually acquired its own language. Members of the secret association were called "agents" or "stationmasters"; their safe houses were called "depots." The fugitives themselves were referred to as "cargo" or "passengers," and this human cargo was transported secretly in wagons or coffins along paths called "liberty lines."[29] Members of the Underground Railroad often used secret codes to communicate with each other. When one stationmaster wrote that "I sent you three bales of black wool," he meant that three fugitives could be expected soon.[30]

Auburn, like the neighboring towns of Rochester and Syracuse, was known to have "a small but fierce abolitionist circle" that offered "a friendly port for slaves on the run."[31] Family histories suggested that one of those ports was the Seward home. In fact, the old kitchen was a likely stop on the Underground Railroad, and a letter between Fanny's father and mother confirmed this participation. "The 'underground railroad' works wonderfully," her father wrote, adding that "[t]wo passengers came here last night."[32]

In fact, one of Fanny's favorite pets likely served as a co-conspirator in the Sewards' Underground Railroad activities. He was a bulldog by the name of Watch, and the animal likely served two purposes: family companion and determined guardian.

First, like all the Seward animals, Watch was valued as a family companion. Returning to Auburn to speak at a Republican gathering as well as vote in the November 1855 election while the rest of the family was away, William Seward found at least one familiar face on the welcoming committee. Watch, he wrote his wife, "would not be put off . . . until he had kissed my face."[33]

Second, Watch's other purpose may have been as stubborn guardian of the house, a particularly important duty during the years when the family was hiding cargo on the Underground Railroad. Seward praised the bulldog's abilities as a watchdog, noting that when "passengers" had arrived in the night, Watch had attacked one of the runaways.[34] Rescued by Seward, the passengers then hurried down to the basement kitchen where they were probably hidden until they could safely emerge to continue their journey to safety in Canada.

Unfortunately, this family guardian would die in the spring of 1856, but he was memorialized by a tiny gray wooden bench placed on his grave. The inscription on the bench, still preserved in the basement kitchen of Seward House, reads:

THIS MARKS THE MEMORY OF OUR PET
OUR WATCHIE WAS
A FAITHFUL GUARDIAN AND A DEAR
FRIEND
April 22, 1856
Aged 3 years
11 months

However, the most compelling evidence of the commitment of Fanny's parents to the cause of abolition was their personal relationship with Harriet Tubman, the "Moses of her people." As Kate Clifford Larson, Tubman's biographer, tells us, Tubman was born into slavery in Dorchester County, Maryland in 1822 as the fifth of nine children. Throughout nearly thirty years as a slave, she suffered many indignities. She hid in a pigpen to escape from an owner's bad temper, fighting the mother pig for scraps of food. She was beaten with a rope that broke her ribs. She suffered a near-fatal blow to the head from an iron weight thrown to injure another slave: the unintentional bludgeoning affected her physical and mental health for the rest of her life.[35] "Slavery," Tubman declared, "is the next thing to hell."[36]

When her owner died in 1849, Harriet and her siblings were in danger of being sold on the auction block to pay his staggering debts. As a result, she determined to escape, and on and off for nearly a dozen years she traveled back to Maryland about thirteen times to free various family members and friends. Approximately seventy former slaves owed their freedom to Harriet's personal efforts; approximately fifty others benefited from her directions.[37]

A number of slaves escaping from the Eastern Shore of Maryland found their way to small villages like Auburn. It is probable that they chose Auburn because of Tubman's friendship with Martha Coffin Wright, the sister of Philadelphia abolitionist and Quaker Lucretia Coffin Mott. In 1860, Martha Wright confirmed in a letter that sympathizers in Auburn were applauding the "seven newly arrived slaves that Harriet Tubman has just pioneered safely"[38] from Maryland. One of those sympathizers may have been Frances Seward; after

4. Harriet Tubman, who directed former slaves to freedom along the Underground Railroad, was a close friend of the Seward family. Library of Congress.

all, William Seward had been a law partner of David Wright, Martha Wright's husband.[39]

In fact, in 1859 the Sewards arranged for Tubman to occupy a seven-acre tract of land located outside of Auburn. The property was part of their inheritance from Frances's wealthy father, Judge Elijah Miller. Finally Tubman could provide a home for her aging parents or for other family members and friends.[40]

Because her husband was so often away, particularly during this period, it is likely that Frances helped negotiate the details of the property transfer with the help of her son, Fanny's brother Will. Following this arrangement, money became increasingly important to Tubman, and she began lecturing in Boston and elsewhere, holding audiences spellbound with her stories of escape told with charm and humor. Even so, payments on the Auburn property often went unmet, and the Sewards appear not to have pressed for them.[41]

Tubman scholar Larson has underscored the unusual and courageous aspects of this transaction. For one thing, Harriet Tubman, a fugitive slave, was not a citizen and could hold, therefore, no rights in property. Furthermore, she was a woman, and property ownership by women was rare during this time. Besides, Harriet was married; even though her husband had stayed in Maryland, he could still return and claim an interest in the property. Furthermore, the Sewards themselves were in a compromised position. They had entrusted property into the hands of a fugitive slave, who was vulnerable to capture. Thus, this property arrangement was precarious for both Tubman and the Sewards.[42]

One of the most baffling episodes involving Harriet Tubman and the Seward family involved a young girl who came to live with the family in 1862. In that year, Tubman volunteered to support the Union war effort in South Carolina. She helped direct supplies to Union soldiers and helped recruit black soldiers into the Union army. Most importantly, in June of 1863 Tubman helped organize and execute an armed expedition for the Union, the first female ever to do so.[43]

Larson reports that some time before she began these efforts on behalf of the Union, Tubman brought to Auburn a ten-year-old girl named Margaret Stewart. The parentage of this child, her relationship to Tubman, and the circumstances of her early life continue to be a subject of debate. Despite these mysteries, Harriet needed the child to be well cared for when she decided to volunteer for the Union cause in 1862. Although originally to live with Lazette Worden, Fanny's aunt, eventually the child appears to have been brought to the Seward house to live.[44] Thus, in the Sewards' entrusting of property to Tubman and in her entrusting of Margaret Stewart to the Sewards, deep bonds were evidenced.

Although neither Harriet Tubman nor Margaret Stewart appears to be featured in Fanny's diaries, Fanny herself, like her parents, became active in her personal support of individual African Americans. When a stranger came to the door with a subscription book in hopes of buying her son from slavery, Fanny immediately gave the woman a dollar. Fanny frequently visited "Aunt Margaret," an elderly African American friend, when Fanny was in Washington. She confessed her admiration for this "good patient christian" woman in the pages of her diary. On one visit, Fanny carried some food to Aunt Margaret in her muff. On another visit, in March of 1862, Margaret was grieving the death of her grandson, a fugitive who had died after only two weeks of freedom. Fanny read from the New Testament to comfort her friend, noting with poignancy that Margaret "wished she had someone to read from the bible—but white folks didn't come to see her, and colored folks couldn't read."[45]

Despite her exposure to her parents' abolitionist views, young Fanny Seward understood that although attitudes between North and South on the issue of slavery were clearly polarized, even those who supported the abolition of slavery occupied warring camps. She would have been aware that radical abolitionists, like her mother, would brook no compromises with slavery and would tolerate no delay in abolishing it; she would have understood that many of their sympathetic brethren, including her father, were more compromising and gradualist in their approach. Such differences led to a great deal of bitterness among even allies in the fight to dismantle slavery.

Not surprisingly, during the wrenching period of 1860–1861 as the nation moved inexorably toward war, those dramatic tensions over the issue of slavery surfaced between Fanny's father and mother. Frances, from the distance of Auburn, felt that her husband moved too cautiously and was too willing to compromise with slavery to save the Union; a Union that included slavery, she believed, was not a Union worth preserving. William, from the tumult of Washington, absorbed his wife's criticism of his "cowardly compromises,"[46] responding that freedom for the slave must not mean destruction of the Union. The strife in the Seward family, of which Fanny Seward was keenly aware, mirrored the strife in the country as a whole.

# 5

# Almost "President" Seward

In November of 1859, fourteen-year-old Fanny Seward watched in horror as Neptune, a German shepherd who was one of the Seward family's favorite pets, suddenly fell down the steps in a spasm of agony.

Three years prior, the dog had followed then-Senator Seward home, and the family lovingly adopted him. Believing him to be a water-loving Newfoundland, Fanny named him "Neptune," delighting in recording snippets about him in her diary. For instance, Fanny observed that Neptune never passed a stream or pool of water without lying down in it and cooling himself. Neppy also loved to run, "chasing after the carriage and racing through the fields with the greatest delight." Young Fanny trained Nep to "love me" with his "dear old paws" on her chest when she commanded "*up*."

As Neppy fell into frenzies of pain, terrified Fanny watched as brother Will and Mr. Miner attempted to doctor the animal, administering warm oil, milk, and salt to make him vomit, but sadly Neppy finally died after two hours of suffering. Inconsolable, Fanny wept at the image of the motionless form on the grass.[1]

Soon, however, came the stark realization that the dog, poisoned by arsenic, had likely been killed as political retribution for William Seward's outspoken positions against slavery.

The timing of the dog's death in November 1859 was more than coincidental. In October, while Fanny's father was away on a tour of European capitals as the most likely candidate for the presidency in 1860, the abolitionist firebrand John Brown raided the Harper's Ferry arsenal in West Virginia, setting out to arm the slaves and mount a slave insurrection against their masters; by the time of Brown's hanging in December, the nation had been seized with fear and fury.

In fact, many laid John Brown's raid at the feet of anti-slavery agitators like William Seward. The *New York Herald* insisted that the likes of Seward, not John Brown, were the real instigators; it was they who should be sent to hang.[2] But Fanny Seward, as the child of committed abolitionists, felt this wrath as well. She concluded in her diary that "we have little reason to doubt that some malicious . . . person poisoned old Neppy for spite to us."[3]

About a year after Neptune's poisoning, a rueful Fanny recorded a new anecdote in her diary: She had passed a homeless little brown dog sitting on a doorstep and looking pitifully at her. She thought to stop and rescue the animal, but she restrained herself, deciding that it was "kinder to pass on." After all, Fanny concluded, "it seems certain death to a dog to belong to our family."[4]

Ironically, not long after Neptune's death, Fanny's father would soon experience a similar rebuff. His lengthy career as a standard bearer against slavery would be an important reason for his losing the presidential nomination in 1860. After all, the speech he gave at Rochester, New York, in October 1858, was not easily forgotten; he had declared that the fundamental differences between the North and the South had created an "irrepressible conflict" that would ultimately compel the country to decide whether the United States intended to become either a free labor or slave labor nation.[5] Thus, adopting Seward as the Republican nominee might not lead to "certain death," as Fanny's adopting a stray dog might have, but it might lead to certain defeat at the polls. Like Fanny looking over but then passing by the little brown dog, the Republicans chose restraint, deciding it might be more prudent to "pass on."

However, in Auburn on May 17, 1860, the townspeople, like many Americans, anticipated a Seward victory for the Republican nomination for president of the United States. Fanny surely watched as friends and fellow citizens hauled a brass cannon to the Seward's South Street house, preparing for a night of jubilation and flag-waving for Auburn's most famous citizen.[6]

In her diary, Fanny had already taken note of the good omen that was Wednesday, May 16: the day the Chicago convention began was her father's fifty-ninth birthday. She chirped that "The New York delegates are all for Father."[7] That much was true; the New York delegation called itself the "Irrepressibles" and was certain that Chicago would witness a "coronation" of their candidate. Others agreed: the presidential election without Seward would be "the play without Hamlet."[8]

But Fanny's conclusion on the following day was inaccurate. She was mistaken in writing that there was no balloting of consequence on the seventeenth,[9] for the momentum of the convention, held in the heartland of Illinois where Abraham Lincoln was its favorite son, was beginning to turn away from Fanny's father.

By Friday, however, Fanny grasped the devastating course of events. After being given the news of his defeat, Fanny's father "told Mother and I—in three words, 'Abraham Lincoln nominated.'" The pages of her diary confirmed her father's devastating political reversal: after the third ballot, her father's fate had been sealed.[10]

Although Fanny recorded her father's projected calm, Auburn was devastated. "The flags were furled, the cannon was rolled away, and Cayuga County went home with a clouded brow."[11]

Although Fanny's father had been a front-runner for the nomination, Lincoln defeated him for several reasons. For one thing, Seward had been in politics far longer than the rail-splitter, amassing a record that was pro-immigrant and marred by rumors of cronyism.[12] From the Senate floor, Fanny's father had argued vehemently against the Fugitive Slave Act, which permitted runaway slaves to be retrieved from any corner of the country, and he had publicly pledged his willingness to defend runaways in court. One irate Southerner wrote to Seward in response: "Now, sir, . . . if we ever find you in Georgia, you will forfeit your odious neck, you scamp."[13] Above all, despite the political back-tracking he engaged in to soften his radical positions on slavery to secure the nomination, few were fooled. Seward was considered a central spokesman of the anti-slavery movement, "its prophet, priest, and oracle."[14]

Seward's lengthy anti-slavery record defined him as too radical for a national audience and unlikely to carry the critical Midwestern states. In addition, whereas Seward's most memorable words—"irrepressible conflict"—raised threatening images of inevitable war, Lincoln's most memorable words—"a house divided"—raised less threatening images of a nation that might yet be united. Finally, although the nineteenth-century political practice dictated that candidates stay away from the convention and let their handlers direct the proceedings, the Chicago convention had been hosted favorably for Lincoln on his home turf of Illinois, and Lincoln's backers simply outmaneuvered the other candidates.[15]

In her diary for May 18, 1860, Fanny recorded that her father took the defeat "with philosophical & unselfish coolness," noting that although "[h]is friend[s] feel much distress—he alone has a smile."[16] Seward's outward calm continued over the weekend. Fanny wrote: "all father's friends disheartened, he alone cheerful."[17]

When no one in Auburn could bear to write up the news for Auburn's *Daily Advertiser*, Fanny's father himself displayed the resilience that characterized his long career. Picking up his own pen, he wrote, "No truer . . . defenders of the Republican faith could have been found in the Union than the distinguished . . . citizens on whom the honors of the nomination have fallen."[18]

But if young Fanny did not understand the truth, Seward's maturer son Frederick did: the blow was "as crushing as it was unexpected."[19] Fanny's father himself later confessed that his public face was at odds with his private feelings, expressing relief that he had not kept a diary preserving "a record of all his cursing and swearing" upon his defeat.[20]

True to form and in spite of his disappointment, in a few weeks Fanny's resilient father was ready to campaign for the candidate who had beaten him. Seeking to broaden his daughter's experience, Seward invited fifteen-year-old Fanny to come along. The trip, which began in September 1860, took four weeks, during which Seward gave ten major speeches and countless minor ones at picnics and whistle-stops. Accompanied by her friend Ellen Perry, Fanny watched each event eagerly as the entourage swung from Michigan into Wisconsin and Minnesota and down through Iowa, Kansas, and Illinois, returning home by way of Ohio.[21]

Although her letters home have been lost, Fanny recorded her impressions of the countryside, of the hosts that greeted the campaign party, and of the atmosphere of this electrifying campaign, in her diary. She provided glimpses of the torchlight parades, the Roman candles, the blazing bonfires, and the whistling fife-and-drum corps. She thrilled to the scores of Republican partisans, called the Wide-Awakes, who greeted the campaign party with wild enthusiasm.[22]

The columns of Wide-Awakes marched in military formations down the streets and boulevards of the North to the rhythm of brass bands and the roar of cheering crowds. But it was the black enameled cloth of their uniforms that caused the sensation. Reflecting the light from torches and lanterns, observers remarked that a column of Wide-Awakes looked "like a beautiful serpent of fire."[23] In stop after stop, Fanny witnessed this innovative feature of the 1860 election that both inspired and increased enthusiasm for the Republicans.

Displaying the pluck that would serve her so well during the war years, Fanny savored these new experiences. She relished her carriage ride up Chicago's Michigan Avenue with its magnificent homes on the lake. She admired the bluffs and prairies of the Mississippi from the pilot house of her steamer. More than once she described herself giddily as a "prima donna": after all, she was escorted into Lansing by two hundred mounted horses and a band, and presented on arrival in St. Louis with gifts of bon-bons and hothouse flowers. Most importantly, during this trip Fanny was rarely tired or sick.[24]

Along the campaign trail, his daughter Fanny in tow, Seward's gregarious cigar-chomping, hand-pumping style was everywhere in evidence. In fact, Lincoln's ultimate victory in the November election owed much to Seward's support. Perhaps Seward himself was thought "too flammable"[25] for the nomination, but Fanny's father, ever the loyal partisan, helped light a fire for the victory of the Republican ticket. Even so, the nation that Lincoln would soon lead was sitting on a powder keg.

After his election to the presidency, a grateful Abraham Lincoln acknowledged the talent and loyalty of Fanny's father by appointing him as his secretary of state. It was no small honor, for the office of secretary of state had a noble history. From the office of the secretary of state had been issued the instructions for the Louisiana Purchase. From the office of the secretary of state had been issued the proclamation declaring the War of 1812. From the office of the secretary of state had been issued the Monroe Doctrine, which prohibited foreign interference in the United States.[26]

However, the months leading to Lincoln's inauguration were fraught with anxiety for both the incoming cabinet and the Seward family. On December 20, 1860, South Carolina voted unanimously to secede from the Union; six weeks later, Mississippi, Louisiana, Florida, Alabama, Georgia, and Texas followed suit. Writing to his wife in Auburn, Seward acknowledged that "[m]ad men North, and mad men South are working . . . to produce a dissolution of the Union by civil war." As Seward biographer Walter Stahr has noted, Fanny's father was the leading player in the political spectacle that winter, attempting to reconcile all parties and all factions. But reconciliation never came. By Monday, December 31, 1860, Fanny observed in her diary that "the clouds seem to darken above the union."[27]

Those clouds of foreboding threatened Lincoln's inauguration day in March. Henry Villard, a journalist for the *New York Herald*, reported on an ominous painting sent to Mary Lincoln from South Carolina as she prepared to leave for Washington. It showed her husband tarred and feathered, his feet chained, his neck roped. An English actress whispered that there was a plan afoot to shoot Lincoln in the middle of the inaugural address with the murderer escaping on horseback. Fanny's brother Fred confirmed that the anxiety in Washington prior to Lincoln's inaugural was "ludicrously intense." In fact, on one particular morning, Washingtonians rushed into the streets half-dressed but flailing firearms; they had not expected to hear such an early beating of drums and failed to recognize what was simply the morning's daily reveille.[28]

The heightened danger was revealed in a letter home from Fanny's father. Lincoln's new secretary of state-elect revealed that a plot to assassinate the president-elect was afoot in Baltimore. In hopes of foiling the plot, Fanny's father dispatched her brother Frederick to Philadelphia, where Lincoln's train had stopped. Fanny's brother delivered an urgent warning letter from General Winfield Scott. That letter and similar warnings from detective Allan Pinkerton, charged with safeguarding Lincoln on the way to the inauguration, convinced Lincoln to change his travel schedule. As a result, Lincoln's train slipped through Baltimore in the middle of the night, and the president-elect arrived in Washington without incident.[29]

As inauguration day approached, Fanny in Auburn anxiously ticked off the days: "Four more days before the inauguration of Mr. Lincoln," she wrote on Friday, March 1, 1861. Like Fanny, the country was holding its collective breath, awaiting news that Lincoln had been inaugurated without incident. In her diary, Fanny underscored the importance of March 4, 1861 both by triple-underlining the date and by describing the anxiety at the family dinner table because there was still no word from Washington.

Hundreds of miles away at the capital, Fanny's father was experiencing an Inauguration Day rife with tension. The day itself, mimicking the nation's nerves, was raw and blustery. Sharpshooters were posted along Pennsylvania Avenue. A security contingent, the nation's first use of a "secret service" for an inauguration, escorted Lincoln's carriage to the Capitol. A special passageway constructed of wood planks had been cobbled together to protect the president-elect as he made his way from his carriage to the steps of the Capitol.[30] Such precautions were essential. After all, rebel flags were flying in Virginia within sight of the White House. Fanny's brother Fred made note of the riflemen aligned along the avenue, atop the houses, and at the windows of the Capitol.[31]

Previously, Lincoln had consulted Fanny's father for suggestions about the inaugural address. Because he still hoped to preserve the Union, Seward suggested that Lincoln tone down some of his language. Lincoln had referred to the ordinances of secession as "treasonable," and Seward suggested the less incendiary "revolutionary." Inaugural commitments to "reclaim" federal property already in rebel hands struck Seward as too bellicose, and he suggested more conciliatory language. And Fanny's father was the author of the memorable phrase about the "mystic chords" of memory that still united North and South, a reference that may have helped Lincoln end his address on a more positive note.[32]

Standing on a makeshift platform overlooking the East Front of the Capitol on March 4, 1861, Lincoln's first inaugural address reminded the nation that though relations between North and South were "strained," their "bonds of affection" must not be broken, and he prayed that "the better angels of our nature" would prevail.

In Auburn, when the newspaper finally arrived with reports that "Mr. Lincoln was inaugurated & no serious disturbance occurred," Fanny shouted "Hurrah-Hurrah" and confessed her "inappreciable relief." She had felt "constant anxiety for Father's safety—& of course joined in the fears so often expressed that Lincoln would never see the 5th of March."[33] When she rose the next morning, she was aware of the day's importance: "The nation wakes under a Republican Government—*The First*."[34]

Soon after the inauguration, Fanny's brother Will returned home from Washington, and he was bursting with news, news that an excited Fanny Seward recorded in her diary. Their father, Will reported, had bought ex-president James Buchanan's bay horses. Second son Frederick had been appointed to help his father as assistant secretary of state. Frederick now had bragging rights, for he had a frank and could be called "the Hon" for "the Honorable." And Will had even met Lincoln himself. In the Seward parlor on South Street, the animated Will dramatized the new president shaking hands "with 25 persons per minute." He imitated the gangly Lincoln even reaching his long arm over the heads of the crowd to shake hands with a very short man lost in the crush of well-wishers.[35]

Still, despite Lincoln's inaugural pleas that North and South must not be "enemies," the rebels ignored "the better angels" of their nature. After they fired on Ft. Sumter on April 12, 1861, the "irrepressible" conflict finally came.

After the Sumter bombardment, a cascade of events now challenged the nation, but life on the home front surged with activity as well. Auburn, like towns all over the North, became a beehive of patriotic activity, and Fanny offered a unique perspective on what life was like on the home front. As Fanny's diary reported, a recruiting office opened in Auburn; flags waved from the churches in town; patriotic songs were sung during services; preachers offered sermons "so glorious that the congregation against all rules burst out into applause."[36]

The efforts of Auburn's women and girls were crucial to the war effort. Within two weeks of the outbreak of the war, more than twenty thousand aid societies had sprung up throughout North and South. Their members stitched flags for the regiments and canvassed subscriptions for money or goods, and Samaritan Societies met to support the work of hospitals. One of the most important and universal activities was collecting lint to be turned into bandages. Fanny reported that lint "pours in in the greatest abundance: the children make it at school, the young ladies out, and the mothers at home—every body [sic] sends a box or a package." Fanny and her mother were engaged in the lint effort, too, Fanny quipping that her mother had practically started "a wholesale lint business. She sends off a barrel a week."[37]

At first, some of the efforts backfired as women found it difficult to connect their enthusiastic stitching to mundane army life. Soon they learned that embroidered velvet slippers were not needed in the army camp or that trousers needed to lap the right way.[38] To her Aunt Lazette, Fanny sent word that sister-in-law Anna in Washington "had asked the Generals what the men most needed, and the invariable reply was *mittens*—Secondly she had enquired . . . what were wanted most in the hospitals, and they said *woolen* shirts."[39]

Throughout the war, these female efforts on behalf of soldiers seldom flagged. In the fall of 1862, Fanny assured her father that some of his dressing gowns had been sent to the local camp hospital for the ailing troops. In the spring of 1863, Fanny's mother sent a box of clothing to Washington for the contrabands, slaves who had escaped or had joined the Union army and who often lived in makeshift "camps" around the capital. As late as May, 1864, Fanny wrote to her father about her mother's making shirts for the soldiers and Fanny's own trips to the Ladies' Aid Society to sew. Even by the fall of 1864, enthusiasm for the war effort had not flagged; Fanny and her friend Mary Titus canvassed house to house for contributions, and the profits from the refreshment tables at the county fair were designated for the Soldiers Aid Society.[40]

Not just in Auburn, but in cities and towns all over the North, the fingers of females were flying. While brothers were flocking to recruiting stations, sisters were flocking to local sewing societies. There they picked up needle and thread and began stitching and knitting on behalf of the troops. In parlors, in church halls, in schools, women made flags, shirts, socks, underwear, mittens, anything their local troops could use. Perhaps female faces momentarily flushed when they realized a pair of male drawers lay in their hands, but such squeamishness was overcome with communal giggling and practice. Throughout the country, in hundreds of communities, women young and old devoted their energies to making blankets and bedding, gathering supplies for hospitals, and scraping lint to be made into bandages. That women and girls admired such work was recognized by a group of Massachusetts stitchers who honored the girl who had knitted the most socks by giving her the military title of "Colonel." As Louisa May Alcott wrote in her diary at the start of the Civil War in April of 1861: "I long to be a man, but as I can't fight, I will content myself with working for those who can."[41]

From Auburn, Fanny wrote to her father about the patriotic fever gripping the town. "All is excitement here . . . the merchants have hung their windows with tricolors—flags are flying from public and private houses—every day there is a presentation of a bible [sic] or a sword or revolver to the captain or someone of the companies."[42]

Fanny's brother Will, like thousands of other young men, was eager to enlist. Edgar Titus, the brother of Fanny's friend Mary, signed up right away, and "Mrs. Titus takes it bravely," noted Fanny. Even pastors were stiffening spines and gathering recruits from the pulpit. Father Creedon of the Church of the Holy Trinity thundered that "every man who did not go was a traiter [sic] and a coward," pointing out potential volunteers in his congregation with "'I want that man,' & 'that man' till when he was through he was able to march fifty recruits to the place of enlistment."[43]

Standing under the awning of the Auburn coal office, Fanny was one of "thousands" who had gathered flowers and assembled to send off those enlistments. When the troop cars appeared, Fanny stood on tiptoe among the crowd, waving her handkerchief and peering at the "out stretched heads and arms, waving hats, and cheering lips" of the departing young men. Each recruit was trying to keep a stiff upper lip, but Fanny saw that the faces were tinged with sadness "at parting with the dearest friends and associations." Too quickly the train passed, and Auburn's young men were "on, over the bridge and out of sight," hurtling, like the nation, toward a future that could not be known.[44]

# 6

# Washington Prepares for War

As she watched the September landscape rush by, sixteen-year-old Fanny Seward was aboard yet another train. This time, she was leaving the rolling hills and sparkling lakes of the Finger Lakes region of central New York, heading through Albany, New York City, Philadelphia, and Baltimore to the makeshift army camp that Washington, DC, had become. In the fall of 1861, her father had finally deemed the capital safe enough for the family to visit.[1]

Fanny was used to trains. She knew their screeching whistles and steaming engines, their brisk conductors and their lively passengers. Reaching Philadelphia, the family changed cars, enjoying the amenities of a private coach that offered a parlor, a bedroom, and a dressing room, as well as a waiter to serve a special dinner complete with large fresh peaches.[2]

Now the view out the window indicated they were nearing Baltimore, which had become the most dangerous city in America. Fanny caught a glimpse of Union flags flying, and she also saw that some along the railroad tracks were patriotically waving their hats at the slowing train; even so, at least one woman, a rebel sympathizer, spat at their car.[3]

Now, in the fall of 1861, Baltimoreans were no longer attacking the rail lines as they had during one dreadful week the previous April, but that didn't mean Fanny's anxieties about her father's and her brothers' safety were any less intense. After all, after the firing on Fort Sumter, there were no troops protecting the capital. One general joked that the capital was protected by "a single old soldier," reliable "only when sober," and that the city could be easily taken "with a single bottle of whiskey."[4] Clearly, Washington's location, sandwiched between seceded Virginia and only marginally loyal Maryland, was precarious.

In fact, on April 19, 1861, the rowdy mob of Baltimore secessionists had prevented Northern troops from reaching the capital by tearing up the railroad tracks. Pelted with paving stones, the soldiers, Fanny wrote in her diary, "bore the ill treatment . . . until one . . . had his gun snatched from him by one of the mob, who shot him in the back—causing instant death."[5] The soldiers then returned fire. By the time the firing stopped, four soldiers and twelve civilians lay dead, and the Civil War had suffered its first casualties.[6]

That spring tragedy had been followed by the summer disaster at the Battle of Bull Run. Hoping to block the Confederate Congress from meeting on July 20 in Richmond, the North was eager for action. Besides, the original Union enlistments were for only ninety days, and Lincoln was afraid his troops would disperse before they had "a chance to smell powder." Consequently, General Irvin McDowell's soldiers were hurriedly marched to Bull Run, with disastrous results. McDowell's untrained men often broke ranks to pick blackberries or rest from the hot sun, gulping all their water in the first few hours with little prospect of getting more. On Sunday, July 21, the day appointed for battle, several congressmen and their wives even took carriages to the battlefield, accompanied by picnic baskets and bottles of wine.[7]

At first, victory seemed possible, but confusion prevailed during the course of the battle, and many of the Northern troops panicked and fled, mixing with the sightseers from the capital and creating pandemonium.[8] It fell to Fanny's father to deliver the bad news to the president. "Pale and haggard," Secretary Seward hurried to the Executive Mansion around six p.m., pronouncing that "[t]he battle is lost . . . McDowell is in full retreat."[9]

Northerners who had assumed the contest would be an easy rout were sorely disappointed. Fanny's brother Fred realized that "what went out an army" was pouring back into Washington as a "disorganized mob"[10]; the North was prepared neither for the defeat nor for the number of casualties.

As the train rolled out of Baltimore, Fanny, like most Northerners, knew now that the war would be neither short nor easy. Ever since New York City, their train had been full of recruits heading to Washington to swell the ranks of the army that was now so critical to the Union's success. Her father, ever the genial host, had invited the boarding recruits to tramp through their fancy private car on the way to their seats, slinging their knapsacks and merry spirits behind them. They had been rowdy and high-spirited, and Fanny noted that the coarser boys had been spending most of their time tipping back bottles and jugs.[11]

As Washington pulled into view, Fanny recorded the way the war had transformed the landscape. Camp tents dotted the hillsides, and Fanny saw squads of men that included her first picket guard, army sentinels patrolling the camp perimeters. She learned to her delight that nearly every regiment had one dog, but to her disgust that some of the ragtag soldiers tamed rats. When the Capitol reared its unfinished dome, the soldiers gave loud whoops and shouts,[12] and the train chugged into a city now teeming with uniformed soldiers and clopping cavalry.

As she eyed the fresh-faced troops getting off the train, rucksacks slung over their strong young shoulders, perhaps Fanny trembled to recall some of the stories about Bull Run and the struggles that awaited these green recruits. One enlistee had written his wife: "I never expected to see you again. The balls was falling around me like hail and . . . the men was falling around me like cornstalks."[13] Mary Henry, a Washington resident who watched the defeated troops drag themselves home, had recounted the story of two wounded soldiers, one Northern and one Southern, "lying side by side, attempt[ing] to bayonet each other" but so weak that they "sank back exhausted and dying."[14] Bull Run, Fanny suspected, meant the war would be longer than hoped. For the sake of these strong and lively grass-green recruits, surely Fanny hoped that prediction would prove wrong.

The Fanny Seward who stepped off the train in Washington in September of 1861 would turn sixteen at the end of the year. She had entered adolescence, a time of great change for any young person moving from childhood to young adulthood. Fanny knew she was privileged. Her father's position opened doors for all his children. There were reserved seats in Congressional galleries, dinner parties with diplomats, outings with senators and representatives. There were private railroad cars provided for the traveling Sewards, like the one she rode in to Washington. Visiting school friends were treated to privileged explorations of the city, in which they attended Mrs. Lincoln's White House receptions, visited the State Department and the Capitol, and viewed the uniform worn by General Washington when he resigned his command.[15] These were privileges unusual even for the daughters of the elite.

But despite these privileges, Fanny shared an unfortunate and universal status with the members of her generation: they were transitioning to adulthood against the background of impending war. As Fanny jostled her way through the crowded and noisy station, she could see that the changes were even more pronounced in Washington than they had been in Auburn. She could not have failed to catch the stench of a city more crowded with everything: soldiers, artillery wagons, even flies. The view from her carriage offered a landscape transformed by warehouses, supply depots, and ammunition dumps. Even the late summer heat, so renowned in muggy Washington, probably seemed even more oppressive than usual.

When Fanny had first become a teenager at age thirteen, her father had written to her that she was blessed to have been born in "so stirring a time, when such great issues faced the people, and when a generation was alive to deal for all time"[16] with those issues. As she bumped along crowded Washington streets transformed by war, the young Fanny Seward, perhaps, wasn't so sure.

When Fanny and her mother and her sister-in-law Jenny arrived for this twelve-day visit to a Washington outfitting itself for war, they were also visiting the house on the east side of Lafayette Square for the first time.

In the square stood the impressive statue of General Andrew Jackson, his horse rearing back on its hind legs. Despite Tad Lincoln's calling it the "tippy toe" statue, there was nothing about Jackson that tiptoed around war or political confrontation. Dedicated in 1853, the statue offered words on its base as relevant in 1861 as they had been in 1830: "Our Federal Union. It Must be Preserved."[17]

Fanny's father had moved into the home in May. The townhouse was a boxy red brick that was tall, narrow, and deep. Containing three stories and a dormer floor,[18] the house was ideally located, close to the White House and the State Department. With the rest of the family, Fanny explored the new home, peeking into the parlors and bedrooms; the library and dining room; the dressing rooms and the pantry; the kitchen, laundry, servants' quarters, and stables. Fanny especially delighted in the garden designed by brother Fred and his wife Anna that now blossomed with geraniums, roses, heliotropes, and passion flowers.[19]

After supper, and still in her traveling clothes, Fanny and her sister-in-law were rushed across the square to meet President Lincoln in the Executive Mansion, the nineteenth-century name for the White House. Fanny was excited to meet the president she had heard so much about. As her father hurried her into an informal introduction in what Fanny described as either an office or a library, Fanny declared that Lincoln "received us very cordially" and that she liked him "very much."[20] Naturally, during this first introduction, Fanny had time to compare Abraham Lincoln, the most important man in Washington, with her father, his second in command.

Historians of the Civil War have often documented the characteristics of Abraham Lincoln and William Seward, but in the fall of 1861 Fanny Seward had the opportunity to assess their differences first hand. Surely Fanny, with her gift for observation, would have been struck by the size differences of these two political powerhouses. Next to her father, a slight and scrawny man whose stature was unimpressive, Fanny must have found Lincoln's size disconcerting. When seated, Lincoln had been described as looking about the same size as most men, but when he unfolded his lanky limbs like a carpenter's rule and rose to greet a visitor, his impressive height was revealed.[21]

Fanny was familiar with her father's ways of walking and talking. He walked with the bouncy gait of a schoolboy,[22] and his voice was husky and sometimes hoarse.[23] But as Lincoln crossed the room to greet Fanny, she would have noticed what at least one historian had observed: there was little spring in his step, as if he preferred plodding to walking.[24] Now, meeting the president for the first time, Fanny would have heard a voice that was thin and high-pitched, carrying what another historian called a kind of "metallic ring."[25] Neither man, she now knew, possessed the grace of a dancer or the melodious voice of an orator.

Fanny's introduction to Lincoln was an unpretentious one. Sharing a love of animals with the president he served, William Henry Seward had given a welcome-to-Washington gift to Lincoln far different from the conventional silver candlestick or crystal vase. Instead, Fanny's father had presented Lincoln with a pair of kittens, and Fanny eagerly watched with her father as President Lincoln showed off the cats. As Fanny observed them frolicking in the grand halls, she learned from Lincoln that he delighted in the cats so much that he willingly encouraged them to climb all over him.[26] Imaginative Fanny could have created a story about a wartime president bent over the latest military orders, one cat perched at his feet, another one perched on his shoulder.

The days that followed were a whirlwind of adventure for Fanny. Her father, ever the welcoming host, took a special interest in his daughter. Fanny visited the State Department offices of her father and brother Fred. There she saw the original Declaration of Independence and was measured at five feet, four and three-quarters inches for her passport; on another visit she would view the large bundle of telegraph messages her father had received every two minutes on the day of the battle of Bull Run. Fanny's father also accompanied his daughter and daughter-in-law Jenny on a special visit to Fort McHenry in Baltimore. Here the young women climbed the ramparts, visited the magazine with its stores of ammunition, saw scores of spikes and spears and mortars and balls, and peered into the gaping mouth of one of the Columbiads, huge cannons that could fire shells weighing

350 pounds.[27] Clearly, Fanny's father was making it possible for her to experience a world far different from Auburn.

During this visit, sixteen-year-old Fanny took almost daily carriage tours of Washington and the surrounding area, witnessing the Northern effort to defend its capital city and recording her observations in her diary. She heard the sound of cannons and saw streams of smoke. She noted that the fortifications all around Washington had so changed the landscape that even long-time residents lost themselves among the earthworks.[28] She saw that the army was even making use of the kitchen in the basement of the Capitol, where a man on the east front side was making bread, "stirring it like mortar in barrels, & bringing water for it by the pailful."[29]

Even more in evidence was the Northern effort to build an army. Following the disaster at Bull Run, General George McClellan, the new commander of the Army of the Potomac, was charged with the defense of Washington. His mission was to turn the rowdy and undisciplined recruits Fanny had seen on the train into soldiers. As Fanny witnessed the ceaseless drills of squads and regiments, she understood that it was a monumental undertaking.

Fanny watched as the raw recruits were taught to use their firearms and bayonets. She observed the dress parades which were held every evening in each regiment. Fanny surely knew that General McClellan was drilling his soldiers so hard that one volunteer was heard to grumble, "For God's sake kill us off in battle, and don't do us to death as jack mules." On a visit with the Twenty-third Pennsylvania Volunteers, Fanny thrilled to the cheering for the president and Secretary Seward, the cheers so loud that they startled the horses. In a more somber review, Fanny faced her first battle-scarred troops. They were members of the Second Wisconsin, which had lost a hundred and fifty men at Bull Run. Sensitive Fanny despaired at the sight of this "broken regiment."[30]

On most afternoons during their visit, Mr. Lincoln accompanied Fanny and her family members on their carriage rides. In fact, by the fall of 1861 on this first visit to a capital at war, Fanny could not have failed to notice that her father and Lincoln had become exceptionally close. During Lincoln's first year in the Executive Mansion, the president spent more time with Seward than with any other person in Washington, including Mr. Lincoln's own family.[31]

As the horses pulled the carriage, kicking up dust as they clip-clopped across the unpaved Washington streets, Fanny and her family would come to learn that Lincoln and Seward had much in common. Both were lawyers and avid readers. Both loved the theatre, animals, and young people. Both men were also keenly ambitious, and as rivals for the presidency, they had every reason to distrust one another. Yet Lincoln, setting rivalry aside, recognized Seward's talent by offering him a place in his cabinet; Seward, uneasy being the subordinate, accepted the appointment, learning to yield to the authority of the president who offered it. Above all, both were matchless politicians, adroit at balancing the fork-tongued serpent of Northern politics: the one-sided passion of the radical Republicans for emancipation, against the one-sided passion of the Democrats for union.[32]

As they rode out in the presidential carriage in the afternoons, observing Washington's preparations for war, Fanny had an opportunity to observe her father and his president at close range. Still, even loyal Fanny could call neither of them handsome. Fanny, of course, was familiar with her father's appearance: his pallid skin, his red hair, his jug-handle ears, and his lively blue eyes. But she also was familiar with the many jokes made about his most distinguishing feature: his prominent hooked nose. Unable to avoid becoming a subject of comic commentary, Seward's protuberance was said to have made him look like "a jocular bird"; a quip circulated that if Seward's face were painted green and his beakish nose tinted yellow, he could be exhibited as a parrot.[33] The parrot analogy applied to Seward's personality as well, for Fanny's father, a garrulous, voluble man, loved to talk.

But now, viewing him at close range, Fanny understood that no one could call Abraham Lincoln good-looking, either. Ordinary soldiers were not afraid to take their measure of their commander-in-chief. One enlistee with the Second New Hampshire Regiment called Lincoln "as homely as a hedge fence," and another soldier offered that he was "not very Pritty." Similarly, the way he dressed did nothing to enhance his appearance. When Lincoln appeared in New York for his famous Cooper Union address, an observer noticed that a trousers leg hiked up about two inches above his shoe, his arms hung much longer than his sleeves, and his hair stuck out "like rooster's feathers." But Fanny was aware that her father was hardly a stylish dresser, either. Even though men's fashions in this era were usually simple, her father insisted on wearing a frock coat, unaware that the laughable addition of a handkerchief tail waving like a flag from the back pocket of his unstylish pantaloons failed to achieve the sprightly effect he sought.[34] The pair of leaders—one short and gnomish, the other tall and giant-like—must have occasionally inspired laughter as they rode together to inspect the troops, young Fanny by their side.

During these and other afternoon carriage rides, Lincoln sought Seward's counsel, often extending those counsels with visits to the Seward parlor in the evenings. During conversations before the Seward fireside, the men reaffirmed their congenial political attitudes. Both men shared a passion for the Union. Both men shared similar ideas about slavery. Both men were indefatigable in their prosecution of the war.[35] Both men benefited from and enjoyed their long relaxed discussions about these and other important issues. Soon the political congeniality blossomed into friendship. On those evenings when Lincoln sought relief from the pressures of war by visiting at the Seward home, it didn't hurt that both men loved to laugh, and as they regaled each other with jokes and stories to relieve the pain of these terrible days of civil strife, the blossoming friendship between Lincoln and Seward became a comfort for them both.[36]

But there was one important person who did not approve of the growing friendship between Lincoln and Seward, and that was Mary Lincoln, the president's wife. In a scene recorded in her diary for September 9, 1861, young Fanny Seward was able to observe Mrs. Lincoln's disapproval at first hand.

The memorable scene opened after dinner on the Monday evening before their Thursday departure for Auburn, when the Seward family attempted to call on Mrs. Lincoln. Fanny recorded in her diary that the president's secretary, John Nicolay, escorted the family to a pre-arranged visit at the White House. They made "quite a party," recalled Fanny, a party made up of family members William and Frances Seward, Fred Seward, Fred's wife Anna, sister-in-law Jenny, and Fanny herself.

After they were shown into the blue and gold room by Edward, the Irish doorman, they were given chairs. Edward then pulled up a chair for Mrs. Lincoln and went to notify her of their arrival. Fanny's father called after Edward to tell Lincoln's young sons, Willie and Tad, that they wanted to see the cats.

"Well," wrote Fanny, "there we sat."

While they waited, Fanny heard "the loud merry laughter of the first children" echoing through the halls. But neither children nor cats presented themselves.

After "a lapse of some time," an usher appeared and said that "Mrs. Lincoln begged to be excused," for "she was *very* much engaged."

Awkwardly, one by one, the family filed out, Edward offering weakly as he ushered them into the carriage that the children could find only one of the kittens, and that one refused to come out without the other.

Honest Fanny was confused. She knew that Mary Lincoln rarely missed an opportunity to entertain; she had heard the gossip that Mrs. Lincoln "sits in state" in the evenings dressed in "ball dresses" in anticipation of "chance callers." Frankly, admitted Fanny to her diary, "it was certainly very rude to have us all seated first." The Sewards had anticipated a pleasant meeting, not a boorish snub.

In the private pages of her diary on the ninth, Fanny attempted to explain "the truth of Mrs. L.'s engagement," positing that perhaps Mrs. Lincoln "did not want to see Mother."[37] Fanny's assessment, however, was inaccurate. Most likely Mrs. Lincoln was not snubbing Mrs. Seward but Mrs. Seward's husband. After all, William Seward had been her husband's challenger for the presidential nomination, and many Americans thought of him as the real power behind the Lincoln throne.

In her book about her White House years, Elizabeth Keckley, Mary Lincoln's dressmaker, confirmed Mrs. Lincoln's disdain for Seward, noting that she had referred to Seward as a "hypocrite" who had wrapped her husband around his fingers as if he were "a skein of thread." Mrs. Lincoln was said to have been threatened by Seward's prominence and had opposed his appointment to the cabinet; perhaps she was jealous that Seward's reputation might overshadow her husband's. When she arrived in rainy Washington for the inaugural, Mary probably considered it a come-down to have had Seward escort her to the fashionable Willard Hotel. The truth was that Fanny's father was simply more familiar with Washington culture than the president-elect, who was ignorant of diplomatic protocol and unpracticed in the social graces. When Seward helped Lincoln with introductions or receptions, Mary Lincoln resented the help.[38]

Still, Mrs. Lincoln had some reason for suspicion. Fanny's father was clearly ambitious. Furthermore, as Lincoln grew closer to Seward, Mary added envy to suspicion. By the fall of 1861, when Lincoln was taking carriage rides with Seward, Mary probably begrudged Seward's inclusion on rides she had intended for the couple only. Mary likely resented the evenings Lincoln spent at the Seward home, evenings she wanted him to spend at home with her. Later, after Seward challenged the First Lady's well-known spending habits, Mrs. Lincoln's dislike for Fanny's father grew so strong that she forbade her coachman to even drive by the Seward mansion.[39]

Although Mrs. Lincoln's rudeness to the Seward family in the fall of 1861 was not justified, it reflected a pattern of behavior. She was rude to Kate Chase, the lovely daughter of cabinet member and Secretary of the Treasury Salmon P. Chase, who hosted social events that rivaled the First Lady's and barely concealed Chase's presidential ambitions. Refusing to attend Kate's 1863 marriage to William Sprague, Mary later boasted that she had not allowed herself to "bow in reverence" before "the gods Chase and daughter."[40] On a trip to visit General Grant at City Point as the war was winding down in 1865, she launched into a tirade against General Ord's wife when she saw the attractive woman riding beside President Lincoln, taking the place that should have been hers.[41]

What was most telling about the Seward family's snub from Mary Lincoln, however, was the way the Sewards reacted to the incident.

Characteristically, Fanny's father overlooked Mary Lincoln's rudeness. Like Lincoln, Seward was neither hateful nor vindictive, and both men could get along with difficult people.[42] But Fanny also overlooked the snub, generously noting in her diary that the woman who had just slighted her family was the same woman who had successfully "begged for the life of the soldier sentenced to death for sleeping at his post."[43] Clearly, Seward's spirit of tolerance had been inherited by his daughter.

Saying good-bye to the house on Lafayette Square after her twelve-day visit must have been difficult for Fanny Seward. Even more difficult than parting from the home with the lovely garden and several parlors was parting from the father who, with brothers Gus and Fred, would be left behind, living at the center of the storm that was the Civil War.

Fanny was lifted into the carriage that would take her through a city in which buildings were now barricaded with sandbags, soldiers were bivouacked in the halls of Congress, and even Mt. Vernon tour boats patrolled the Potomac as river pickets.[44] As the hooves of the horses began to clip-clop down Washington's unpaved streets, dodging soldiers on foot and officers on horseback, passing artillery and supply wagons, perhaps Fanny turned back to catch a last glimpse of the statue of President Andrew Jackson, the one that greeted her daily from Lafayette Square. Perhaps she shuddered, remembering the prescient words at its base, the words that held so much importance and so much danger: "Our Federal Union. It Must Be Preserved."

# 7

# 1862: The Dismal Year

On Sunday, September 21, 1862, Fanny Seward was facing the most miserable day of this most miserable year: her brother Will was departing for war in the morning. She had skipped church in order to extend her time with him. She had busied herself with helping him pack his trunk. Now it was Sunday evening, and Aunt Lazette and others had departed after saying their good-byes. Finally Fanny and Will had a few private moments to themselves.

Will's departure was a wrenching one for Fanny. After all, Will was the brother closest to Fanny in age, and this confident and attractive young man had always buoyed the spirits of his shy little sister. Even as a child, Will shared his father's lively vitality; seized with Gold Rush fever, the adventurous nine-year-old had hankered to follow the prospectors to California. Perhaps because he had trouble with his eyes, Will was never much of a student. More interested in building his hen house than in learning dead languages, Will preferred riding horses[1] to galloping through the pages of a book.

But William Henry Seward Jr., had matured into a responsible young man. Now it was Will who clambered to help whenever Auburn's fire alarm was sounded. It was Will who faithfully met family members at the depot on their returns to Auburn. It was Will who made nightly trips to the Auburn telegraph office awaiting war news. It was Will who looked out for the family interests in Auburn while his father and brothers were away.[2]

Naturally, when war came, this high-spirited and energetic young man desired to serve. But there were complications. Three men of the family—father William Seward and sons Augustus and Fred—were serving the war effort in Washington, so Will was the only son remaining in Auburn to watch over the increasingly fragile Frances and delicate Fanny. Furthermore, soon before the war broke out, Will had married Janet (Jenny) Watson; after June 27, 1860, Will now had responsibilities as a new husband and, not long afterward, responsibilities as a prospective father.

In fact, only ten days before Will's departure as a Lieutenant Colonel with the 138th New York Regiment, came a rare moment of joy in this dismal year: Jenny had given birth to a baby girl, Cornelia (Nelly) Margaret Seward, the family's first grandchild. "At or near seven o'clock," wrote her proud aunt Fanny, "a dear little girl was born to us." Fanny could not resist taking "sly peeps at the odd little bundle on the sofa." The proud aunt thrilled to her niece's black eyes and "long slender hands and filbert nails" like her father's.[3] Thus, when Will departed for service, he was leaving behind Fanny, his mother, his wife, and a newborn daughter.

In the spring and summer of 1862, General George McClellan's Peninsula Campaign, with its intent to take Richmond, collapsed. With alarm, Fanny's brother Fred noted that the army was suffering not only from battle casualties but from desertion, discharge, and demoralization.[4] The situation necessitated a call for three hundred thousand more troops. Will Seward, Junior, determined it was now time for him to volunteer, too.

By the fall, Will's leave-taking was particularly wrenching for Fanny because it took place while some of the bloodiest battles of the war were raging. The Southern success at Harpers Ferry, part of Lee's strategy to invade the North through Maryland, was followed quickly by the battle of Antietam. That contest, with its twenty-three thousand casualties, was considered the single bloodiest day in American military history. In it, Hugh McNeil, one of Jenny's favorite cousins, was killed, bringing the fighting home to Auburnians in a deeply personal way. Sadly, Will's departure would coincide with the solemn and emotional military funeral for young Colonel McNeil. That tragedy made Fanny's loss of Will "doubly hard to bear."[5]

Adding to her anxiety, the fresh reports of recent corpses piled like sheaves of grain had been preceded by tales of the harrowing experiences of Union soldiers which had reached Fanny's ears earlier in the year. In the spring of 1862, Fanny had heard first-hand reports of the injured recuperating from a battle at Kernstown, Virginia. Although Fanny herself had been too ill to travel there, her father, her sister-in-law Anna, and Anna's mother had visited the battlefield and the wounded soldiers being treated at nearby Winchester. Fanny's diary record of their reports was horrific:

> The wounded men were miserably provided for— . . . with no better beds than straw thrown on the floor—no food but soldiers rations [salt pork] and no ventilation . . . the only nurses were men from the ranks, to whom the work was so distasteful that a guard was necessary to keep them from running away. An effort was made to construct bunks by nailing boards together but failed, for there was not a nail to be had in all Winchester! . . . The wounds of some of the men were horrible—with one man a ball had entered his head on one side and traveled round under his forehead to the other side, forcing one eye out on a level with his nose—and this poor being yet lived . . . Such are the heart-rending details of war! Oh how long?[6]

Later, in May, Fanny recorded rumors she had heard about the treatment of Northern soldiers who had fallen into the hands of the Confederates. She told her diary that many of the wounded had been "bayoneted," one even having a leg "*actually wrenched off.*" She learned of a captain who had been "*crucified*—nailed hand & foot to a cross—by the confederate fiends—and in this state he lived a week, & when found by unionists—was still alive but died soon after."[7]

Now, on the eve of Will's departure, Fanny and Will participated in a tearful scene. Will opened his Bible and read aloud from the fourteenth chapter of St. John, the passage in which Jesus prepared his disciples for His death. "I wanted to keep a cheerful face," Fanny confessed, but in listening to her brother she was overcome by emotion. Before Will could finish his reading, the young girl who had been pained by family separations all her young life began to cry. Then Fanny escaped to the dining room where she paced up and down until she had "choked down the crying spell."[8]

Hers were not unrealistic tears. Fanny was more keenly aware of the dangers of the battlefield than most girls her age because her father had exposed her to life in the army camps around Washington. Often, Fanny knew, sons, brothers, fathers, nephews, or cousins belonged to the same company or regiment. These kinship bonds helped build morale and foster cohesion, but when such a regiment suffered battlefield casualties, both soldiers in the field and families on the home front were especially devastated.[9]

In fact, in Washington during the previous March Fanny had helped send off an Auburn regiment to join General Burnside's amphibious campaign along the North Carolina coast. Heightening her anxiety for these local boys like Edgar Titus, John Ammon, and Fred Dennis was the fearsome introduction of new iron-clad vessels like the *Merrimac* into the arsenal of Southern naval weapons. Her brother Fred had remarked on the *Merrimac*'s "huge beak, her great guns, and her invulnerable plates." To her diary Fanny confessed to visions of personally begging President Lincoln to scuttle this campaign.[10]

That same fall, on the evening of September 21, 1862, the family retired to bed, dreading the next morning, when their youngest son Will would depart. Fanny, struggling to sleep, tried to comfort herself by reading her Bible. Her eyes alighted on a random passage from Romans: "Now [may] the God of hope fill you with all . . . peace." But peace was in short supply that sleepless night.[11]

The next morning, family members steadied themselves with departing rituals. Fanny's mother helped her son on with his coat. Brother reminded sister to "Keep Mother feeling as well as you can." But as he kissed his sister good bye and walked to the gate, Will's eyes, wrote his sister, were "full of tears." Fanny's anxious eyes tracked the departing Will until he rounded a corner and she could see him no longer. Then she gave vent to tears "long repressed."[12] To separation from a father and two brothers had now been added separation from her dearest sibling, who was sent onto distant battlefields where, day and night, night and day, death or the threat of it hovered.

To Fanny's worries about Will were added her worries about her father. The month before Will's departure, Secretary Seward returned to Auburn for a respite from war during that dismal year. Fanny was alarmed, for her father looked exhausted and sick. It was Fanny to whom Seward turned during this brief trip home, spending an entire day with her by driving to Cayuga Lake, lunching along the lake shore, then visiting into the evening at Aurora and Owasco. Fanny understood that in the quiet of pleasant Auburn, he could escape the din of rumbling army wagons, clanking swords, galloping cavalry, and marching boots. But Fanny noted in her diary that her father's visit had to be cut short; he would have to rush back to Washington after only a few days' visit, having heard of another disastrous Union defeat at Second Bull Run.[13] It seemed there would be no end to the dismal year of 1862.

Since birth, however, Fanny's role in the family had been to cheer, to provide solace, and she filled that role in abundance during 1862. The public was furious at the battlefield incompetence displayed by Northern generals, and Lincoln and Seward were under bitter and unrelenting personal attack. Fanny, the young daughter to whom William Seward had always been devoted, was a critical source of comfort for him.

In fact, Fanny's father especially needed the solace of her youth and optimism during the desperate summer of 1862. He pleaded with her to write to him "cheerfully, as you are wont to do," of "boys and girls and dogs and horses, and birds that sing, and stars that shine and never weep." He added that he wished for her to "be blessed for all your days, for thus helping to sustain a spirit."[14]

Sustaining her beleaguered father's spirit had been a mission willingly undertaken by Fanny since the war began. During the fateful winter of 1860–1861, Seward had hardly had a minute to spare. He was preparing for Lincoln's inauguration and attempting to prevent civil war at a time when Southern states were seceding from the Union. Still, Seward made time to write to Fanny, even though his official correspondence numbered nearly eighty letters each day.[15] Explaining that he had no leisure at a time when "treason" was at work, he still confessed his need to hear from her, insisting almost pleadingly that "You must write to me often."[16]

While Fanny's father was working furiously with foreign diplomats to keep their nations from siding with the Confederacy, Seward wrote to Fanny about the newspaper accounts of the "great people" he had been "carrying on with," declaring to her that he loved them "much less than I do you."[17] Although he was writing to the likes of kings, queens, and ministers, Seward averred to Fanny that he valued a letter from her "more than one from any of them."[18] Clearly, the sustaining bond between father and daughter helped him endure the crippling pressures he was facing.

Fanny responded to her father with equal devotion. The teenaged Fanny was still tenderly signing her letters as "your affectionate little girl." Although still a very young woman, she was keenly aware of her father's pressing responsibilities, and she seemed to sense the sustaining power of images of home and family. In letter after letter, throughout the war, she provided him with comforting descriptions of home. As Southern states were seceding from the Union, she wrote that the horses were "fat & gay," and the squirrels, in possession of the woodhouse, had been making "a great chattering." During the period when the April crisis of Fort Sumter was mounting, she offered a vision of the song birds and the crocuses and the growing calf and the crowing chickens and the nice large eggs laid by brother Will's geese. After Sumter was surrendered and war commenced, she wrote encouragingly of the patriotic response on the home front and the Auburn citizens who wore tricolored ribbons and bonnet strings tipped with flags.[19] Her support in the dismal year of 1862, and her father's request for it, testify to the ongoing devotion between daughter and father.

Through her letters, Fanny nurtured her father's spirits in the same way that thousands of women on the home front nurtured their husbands and sons and nephews who had left for war. She was doing what a writer advised from the pages of *Atlantic Monthly*: "Fill your letters with kittens and Canaries, with baby's shoes, and Johnny's sled, and the old cloak which you have turned into a handsome gown. Keep him posted in all the village gossip, the lectures, the courtings, the sleigh rides, and the singing schools. Bring out the good points of the world in sharp relief.[20]

Still, in the melancholy year of 1862, the good points of the world were hard to find.

# 8

# Two Emancipations

Fanny was hurrying herself into her new blue silk dress, readying herself for President Lincoln's New Year's reception. The end of the year had been a blur. There had been the military disaster for the Union at Fredericksburg only two weeks earlier. That catastrophe had been followed by a political crisis that threatened to oust her father from the cabinet. From Auburn, Fanny was unclear about the details of these political machinations, understanding only that they had forced the postponement of the family's 1862 Christmas reunion. However, the doctor that was treating Jenny for a sore throat declared that her father's political enemies had engaged in a "damnable performance."[1]

On New Year's Day, 1863, as she began her morning at the White House, perhaps Fanny tried to shrug off her gloom. After all, a New Year was supposed to offer new beginnings. But gloom was something she had tried and failed to banish all last year. On a Saturday the previous spring, she confessed to "Blues yesterday & today & the day before too." A week later, she still felt "very insufficient for myself." Today, however, her father's welfare was likely uppermost in her mind. Perhaps she offered a silent New Year's wish to him, one like the wish for "happy returns" she had sent on his last birthday in May, one wishing him days "more peaceful than these."[2]

Now, readying herself for the president's New Year's reception, perhaps she silently repeated the names and countries of the diplomats who reported to her father, the secretary of state. The diplomats had grand titles like "Envoy Extraordinary and Minister Plenipotentiary," and at New Year's they appeared in their official regalia, embellished

5. Young Fanny Seward grew up within a progressive political family, coming of age during a turbulent period of American history. Collections of the Seward House Museum, Auburn, NY.

with multi-hued sashes and sparkling medallions.[3] Fanny would surely want to make her father proud by remembering details about these ministers despite their "unpronounceable names."[4]

Perhaps Fanny gave herself one final turn before the mirror, adjusting the white hat on her head. The flowers that trimmed it were of a deep, dark blue,[5] but Fanny was perhaps too rushed to notice how well the flowers complemented her blue silk dress. Forcing her lips into a smile, she concentrated on putting on her best face for her father and Mr. Lincoln's distinguished guests.

They knew not to be late, for President Lincoln's New Year's reception started promptly. Crossing Lafayette Square at eleven a.m. with her black cloak around her shoulders, Fanny was grateful to Anna and Fred for the gift of the fan; it was a lovely ivory with pink silk and spangled with steel,[6] and it might give a shy young woman something to do with her hands.

As she entered the White House, Fanny saw the long lines made up of the general public crowding the walks and snaking around the side of the building; the citizenry stamped their feet and rubbed their hands against the January cold. Fanny admired their patient waiting: they would not be admitted to shake hands with the president until the more formal part of the festivities had been concluded.

Inside the Blue Room, Fanny reminded herself to smile, wondering absently if her cheeks would hurt at the end of a day that promised much forced cordiality. Although Fanny had attended this reception before, she silently reviewed the order of events to help her remember: the first to be received was the cabinet and the diplomatic corps; the second to be admitted was the army and the navy; finally the general public was admitted.[7] If she had remembered how the motley assortment of citizens representing the Civil War public often snipped off a curtain tassel or a drapery swatch as souvenirs,[8] Fanny likely suppressed a giggle. A giggle would have been welcome; it might have muted the worries that had plagued her all year.

New Year's Day 1863 was also a day that coincided with Fanny's own "coming out," a rite-of-passage for young women of Fanny's station, an event marking Fanny's arrival at the door of womanhood. But Fanny was apprehensive about this celebration. The previous October, she had shopped for clothes for the occasion, purchasing a beaver cloak and two dresses, one a white embroidered muslin and the other a reddish purple silk. But, with the nation at war, sensitive Fanny felt guilty about buying "new and gay things for my own wear."[9]

For a shy young woman like Fanny, this formal introduction to the social world must have generated anxiety. After all, her most significant female role model had been her mother, and Frances Seward had plainly disliked prescribed socializing. "Visiting and receiving visits," she confessed to Fanny's Aunt Lazette, was "not the kind of life adapted to my taste, feelings, or constitution either physical or mental."[10]

Frances's reclusiveness, especially when in Washington, was carefully recorded in her daughter's diaries. Fanny made note of a number of social engagements which her mother refused, whether for health or other reasons. When an elaborate Washington ball was given by the departing Lady Napier, wife of the British ambassador and one of William Seward's closest diplomatic friends, Fanny, Anna, Will, and her father attended the grand occasion, but Fanny's mother did not[11]; when the family attended a hop at the Willard Hotel, they went without Frances.[12]

Even when Frances did make an appearance, she was described as "pale and withdrawn." Many were the times when distinguished visitors came to the Lafayette Square house and Frances stayed upstairs or "received in her room." Fanny's diary remarks took note of her mother's being "up but not well." This condition presumably implied that Frances was feeling better, but not so well that she would be expected to socialize.[13]

Such attitudes cannot have been helpful to the quiet girl "coming out" in January of 1863. Her mother had described previous New Year's celebrations as "the turmoil."[14] She had characterized the round of socializing in Washington as "the life to which I am doomed."[15] If so, perhaps her attitudes doomed her daughter as well. Torn between her garrulous father and her retiring mother, Fanny must often have felt conflicted.

Even so, Fanny gamely received the guests in her new plum-colored dress at her family's own reception on Lafayette Square. They included countless senators and government officials, scores of generals conducting the Northern war effort, and heaping handfuls of foreign ministers. At the end of a day of importance in her young life, a day marking her transition to womanhood, shy Fanny scribbled only a modest notation about it in her diary. "Today," she quietly wrote, "was my 'coming out' occasion."[16]

But Fanny's coming out on January 1, 1863 coincided with a more momentous event, an event of historic significance: the official signing of the Emancipation Proclamation. That morning, Fanny's father and her brother Fred had brought the document from the State Department for Lincoln's official signature at the White House.[17] According to Lincoln's young secretaries, John Hay and John Nicolay, the signing of the document itself was an informal event. In fact, Lincoln had not finished revising the document before the White House reception began.[18]

But if the signing itself was calm, the political events that preceded it had been tumultuous. For decades before the war and in the years after it began, what to do about slavery was the vexing problem that yielded no solution. The slavery question, noted Fanny's brother Fred, was like "the flourish of the red cloak at a bullfight."[19]

After the Northern battlefield defeats during the summer of 1862, Lincoln recognized that the purpose of the war needed to be enlarged beyond that of restoration of the Union. To that end, Lincoln had held a Cabinet meeting in the summer of 1862 to discuss the idea of freeing the slaves by proclamation. After heated debate, Lincoln decided to proceed, but Fanny's father opposed issuing such a proclamation immediately. To Seward, timing was everything. Issuing the proclamation after so many battlefield defeats, he argued, would look like the desperate act of a desperate cause. More politic, Seward suggested, would be to withhold the act until after another Union victory so that the proclamation could be "borne on the bayonets of an advancing army, not dragged in the dust behind a retreating one."[20] Lincoln agreed to wait.

Signing the document on January 1, 1863 would make freedom for the slaves official, and the witnesses to Lincoln's signature included Fanny's father and her brother Fred. At noon they had carried the historic proclamation in a portfolio to the White House, wending their way through the crowds outside, joining the president upstairs, and spreading the document before him on the Cabinet table.[21]

All morning, however, Lincoln had been on duty in the Blue Room, vigorously shaking hands before he had to affix his signature to the critical document.[22] Fanny's brother Fred reported that Lincoln hesitated after first dipping his pen in the inkwell; he had been shaking hands for so long that his arm was now numb and stiff. Fred recalled that Lincoln hesitated because he didn't want to leave any signs that his hands might have trembled. After all, Lincoln's signature on this historic document would be scrutinized for generations to come, and he did not want them to detect any "reservations in the handwriting." For posterity's sake, Lincoln wanted the signature to be unwavering. After a good laugh at this predicament, Lincoln made a clear signature, and Fanny's father, the secretary of state, affixed the seal to one of the most important documents in American history.[23]

Ominously, however, on the very morning when Fanny was presented to Washington society and the Emancipation Proclamation was presented to the world, she had heard a rumor circulating about an event of the night before. Although no foundation for the event was found, Fanny was sufficiently alarmed to record the rumor in her diary. "[A]n attempt," the rumor suggested, had been made "to assasinate [sic] the President, in his carriage & his coachman killed."[24]

The consequences of the Emancipation Proclamation, issued as Fanny Seward was coming out on January 1, 1863, changed the course of the Civil War. It expanded the war aims to include two goals: union *and* freedom. It also established former slaves in the rebellious states as free men and provided them with the opportunity to volunteer as Union soldiers. "After the emancipation proclamation," observed a Michigan soldier, it was generally agreed that "a black man could stop a bullet as well as a white man."[25] In fact, the Emancipation Proclamation prepared the way for the heroic military exploits of the first black Northern regiment, the heralded 54th Massachusetts Colored Regiment, famously listing two of Frederick Douglass's sons on its rolls.[26]

Throughout the war, makeshift camps had been springing up to house "contrabands," blacks who had walked away from their masters, escaped behind Union lines, or been captured by Union soldiers. Now these camps swelled with scores of African American contrabands newly freed by the proclamation. Established on an acre of ground in the fall of 1862, one camp near Washington, DC housed over a thousand contrabands in converted cavalry stables.[27] In her diary for January 4, 1863, Fanny made note of a little group of such contrabands that she saw on the way home from church. Her awareness heightened by the signing of the Emancipation Proclamation of only a few days before, Fanny was drawn to this group making its way from Virginia to a Washington camp, each person carrying a "very touching little bundle of worldly possessions." Each woman, Fanny observed, "carried a baby," and half-grown children "trotted" along behind. A few soldiers marched along with them, and bringing up the rear was a wagon laden with goods, "a lively little black face peeping out from the topmost layer." This march was undoubtedly the "[r]esults of the proclaimation [sic]," concluded Fanny, whose diary celebrated this poignant picture of "[t]he old & young, the strong & hale, the broken & feeble" all tramping along to "Freedom."[28]

In March, Fanny learned more details about the contrabands and their camps during a visit with Emily Howland, a former teacher at Washington's School for Colored Girls and a former Christmas dinner guest of the Sewards. Howland had begun teaching in a Washington contraband camp in January of 1863, witnessing first-hand the suffering of the African Americans who found their way there. She was acquainted with the leaking stable roofs, the lack of heat and clean bedding, and the outbreaks of tuberculosis and smallpox.[29]

On Howland's visit to the Seward home, she provided details about the camp and anecdotes about the mistreatment of some former slaves. Fanny recorded these incidents in her diary. One mistress, Howland reported, had pinched their noses with "red hot tongs," blacking over the burns to keep them undetected. She had also used her scissors handles to pinch their ears "till they were all worn and slit." In addition, Fanny recorded with horror another incident involving a Southern lady who was reputed to have beaten a girl "till her back was covered with blood" for the offence of reading a book, her mistress threatening to kill her if she attempted to read again.[30]

Thus, Fanny Seward's entrée into the social world in January 1863 coincided with a sweeping political event. On her coming-out day in 1863 she had rubbed elbows with President and Mrs. Lincoln; Generals Butler, Halleck, Heintzleman, Stone, Hamilton, Thomas, and Ripley; John Nicolay and John Hay, the president's secretaries; the artist Emanuel Leutze; foreign ministers and diplomats; and Senators Trumbull of Illinois, Howard of Michigan, Wade of Ohio, and Foster of Connecticut.[31] But, more importantly, the slaves for whom all social progress had been blocked were now liberated. Fanny enriched the historical record by recording her experiences as she stepped into the receiving lines, the parlor gatherings, and the handsome carriages of Washington's social and political elite; at the same moment, former slaves, miraculously, also stepped into history for the very first time.

# 9

# Turning Points

Fanny's own emancipation would prove less exhilarating than that of the slaves whose emancipation she celebrated, for she was now engaged in a grinding round of receptions, open houses, or "at-homes," scheduled like clockwork throughout the week. The social world in which Fanny traveled after her debut in January of 1863 was more like sentry duty: long hours spent at a post that consisted of standing, feigning alertness, and making small talk. Her engagements paraded with almost military precision across her calendar: the president held his weekly receptions on Tuesday evenings; the First Lady received guests on Saturday afternoons; the Speaker of the House greeted guests on Friday nights. The Sewards' own weekly "at-home" receptions took place on Wednesdays at one o'clock. On one Wednesday reception day, Fanny counted over one hundred visitors. "I was exceedingly tired," she confessed to her diary, admitting that "such days are *working* ones."[1]

Such days were often boring as well. On hand along with the dignitaries were the invariably "sour looking" maidens or those who were "fat, fat, fat" and "indiffer[ent] to all efforts at entertaining" them. Often tolerance was required of those whose tongues were "never allowed to rest." Patience was necessary when seated near General Barnard at dinner; Fanny had to scream to be heard, for the general was "exceedingly deaf." Frequently, indulgence of the downright vapid and silly was expected; in this category fell Miss Lisboa, who had "a bunch of curls or frizz on the top of her head, a quantity of flowers on that, and the whole crowned by a hummingbird."[2]

Thankfully Fanny's entrée into the social world was eased by her sister-in-law Anna, her brother Fred's wife. Since 1857, Anna had become the Seward family's official Washington hostess. Anna and Fanny had grown fond of each other, and Anna, reliably gracious, helped Fanny adjust to social Washington by offering advice about small talk. When tongue-tied, Anna suggested, Fanny could always speak of the fire in the hearth or the paintings on the walls,[3] which, in the Seward home, included portraits of Washington, Jackson, and Webster, borrowed from the State Department.[4]

However, like the well-mannered young woman that she was, Fanny rarely confessed to the wearisome nature of socializing. When asked by a distinguished guest "if I did not tire of all this," meaning formal social events, Fanny responded tactfully that "we never stayed late."[5]

But leaving early was not always an option, for Fanny's attendance at grand affairs was now expected, and sometimes a single evening involved several receptions or parties. At these affairs, ladies paid special attention to dress, and Fanny's diary often captured their finery. In February of 1863, Fanny attended an elegant party given by Madame Mercier, wife of the French minister. Before the party, a hairdresser came to arrange Fanny's hair, and as the ladies passed by like jeweled flowers in their necklaces of rubies and topaz and their silks dressed with lace and diamonds, the guests sampled ices in the shapes of birds and rosebuds displayed on glass grape leaves.[6]

Now, as her own social experiences were expanding, Fanny's responsibilities in that world were intensifying. Those responsibilities sometimes included hostessing. After Anna's grandmother died, Fanny took Anna's place by presiding at a dinner party as hostess. At this affair were diplomats, generals, and senators, not to mention Henry Raymond, the influential editor of the *New York Times*. Shy Fanny attempted to fulfill her hostessing assignment competently. By her own account, she made a great effort to keep up her end of the conversations, an effort that was "quite a stretch for my tongue, which is a little unpliable by nature."[7]

But the shy girl with the unpliable tongue must have been challenged to rise to her increasing social commitments. An illustration is provided by an incident that occurred not long after her coming out. It involved John Nicolay, one of President Lincoln's young secretaries.

Although Fanny had been suffering from a queasy stomach, she was not able to put off attendance at an evening reception at the home of Lyman Trumball, senator from Illinois. The genial appearance of the familiar Mr. Nicolay heartened Fanny, for Fanny was comfortable around him. He, "like most Western people," was "always very cordial," she wrote.[8]

Cordiality would not have been a word most Washingtonians would have chosen to describe young John George Nicolay. A sober-sided native of Bavaria with only a year of formal education but with a motley assortment of experiences in print shops and newspapers behind him, he began serving as Lincoln's private secretary during the summer of 1860. Soon the job grew too large for even the diligent Nicolay, and he hired a young friend as his assistant, the sprightlier, better educated, and more cordial John Hay.[9]

After Lincoln's election, both young men went to Washington to serve Lincoln. They lived in the White House, got to know Lincoln personally, and experienced first-hand every aspect of the Lincoln presidency. By all accounts, Nicolay served his president well. To see the lion Lincoln, a visitor had to pass through the den of his secretary, the notably uncordial "bulldog in the ante-room"; indeed, the young man was often referred to as "the impassable Mr. Nicolay."[10]

Fanny met Nicolay on her visit to Washington in the fall of 1861. As her father rushed Fanny and Jenny to the Executive Mansion to meet the president, she spoke with Nicolay, "whom," she jotted in her diary, "I liked quite well."[11] The very next day, on a visit to an army camp in the company of the president, Nicolay rode in a carriage with Fanny as part of the party. In addition, it was Nicolay who escorted Fanny and her family to the infamous Mary Lincoln snubbing[12] at the White House.

Based on Fanny's frequent visits to Washington, the two young people had the chance to make each other's acquaintance, and Nicolay made occasional appearances in Fanny's diary. On the morning of her "coming out," Fanny glimpsed Nicolay at the White House reception,[13] and at another gathering about a week later, they engaged in

6. John Nicolay (to Lincoln's right) and John Hay (to Lincoln's left) served as secretaries to President Abraham Lincoln. Library of Congress.

conversation, Nicolay hinting to Fanny and Anna that he might no longer be appearing at Mrs. Lincoln's morning receptions, implying that "he & Hay were tabooed there." Understanding that Mrs. Lincoln could be "very odd," Fanny also learned from Nicolay that the First Lady would only allow the two young secretaries to sleep at the White House, insisting that they take their meals at the Willard Hotel.[14]

There is every evidence that Nicolay was attentive to Fanny and her family, and one biographer hinted that the family thought Nicolay might possibly be interested in her. This was unlikely, given that Nicolay was thoroughly absorbed in his work for President Lincoln and also quietly engaged to Therena Bates back in Pittsfield, Illinois, to whom he wrote twice a week throughout the war. Furthermore, as a suitor, Nicolay had little to recommend him. Tall but "thin almost to emaciation," John Nicolay was "hawk-faced, with thinning hair and a scraggly goatee." Nicolay was also quiet and slow to laugh; unlike his associate, the more lively and verbal John Hay, he "never said anything worth quoting." Still, Nicolay's very quiet reliability might have appealed to the equally quiet Fanny Seward, and she may have reminded him of his absent fiancée, who was also dark-haired and dark-eyed. However, in the unlikely event that Fanny herself harbored some flicker of interest in this young man, that interest was likely doused when Nicolay mistook her for a "Miss Boyd" at the president's New Year's Day reception at the White House in 1862. "[V]ery glad to [see] you, Miss Boyd," Nicolay said, Fanny explaining in her diary that he had confused her with Anna's cousin.[15]

Recognizing Fanny at the affair at Senator Trumball's, Nicolay asked if she had been in to supper, and as Fanny was stammering out a "no" and wondering how to explain her upset stomach, he offered his arm, an invitation to escort her in. Awkward Fanny hung back, stuttering that she didn't wish any supper but if she did wish it, she would be "happy to go with him," a remark Nicolay didn't quite hear. Fanny feared that she had been rude and that Nicolay might have felt rebuffed.

Making small talk after that with some other guests, Fanny continued to be aware of the proximity of Mr. Nicolay. She noticed that he was still talking nearby, standing with a young lady at the center table.

Before they could reconnect and before she could clarify the reasons for her rejection of his invitation, Senator Trumbull swept in, inviting Anna in to supper, and Senator Arnold swooped down to invite Fanny to go in, as well. Fearing being left alone, shy Fanny mumbled to Senator Arnold an inaudible remark about not caring for any supper, but was nevertheless swept along on his arm, anyway. Embarrassed and uncomfortable, Fanny spent most of the meal trying to avoid the oysters that the senator plied her with and the teasing that resulted from her refusals.

On the way out, however, John Nicolay was nowhere to be seen, and Fanny was distressed at "how rudely I must seem to have treated Mr. Nicolay." Embarrassed that the self-possession she was expected to have acquired had been "quite destroyed," Fanny poured out to her mother at home the story of her "blunder."[16]

In the faux pas with John Nicolay, Fanny's parents only made the awkward situation worse for Fanny when they decided that she must make things right with the young man. Her father intended to invite Mr. Nicolay to dinner so that Fanny could give an account of her actions to him personally. Wishing to apologize, yet dreading that humiliation, Fanny, still "sick & nervous," felt like "mountains" were being made "of all the molehills I could find."[17]

Still, Fanny's oversensitive nature also magnified the molehills. Like Hamlet, she tied herself up in knots, declaring that she felt "stale, flat & unprofitable."[18] She was castigating herself for what was a minor and forgivable awkwardness. However, because of confusion about previous dinner engagements, Seward did not have time to extend an invitation to Mr. Nicolay, and explained to Mr. Nicolay about the mistake himself. Fanny, for her part, was "heartily relieved."[19]

Soon after, however, at another party, the first gentleman she spoke to was Mr. Nicolay. With relief, she confessed to her diary that "[w]e did not allude to my performances at the Trumbulls."[20]

Although Fanny's acquaintance with John Nicolay never blossomed into romance, their sporadic friendship continued. Their paths crossed at other receptions, where they danced and agreed on their mutual admiration for Lincoln, she sharing an incident in which

Lincoln made a point of greeting a wounded soldier, he confirming that "all the president's cordiality was sincere."[21]

As Fanny prepared to leave for a summer in Auburn in May of 1863, John Nicolay stopped by to say his good-byes and leave a photograph of himself for Fanny and Jenny and Anna.[22] The Fanny Seward of whom this young man took his leave had passed through a challenging "coming out" season. It remained to be seen how well she, and the nation in which she lived, would weather the season to come.

On April 26, 1863, Fanny Seward was finally being delivered from the obligations of Washington parties. She was arriving into the heart of the Union army camp by army ambulance. As the horses slowed, Fanny had already observed recruits napping on boards and rails, an army wagon nearly upset by a pair of frantic horses, and soldiers everywhere aligned across the north bank of the Rappahannock, preparing for a move.[23]

As the snorting horses pulled up so Fanny and her sister-in-law Anna could alight, the young women learned they would be sleeping in a tent to the right of the general's. Inside, they found camp beds furnished with sheets, pillow cases, and plenty of army blankets. Fanny, with her keen eye for details, observed that they even had "a candle in a candlestick made of a turnip."[24]

During the war, Fanny's father had often exposed her to the camps and soldiers around Washington. She had sat on camp stools, wrapped herself in buffalo robes, witnessed mock skirmishes, and recorded her observations of camp life right down to the hanging newspaper and pair of pants that served as soldiers' "curtains."[25]

But this camp was different. This was no ordinary encampment; it was the camp of the Army of the Potomac, commanded by a new general and poised for fighting on the eve of battle. Fanny's father was continuing to expose her to a life far from the confines of Auburn, and Fanny Seward was thrilled.

The large party that left on Sunday, April 26, 1863, included several foreign ministers who departed for the Peninsula on the *Carrie*

*Martin*, a steamer used as a government dispatch boat to ferry President Lincoln and others to and from Washington and the army. With a comfortable cabin devoted to the ladies, the steamer first delivered the party to Aquia Creek, a military supply center. There they saw waiting transports, puffing steamers, and storehouses crowded with army supplies like muskets, ammunition, provisions, and clothing. Then the party continued to the Falmouth depot, where the spires of Fredericksburg, witness to so much bloodshed only a few months before, could be seen in the distance.[26]

Now, having been deposited via ambulance with the Army of the Potomac, Fanny and Anna laid aside their bonnets and brushed their hair. Soon "a handsome hand" reached under their tent cloth, found the supporting pole, and knocked politely. It was the hand of General Joseph Hooker himself, inquiring if the ladies were comfortable and ready for supper.[27]

Hooker was the newest commander of the Army of the Potomac, whose previous commanders had presided over military disasters. To his credit, Hooker would show skill in improving the cavalry and intelligence-gathering operations,[28] but Lincoln and Seward knew that appointing Hooker to command entailed risk. After all, the general had never been afraid to criticize his superiors, and his fondness for alcohol and women had earned him a shady reputation.

To Fanny Seward, the general who came knocking at her tent pole was, frankly, captivating. Renowned for his sparkling blue eyes, copper hair, and handsome head, Hooker was carefully appraised by Fanny. She took in the broad chest, narrow waist, and erect posture of a general who reminded her of the dashing portraits of Sir Walter Scott, adding that "Gen. Hooker is handsomer." She also confirmed the spirit of a general who had been called "a gay cavalier, alert and confident . . . and cheery as a boy." That boyish good cheer was documented by Fanny, for the hearty Hooker boasted to her that he loved sleeping in a tent or the open air, and only "took cold" by "going to Washington and occupying a bed-room."[29]

With the general in his dining tent, Fanny dined on fish, ham, bread, and warm biscuits. While they ate at a table waited on by contrabands, a band played, and the music was still playing when Fanny and Anna retired for the night.[30] Later, Fanny marveled at General Hooker's ability to serve as such a gracious host while he was plagued with so many "distracting cares, hourly increasing."[31] A major battle was only days in the offing.

The next morning, Fanny and her party were treated to the sight of an ascending army balloon and a military review of a huge camp that occupied a circumference of one hundred miles.[32] Describing the review of Sickles's corps, Fanny noted that General Hooker and his staff rode rapidly from one end of the front to the other. As they galloped across a line of soldiers that stretched for a mile and a half, each regiment in turn gave three enthusiastic cheers that were "loud and hearty." In the review, Fanny was able to see the infantry of the famous Berdan's Sharpshooters, in their dark green coats. They were led by General Berdan himself, the legendary crack shot as well as the inventor of ingenious armaments. Fanny also recorded the striking and dramatic dress of the Second Fire Zouaves.[33]

As part of the review, Fanny was regaled by the swelling music of familiar patriotic songs like "Hail to the Chief" and "The Girl I Left Behind Me." She was touched as the tattered flags and banners fluttered by, "stained, torn to ribbons, hanging in fragments—glorious with the marks of many battles." Although she delighted in the dogs that accompanied several of the regiments, ominously she noted the presence of long rows of army wagons, the ambulances with their drivers and medical assistants, and the stretchers loaded with "the painful necessities suggestive at once of suffering and relief."[34] All too soon, Fanny realized, suffering would commence, and relief would be desperately needed.

As the party departed for Falmouth and the *Carrie Martin* again, Fanny and Anna said "affectionate and regretful" good byes to their "dear tent," Fanny telling General Hooker at departure that she "never enjoyed anything more." General Hooker asked the party to "pray for pleasant weather for the army."[35] Soon Hooker would need more than pleasant weather to guarantee success.

Anchored off of Fort Monroe on the night of April 30, 1863, Fanny spent the evening twilight on the deck of the *Carrie Martin.* She was exhilarated by the air; the red, purple, and golden sunset; the gentle passing of a fishing boat; and the twinkling appearance of stars overhead. Fanny's heart was full of "joyous happiness" as she listened to the music of the Negro waiters, singing, significantly, "When This Cruel War is Over."

Sailing for Washington the next morning, Fanny learned that Hooker had crossed the Rappahannock and that firing had been heard. Fanny and the others of the party had high hopes for the army's success as they passed operations on the wharf at Aquia Creek, where camp equipage like kettles, chairs, saddles, and clothes had piled up, having been sent back by soldiers preparing to march.[36]

That night, Fanny described a blissful evening aboard a ship whose path was lit by a brightly shining and nearly full moon. The brigs and schooners, their white sails puffed with wind, floated by "like phantoms or the shadowy creations . . . in dreams." Fanny admitted that she had spent six of "almost the happiest days" she had ever known, days with a tempo and a meaning that were not lost on her. Concluding her final entry about this journey, she exclaimed: "Oh! How happy, happy, happy, we were."[37]

But whether such happiness could last was about to be tested. May 1–4 would engage the Army of the Potomac in the fearsome Battle of Chancellorsville. Even so, prospects for the Union were bright. The North had twice as many soldiers as the Confederates. The Southern forces and their animals were hungry, and it was said that the Confederates foraged for food just as their horses foraged for grass.[38] But General Hooker, who intended to surround Lee at Chancellorsville, was confident. He had bragged that "My plans are perfect . . . may God have mercy on General Lee, for *I* will have none."[39]

From Washington, Fanny worried. She spent an anxious day on Sunday, May 3, with no news from the Army of the Potomac. Eventually, the news would be grim. Soon after her return from her trip to the army, Fanny took ill, but despite her chill and high fever, she followed the news from Hooker's army that now reported "painful lists of the killed."[40] Fanny's hopes, so recently high, were dashed.

Although Hooker had planned to launch a coordinated campaign across a wide landscape that would send Lee into a retreat, Lee fiercely stood his ground, and Hooker's grandiose confidence collapsed.[41] Lee's superior tactical strategy at Chancellorsville led to a Northern defeat that was simply a slaughter.[42]

In Washington, journalist Noah Brooks said he would never forget the image of Lincoln holding a telegram and shutting the door behind him. "His face, usually sallow," the reporter noted, "was ashen in hue," like the French gray wallpaper in the room. "My God! My God!" the president cried. "What will the country say!"[43] An army surgeon was less distraught and more disgusted, declaring that the North had "an army of lions commanded by jackasses!"[44]

Fanny now returned to Auburn for the summer of 1863, where she confided to her diary about the rumor she had heard mid-June: the wily Lee had launched a "rebel raid into Penn." In fact, there was much panicked whispering about a military assault on the North. Both Fanny's brother Will and Will's friend and partner Clinton MacDougall were on furlough in Auburn. The young soldiers knew something serious was about to happen. As both Will and "Mac" prepared to scramble back to their regiments, Fanny now understood that the threat of Lee's army in Pennsylvania was real. Coming on the heels of the Chancellorsville defeat, Fanny's anxieties about the season to come were compounded during the summer of 1863.[45]

General Hooker, now relieved of his command, was replaced by General George Meade, famous for his temper. Colonel Theodore Lyman likened him to a firecracker, "always going bang at someone," his subordinates operating in a "semi-terrified state."[46] Even so, Meade was soon to prove himself a thoroughly admirable leader at Gettysburg. But until the battle was launched, Fanny worried over the "[d]iscouraging news" about the rebel invasion of the North, which continued until the end of June.[47]

Again, Fanny churned with anxiety for the safety of her brother as she watched Will and his friend preparing to depart, the two young comrades "walking down the lane together, in their citizen's dress." Fanny indulged in another moment of wishful thinking, longing for the war to be over and "things as they used to be." But the war was definitely not over, and early in July Fanny knew only that a battle was supposed to be underway. Maddeningly, however, by the Fourth of July, there was little news in the paper. In fact, Fanny called it "the gloomiest Fourth I ever knew." When Will's wife Jenny received a worrisome letter from Colonel MacDougall, scratched out in pencil and paper on his saddle, she surmised only that he and his regiment were in the ongoing battle. Later on, however, after a very anxious day, a newspaper extra offered happier news; now all in Auburn could hope that "the affairs of our country begin to brighten."[48]

Brighten they did. By Monday, July 6, family friends had rushed to the Seward house to bring the latest "telegraphic heads." Those short, staccato phrases, recorded by Fanny in her diary, confirmed that victory was at hand: "Lee ordered to retire from Penn. We hold Gettysburg—Rebels retired to Cashtown." That good news of the sixth and seventh lifted Fanny's spirits, especially as it was accompanied by word that Grant had finally captured Vicksburg as well. "*Vicksburg surrendered*," she double underlined in her diary, "*on the 4th of July*." The streets of Auburn, Fanny noted, were exploding with the joyous firing of guns and the passionate waving of flags over the news of simultaneous victories at Vicksburg & Gettysburg.[49]

Yet despite the victory at Gettysburg, the North was roiling with turmoil, and flames of anger would scorch even quiet Auburn during that hot July summer. A large stone had been thrown through the window of the north back side of the Seward house, near where it was Frances Seward's custom to read in the morning. Had Fanny's mother not arisen later that morning and had instead been sitting in her usual chair at the usual time, she would have been injured by the flying glass.[50]

The danger arose from the draft riots. Reverses on the battlefield were continuing to lead to shortages of soldiers, who were deserting or being killed in record numbers. As a result, on March 3, 1863, Congress ordered a draft. These calls for conscription as well as inclusion of abolition as a war aim were feeding the flames of a peace movement that was growing ever more strident. In fact, the North's own internal conflicts were an important source of Southern hope.[51] The discord reached its height in the summer of 1863 with a draft riot in New York City that ranks among the bloodiest urban riots in American history.[52]

The restiveness that was sweeping the North was particularly strong in the working classes, especially among the Irish in New York City. Fearing that the Emancipation Proclamation signaled they could lose their jobs to newly freed African Americans, they were also angry over the draft. After all, it exempted African Americans from the draft and permitted the well-to-do to escape conscription with a three hundred dollar payment. On Monday, July 13, a mob set fire to the draft office, the *New York Tribune* headquarters, and the homes of affluent New Yorkers. It set the Colored Orphan Asylum ablaze, completely destroying the building.[53] Five days of rioting and bloodshed ensued. Fanny's brother called it "anarchy" and a "reign of terror" in which the mob seized boats and railways and in which "peaceable citizens barricaded themselves in their houses." The atrocities mounted and included the "shooting of public officers, the burning of hospitals, asylums, and private houses, the murder of unoffending negroes, and indiscriminate pillage."[54]

The rioting even threatened small towns like Auburn, where Fanny and her mother huddled during the frightening July of 1863. Even before the draft law had been formed in the county and even before the law passed Congress, Fanny's mother had alerted her husband to the organized resistance that was mounting. In addition, vulnerable Auburn, lacking a local police or military authority, would be "at the mercy of the excited . . . multitude."[55]

Late in June, the tension between white and black in Auburn had begun to mount. It had been ignited when Dennis Scollins provoked a fight with a black servant named Williams. The resulting injuries to

Scollins, a member of the Third Artillery, were serious; they included cuts, bruises, and a concussion that the doctor predicted might be fatal. As a result, the Irish in town were furious and promised retribution. Frances Seward feared the "bloodshedding" that would follow should Dennis Scollins die.[56]

In fact, in their fury about Scollins, the Irish in Auburn made their ire personal: they threatened to burn down the Seward's South Street house because the family was "a friend of the negroes." Frances feared that some of their neighbors would wish for the Irish to "execute their threats." Fanny shuddered at the irony of her former hopes that her father and brothers might ride out the war "safe at home in quiet Auburn."[57] Now, even Auburn was no longer safe.

But Frances refused the offer that Fanny and she stay with friends until the storm blew over, determining to stay with the home that she so loved. Despite the personal danger to themselves, of greatest concern to both women, however, was the fate of "the poor colored people" who lacked protection since "few persons are willing to assist them." Fanny echoed her mother's anxiety about Auburn's black population "to whom, with all our pity, we could offer no protection."[58]

But Fanny's mother, true to her principles, moved beyond pity to outright defense, and Fanny moved with her. Frances sent her servant Nicholas and his family into the country for safety. In a daring act that showed both her alarm and compassion, Fanny's mother furnished another servant, coachman William Johnson, with a pistol to defend himself if attacked.[59] Anticipating July 23, 1863, the day of the Auburn draft, with apprehension, Frances sighed that "if all the coloured [sic] population escapes with their lives I shall be content—."[60]

Fortunately, draft day passed peacefully. Fanny credited Auburn's local citizens with the organization of a citizen's police force which contributed to the "orderly behavior" on draft day in Auburn.[61]

But now the wounded from Gettysburg had started to limp home. The citizens of Auburn were facing the grim news about the local boys wounded in the carnage. Willie Wright, a lieutenant in the Auburn unit known as Kennedy's Battery,[62] was in a very dangerous condition; he would soon be mustered out for his Gettysburg injuries. Earlier in the year Fanny had been saddened by the death of another Auburn boy, a Lieutenant Whiteside, who had been "the partner of many a pleasant dance . . . so modest & gentlemanly." Fanny felt great sympathy for the boy's mother, who had yielded "all her sons to the country's service."[63]

In the year to come, Fanny would learn of the death of another young Auburnian, Theodore Van Rennsalaer. Wounded in battle, he died the next day with his brother by his side. His death, noted Fanny, was "a sad blow to the family— . . . he was . . . not more than nineteen."[64] Later, in 1864, Fanny would also learn that Robert Perry's arm wound was worsening and that "a long bone" would be removed, making his arm "useless for the rest of his life."[65] Sadly the war was wreaking its toll of death and injury on the acquaintances of Fanny's girlhood.

But Colonel MacDougall's injuries were especially alarming. He was no mere acquaintance. He was Will's friend, banking partner, and a family favorite. Wounded at Gettysburg, "Mac" was sent to Auburn to recover. His left arm in a sling, Will's friend and business partner was able to tell the family about the battle, and Fanny provided details about his battle injury in her diary. "[H]is men were all lying down when he was struck, his height making him a prominent mark. When he felt a 'stinging' sensation in his left arm, . . . it dropped suddenly, as if broken." Binding it with a handkerchief, Mac "thrust it into his pocket, & continued in the fight, commanding a brigade, four hours—until the battle was over." Then, because he was too faint to go on alone, a comrade supported him on the mile-long walk to the field hospital, the two men dodging shells all the way.[66]

In spite of her worry about the welfare of the soldiers, Fanny and others in the North took comfort in the knowledge that Lee's greatest success at Chancellorsville was followed by his greatest failure at Gettysburg. Still, there were ominous signs yet to be understood. On the second day of Gettysburg, Mary Lincoln suffered a serious head injury from a carriage accident. Someone yet unknown had taken off the screws securing the driver's seat to the carriage in hopes, perhaps, of injuring the president.[67] Similarly, a young Confederate by the name of Lewis Powell would be wounded and captured at Gettysburg.[68] Later, on April 14, 1865, Fanny and her family would receive a menacing introduction to him.

The war may have reached a turning point, but it was hardly over.

# 10

# Loss and Consolation

Sensitive Fanny Seward would later claim that "any recital of suffering affected & haunted me." Now, growing up against the backdrop of civil war, Fanny had experienced unending recitals of suffering for both the dead and the living. Among the dead were those buried in a half dozen modest graves witnessed when visiting camps surrounding Washington during 1861; only one or two were even identified by a headboard or a name painted in black letters. Among the living was the Wisconsin soldier whose experience in battle cost him both arms but whom Fanny heralded as "young, strong & stalwart." Fanny's deepening compassion now extended to those beyond her own family. She recognized that, to their own "stricken households," the fallen were "precious."[1] Clearly, Fanny's natural sensitivities had intensified under the pressures of war.

Despite the fact that the tide was turning and that the North was likely to be the victor in the American Civil War, that victory was compromised by the calculus of loss. Loss was felt everywhere: in churches, in shops, on street corners, in fashionable parlors, and in humble farmhouses. Americans were daily bombarded by unceasing telegraph or newspaper reports about the deaths of soldiers on battlefields from Bull Run to Gettysburg. While Fanny Seward was growing up, the statistics in the record books mounted: soldiers at Gettysburg suffered the highest number of casualties; Antietam experienced the greatest number of deaths for a single day; at Cold Harbor, it took only a heart-wrenching twenty minutes for seven thousand soldiers to die.[2] Eventually, approximately 620 thousand men would die in the Civil War, more than in any other war in American history.[3] Enumerating the deaths of legions of men snuffed out in their prime like thousands of brief candles, those reports haunted not just the daughter of Lincoln's secretary of state; they haunted everyone, North and South.

Fanny Seward was only sixteen when the Civil War began, part of a generation of children and young adults growing up amid the anxiety of war and deeply affected by it. Tragically, the war had stolen the childhood innocence of Fanny Seward and others of her generation. Boys had not brandished play guns and swords; they had fired real weapons. They had not dragged wagons across the family yard but commandeered ambulances across battlefields. Girls had put down their needlework samplers to stitch blankets and socks for soldiers. They abandoned the make-believe world of the doll house and assumed the real work of managing homesteads after fathers and sons left for the battlefield.

In fact, as Emmy E. Werner has pointed out in her studies of Civil War children, thousands of young people in their teens or younger had shown up for battlefield duty. Although a minimum age of eighteen was required for all Union enlistees, between ten and twenty percent of Northern soldiers were underage. Wearing government-issue shirts with neck sizes too large and trouser legs too long, they responded to the needs of their region in outpourings of patriotic fervor. "The Star Spangled Banner" was "whistled by juveniles, . . . hammered on tin pans by small boys," . . . and even "barked" by their dogs. But both Union and Confederate war aims were served by young troops. Between 250,000 and 420,000 enlistees were estimated to have been boy soldiers.[4]

However, children experienced the Civil War from places other than battlefields. Scores of boys like fifteen-year-old Billy Bates of Ohio became prisoners of war at Andersonville, surviving on a few tablespoons of beans and some cornmeal each day. Their drinking water was from a polluted creek that doubled as a sewer. While their town was subjected to merciless shelling, more than a thousand Vicksburg children hid out with their parents in "prairie dog villages." These were caves dug into the hillsides to shelter the families of this beleaguered city. Young Lida Lord, the daughter of a Vicksburg clergyman, was terrified when a shell exploded in the middle of the rectory's dining room. The bomb crushed "the well-spread table like an eggshell, . . . making a great yawning hole in the floor, into which disappeared supper, china, furniture . . . and our stock of butter and eggs."[5]

Naturally, Southern children, whose family fields and farms served as battlefields, suffered alongside their starving parents. A Virginia girl watched her mother toast rye to extend the stores of coffee. Others made bread of ground peas. The children of a Richmond refugee subsisted on boiled turnip tops. Sadly, even the jaybird brought to entertain a sick little girl had to be turned into her dinnertime soup. Recognizing the particular suffering of children, even President Lincoln wrote a letter of sympathy to young Fanny McCullough, whose father was killed in the war. "In this sad world of ours," he wrote, "sorrow comes to all; and, to the young, it comes with bitterest agony, because it takes them unawares. The older have learned to ever expect it."[6]

But few children experienced the horror of war like that of fourteen-year-old Sue Chancellor, a Southern contemporary of Northern Fanny Seward. In 1863, Sue and her six siblings saw their house first established as headquarters for Union General Joseph Hooker and then turned into a makeshift hospital. As Confederate General Stonewall Jackson eviscerated the Union's flank, the Chancellor family cowered in the basement, hearing the screams of the dead and dying upstairs as the piano on which the children practiced their music was turned into an amputating slab. Fleeing through woods engulfed in sheets of fire, dodging gunfire with every step, they turned back to see their beloved homestead consumed by flame in an inferno called Chancellorsville, a devastating defeat for the North which would bear their family name.[7]

The Chancellor children would be forever changed by their wartime experiences. Likewise, Fanny's diary entries would record the way the Civil War wrought changes in her own adolescence, exposing her to battle-weary soldiers, wrangling politicians, chaotic events, and the turbulence of a society in the throes of war. Although Fanny's experiences would be played out in the arena of politics and not on a battlefield, the night of April 14, 1865, would rival anything witnessed by a young person during the Civil War.

That the war changed Fanny Seward as it had so many young adults of her generation was evidenced in her diary. She was no longer the puckish adolescent substituting salt for sugar at the dinner table.[8] She was no longer the carefree youngster happiest when romping with her brother Will. She no longer wrote in a neat, even schoolgirl hand but in a script that reflected a busier, sometimes frenzied, pace. By 1864, the war had brought rapid maturity to a Fanny who had come face-to-face with the tragedy of human death. Like an epidemic spreading through a neighborhood and sparing no one, the war had turned out to be "not the fine adventure . . . represented . . . by novelists and historians, but a dirty bloody mess, unworthy of people who claim to be civilized."[9] Young and old, male and female, slave and free, powerful and humble: all had to figure out how to survive the emotional chaos of war. How, one wonders, did young Fanny Seward manage to cope?

For one thing, Fanny was comforted by friendship. Her friends included Sarah How, whose family donated land for Auburn's Fort Hill Cemetery; Mary Titus, a close friend from Auburn whose brothers Edgar and Henry were also friends; and Mary Woodruff, the daughter of a prosperous Auburn merchant.[10]

But Fanny's closest and most lasting friendship was with Ellen Perry, the Auburn friend who accompanied Fanny on her father's campaign tour as he stumped for Lincoln's election in 1860. During the war, when Seward took a group of foreign dignitaries on a tour extolling the wonders of New York State, Ellen and Fanny went along, too. Fanny's diary also captured their lives in Auburn, the two friends making candy and, together with Ellen's sister Esther, playing checkers and backgammon and gazing at fashion plates. As young adults, Fanny and Ellen shared time together by looking at photographs.[11]

Ellen Perry was a friend who could be counted on for support. When the Seward family was anxiously awaiting the arrival of William Seward from his European tour in 1859, Ellen Perry visited Fanny, offering reassurances that her father would be safe. On the afternoon of the funeral of Sue Ward, Fanny's friend from boarding school, it was to Ellen Perry that the grieving Fanny wrote. Fanny attended the Auburn services when Ellen and her sister Esther joined the Baptist Church, and Ellen visited Washington when Fanny took her first communion. When Fanny confessed her loneliness to her diary, feeling she had "no human friend at hand," the remedy was a visit with Ellen. "When I see Ellen," she wrote, "how we will talk!"[12]

In addition to the solace of friendship, Fanny also found relief from the anxieties of war in reading, a comfort shared with other young people of her generation. Dora Miller, a young Vicksburg girl, sustained her spirits by reading Charles Dickens. Emma LeConte, from Columbia, Missouri, confessed to her diary that her books were "a refuge . . . from the sadness all around." In her diary, the naturally introspective Fanny confirmed that reading was a great help in "distracting attention" from the anxieties that beset her.[13]

Reading was a consolation to others of the Civil War generation who also needed distractions from the cruelty of war. Civil War-era reading material flourished. Newspapers like Horace Greeley's *Tribune* sold 176 thousand weekly copies in 1857, and magazines like *Harper's* issued 175 thousand copies per month. Books were also increasingly abundant in Civil War America. In 1834, only 449 books had been published; by 1863, nearly four thousand titles had been published.[14] During the Civil War, reading flourished.

For young women like Fanny, reading was a double blessing when it was accompanied by the presence of a friend. On her visit with the Sewards in February of 1863, Sue Ward read aloud in *Les Miserables* with Fanny. In 1861, Fanny and Ellen Perry were spending every Tuesday and Friday morning reading history together. Fanny and Ellen had long shared a habit of reading together, marking passages in poems like Tennyson's "In Memoriam," in which some parts struck Fanny as "*almost inspired*."[15]

Like others of her generation for whom publishers supplied burgeoning stacks of reading materials, Fanny was enthralled by stories of patriotic heroism, and her favorite author, Theodore Winthrop, inspired rhapsodies of praise. At the time, the heroic life story of Winthrop, now considered a minor author, captivated the American public, Fanny Seward included. Prior to the war, the handsome Winthrop had written several modestly successful books, but still seemed unsure of his destiny. After he volunteered with the Seventh New York Regiment at the start of the war, Winthrop found his calling.[16]

In his writing about the Seventh's thirty-day experience in Washington, Winthrop covered a subject that inspired ecstasies of patriotism in Fanny Seward. Winthrop described his regiment's send-off and the female handkerchiefs which "came floating down . . . from the windows, like snow," and the "pretty little gloves pelt[ing] us with love-taps." Housed in the Capitol as quarters, the young soldier quipped that the dome had been conveniently left off to provide the troops with ventilation. At the mustering-in ceremony, Winthrop beamed with pride at his fellow soldiers who had "whitened" their belts, "burnished" their arms, "curled" their moustaches, and scowled their "manliest" in order to pass muster for Uncle Sam.[17]

Sadly, Winthrop's life was cut short early in the war. In mid-June, 1861, an expedition that included Winthrop set out from Fort Monroe to confront the Confederates at Big Bethel, located between Hampton and Yorktown. At the end of the rout, the Union troops retreated, but not before a young officer tried to rally his brother soldiers. Climbing a log, the man whose hands had been made for writing, not for fighting, tried to rally his brothers. An easy mark for a Confederate sharpshooter, Theodore Winthrop became one more Union casualty.[18]

As a result, his heroic sacrifice rekindled interest in his work, and Fanny was as captivated by the young man, his writing, and his photograph as any modern teen swooning over a celebrity. Thus, in books like those by Theodore Winthrop, Fanny found an outlet for her patriotic anguish; even better, she was doubly consoled by sharing such books with a friend.

But most Civil War Americans entertained themselves in less intellectual ways. Other enticements included prize fights or lectures or amusement galleries where they could ogle snake charmers or test their firing power against fake Confederates at the "Jefferson Davis shooting gallery." They could buy sheet music and whistle tunes like "John Brown's Body," "Yankee Doodle," or "The Battle Cry of Freedom." War-weary Northerners could also visit museums, eclectic collections of everything from the sacred to the profane and far different from the museums familiar to people today. P. T. Barnum's American Museum, for instance, was renowned for its parading sideshows of freaks and curiosities. During the Civil War, however, Barnum's showmanship reached its height when he brought a captivating celebrity to public attention: Tom Thumb, the midget whose marriage held the nation spellbound. The miniature bride and groom, on their honeymoon, were honored at a reception by President and Mrs. Lincoln at the White House on February 13, 1863.[19]

Fanny, in fact, eagerly listened to all the talk of the bride and groom, both barely a few feet tall, as she substituted for Anna at a dinner party, revealing that she had been invited to a reception for the little newlyweds at the Willard Hotel the night before.[20] Fanny knew that General Tom Thumb and his bride Lavinia Warren made a sensational impression. Guests at the White House on Valentine's Day, the tiny couple only reached Lincoln's pants pockets. Even stoical John Nicolay was impressed by the way Lincoln introduced his wife to Tom Thumb and his bride. With "gentleness," reports Nicolay's daughter Helen in her biography of her father, Lincoln "took their little hands into his great one, as though they were fragile birds' eggs."[21]

However, the visit of Tom Thumb and his bride was only a momentary entertainment; when John Nicolay shared his photograph with the young Seward women in the spring of 1863, he was highlighting one of the most universal delights of the public during the Civil War era: the photographic studio. In the photographic studio, human vanity combined with technological innovation to produce one of the most appealing amusements of Fanny's time.

In 1858, Mathew Brady, whose popular studio in New York City exhibited the portraits of many famous Americans, opened a new photographic gallery on Pennsylvania Avenue in Washington.[22] Fanny Seward often visited there to view or buy photographs.[23]

When Brady was born, photographs did not exist, but by the time he died, photography had entered every facet of nineteenth century American culture.[24] His photographs of generals and politicians and artists fascinated the public and provided an important historical record. That record included the first ground-breaking photographs of war. Brady and his assistant Alexander Gardner took portraits in army tents, before field cannons, on the decks of vessels, and on bloody battlefields, bringing the Civil War to the American public in a more immediate way than newspaper reports ever could.[25]

In fact, Fanny and Gardner would eventually be connected in a chilling way: he would be the official photographer at the hanging of the Lincoln assassination conspirators, one of whom was the strapping young man who came to the door of the Seward house on the evening of April 14, 1865.

But the form of entertainment Fanny Seward enjoyed most, an enjoyment she shared with scores of Civil War Americans, was the theater. Fanny had been enamored of the theater since girlhood when, only eleven years old, she begged her father for a play theater; after it became her Christmas gift, she enjoyed drawing pictures of little actors, possibly as figures to accompany it.[26] Fanny shared her passion with her contemporaries, for in a time without radio or television or computers, the theater offered itself as the most gripping and absorbing entertainment available.

Over the years, in the company of her father or Will or Anna or Jenny or the actress Charlotte Cushman or even housekeeper Kate Barrett, Fanny collected playbills from an assortment of theater pieces: *School for Scandal*, *Othello*, *Macbeth*, and *Richard III*.[27]

In fact, Fanny's love of theater rivaled her love of books, and her critiques of the plays she attended attested to the intensity of her devotion and her ability to learn from what she saw on stage. Affected by a production of Shakespeare's *Much Ado About Nothing*, she pondered the quality of the acting well into the next day.[28] Discussing Edwin Forrest's portrayal of Othello, she noted that his performance gave "dignity" and "feeling" to a character whom Fanny had previously misjudged as only a "raving maniac." In the hands of a skillful actor like Forrest, Fanny now grasped that Othello was "a noble strong brave man—wrecked by a demon" and Desdemona, who had earlier seemed only a weak and frivolous character, emerged as a fully developed woman whose subservience could be understood as based on "custom more than weakness."[29]

Fanny was fortunate to have been born in an age when some of the finest actors and actresses of the theater flourished on the American stage; she was also fortunate enough to have either seen, met, or known a handful of them. When she saw James Murdoch perform as Charles Surface in *School for Scandal*, she was witnessing an actor near the height of his fame. On another occasion, Fanny's father called her downstairs to meet the pretty actress Jean Margaret Davenport, famous for her London performance in *The Hunchback* as well as for roles like Hester Prynne and Mary Stuart. Another well-known actor was James William Wallack Jr., whom Fanny had seen as Macbeth.[30]

Edwin Forrest, whose portrayal of Othello so impressed Fanny, was the most important male actor of the pre-Civil War era. Preeminently a Shakespearean actor whose accomplishments gained respect for the fledgling American theater, Forrest was closely identified with his interpretation of King Lear. A well-known anecdote circulated at the time about his grip on that role. When flattered for his "playing" of Lear, he immodestly proclaimed, "By God, I *am* King Lear!" Ahead of his time in the way he developed his characters, Forrest visited an insane asylum if he was to portray a madman or followed the elderly around to study their mannerisms for a more convincing portrayal of the aged. But Forrest was identified with a flamboyant, bombastic style of acting, and by the Civil War period such excesses had fallen out of favor.[31]

The theater, at the height of its popularity during the Civil War years, could count as its most enthusiastic patron President Abraham Lincoln himself. Like Fanny, he loved the theater. Like others of his time, he recognized its value as escape. As one Civil War theatergoer put it, "When we were profoundly miserable and frightened, what a relief it was to go and see Edwin Booth in *Hamlet*."[32]

In Lincoln's case, the theater became a kind of oil to pour over the troubled waters of the war. One historian described his attendance as "therapeutic theater-going."[33] In the theater, Lincoln could escape the images of young men crying out in Washington hospitals; in the theater, Lincoln could escape from the machinations of politicians and generals; in the theater, Lincoln, whose agitation over the war was constant, could put his mind at rest. "I *must*," he confessed, "have some relief from this terrible anxiety or it will kill me."[34] That relief came at the theater.

As Fanny's playbills pointed out, Shakespeare was by far the most popular playwright. President Lincoln, whose personal copy of Shakespeare's works was well-thumbed, was an especially ardent fan. In Shakespeare, as historian Doris Kearns Goodwin has noted, Abraham Lincoln found themes that mirrored the struggles of the day: "political intrigue, the burdens of power, the nature of ambition, the relationship of leaders to those they governed, . . . the dire consequences of civil strife, the evils wrought by jealousy and disloyalty, the emotion evoked by the death of a child, the sundering of family ties or love of country."[35] But those themes resonated with the broader Civil War public as well. Acted out on the stages of the Washington theaters, surely those plays confirmed for Civil War Americans like Fanny Seward and her family that they were not just observing the drama of war: they were living it.

The most significant way in which Fanny Seward coped with her difficult wartime experiences was by keeping her diary.

Fanny kept a diary for several reasons. First, as a devoted daughter, she was unusually attached to her family, and she wanted to preserve a record of her family and its life. This record-keeping impulse for diary writing had a long history. One touching example was penned in 1782 by Mary Vial Holyoke: "My Dear Child Died," she wrote, "9 A.M., which makes the 8th Child." Happier accounts were written by two nineteenth-century diarists. Jane Fiske recorded the vital statistics of her new baby Willie: "Baby weighs 12_, girth 15 inch & measures 21_." Similarly, Sarah Edes, writing on the last day of the year in 1853, attested to the fact that her son Hal "had his first bath."[36]

Fanny also used her diary to record significant events in the life of her family: the birth of Will and Janet's daughter Cornelia, the family's first grandchild; the death of Aunt Clara, the last family link to Judge Miller's era; the birthdays of her father and other family members; several family Christmases. Many of these records were embellished with Fanny's loving observations. New aunt Fanny recorded that she sang her just-born niece Cornelia "the first song she ever heard" when her little niece was less than a few days old.[37] Fanny also recorded the gift of a formal diplomatic dispatch, signed by the secretary of state, offering congratulations on the birth of his grandchild.[38] Like women before and since, Fanny took on the role of family historian.

Furthermore, Fanny's record-keeping instincts were bolstered by an age obsessed with collecting and recording. Everything from photographs to insects was gathered, arranged, documented, and shared by people living in the nineteenth century. In the Seward family this impulse was raised to an art form. The Sewards left behind important official papers, letters, mementos, photographs, paintings, silverware, and gifts from foreign visitors. Although they saved a signed letter from Abraham Lincoln and a famous painting of the signing of a treaty for the purchase of Alaska, they did not ignore more humble artifacts like a stool that became a memorial to a family dog. Aware that their possessions had historical value, they carefully labeled their photographs of visiting kings, queens, emperors, empresses, and ambassadors, photographs of those that Fanny's father had laughingly called "my tormentors."[39] Such careful cataloguing enabled future visitors to the halls of Seward House to identify those tormentors, too.

However, although Fanny dutifully took note of the letter-writing, visitor-receiving, scarf-knitting, and whist-playing that made up her days, those entries were mere asterisks in her diary. The majority of the entries described important events or people, confirming her awareness that, as the daughter of the secretary of state during a pivotal period in American history, she was living through days filled with a significance beyond the ordinary. Fanny understood that a visit to a general's army camp or a ride in a president's carriage was a remarkable opportunity. Indeed, Fanny was keenly aware that Washington, not Auburn, provided the richest material for her diary. When she was at home in placid Auburn, she often abandoned the diary, resuming it when she returned to bustling Washington where "every day has some memorable occurrence."[40] Thus, when Fanny Seward recorded her first-person experience of episodes like Hooker's camp preparations prior to Chancellorsville and Washington's victory celebrations as the war came to its blessed end, she was keenly aware of their historical import.

Although the record-keeping purposes of Fanny's diaries were evident, nineteenth-century diaries were not considered vehicles for self-discovery in the way that modern diaries are. In Fanny's day, diaries were not confessionals. They were often "semipublic documents" available to be read by an audience.[41] Diaries did not serve a private function; they were not kept under lock and key or hidden under mattresses as a secret place for revealing repressed emotions or secret assessments about other people. Only occasionally did Fanny engage in reflections that could be considered personal or private, and not a single passage offered a whiff of criticism about any of her family members. Even those not members of her family, such as Mary Lincoln or Kate Chase, were discussed with well-mannered reserve. The truth is that diaries in Fanny's day rarely remained solely in the diarist's hands; instead, they were often shared among family or friendship groups. Like the communal reading, sewing, and visiting that abounded, Civil War Americans "made virtually all their literary experiences"—even diary-writing—"into social ones."[42]

Still, a diary is always a rough sketch of an unfolding life, and Fanny's diaries marked her evolution from innocent young teen to self-aware young adult during the war years; in them can be seen the silhouette of the woman Fanny Seward was becoming. As she changed from a young girl into a young woman, the tone of her writing also changed. The sprightly young girl of the earlier entries had turned into a serious and sober young woman. For instance, a more self-aware Fanny Seward greeted her eighteenth birthday, describing it as "[a]n occasion to which I had almost insensibly looked foward [sic] as one that would change me completely, in all respects." With wry maturity, Fanny acknowledged in her diary that when the day arrived, no "alarming improvement had taken place."[43] Furthermore, as her youthful idealism was tempered by war, she came to the mature recognition that most people possess both good and bad traits and cannot be expected to have only "lofty and generous" impulses.[44]

Fanny's diaries also provided evidence of an evolving personality, one that was beginning to chart its own course. In Washington, she was now presiding over the occasional dinner or at-home with her sister-in-law, often enjoying the functions for which her mother expressed utter distaste. In addition, her diaries painted a portrait of Fanny's mature acceptance of her ill health and a desire to live well despite its interference with her happiness. Not a single passage in Fanny's diaries suggested self-pity in the face of illness; instead, her diaries revealed a kind of stalwart acceptance, an attitude that suggested that poor health was an inconvenience rather than an incapacity. Fanny shrugged off with a kind of mordant wit the infirmities of her body, unlike her mother, who rarely minimized her symptoms. Her approach to her illnesses was universally plucky. It was similar to her attitude during a drive through Rock Creek with a careless coachman threatening to upset the carriage. Unlike her mother, Fanny refused to be alarmed. She had "some fears of upsetting," she confessed, but she "contrived" to make the best of things.[45]

Another change in Fanny that occurred during the war was her attitude toward the family home in Auburn. She was still her mother's main source of solace there, but she was feeling the pull of the nation's lively capital. By 1864 she was confessing to her father that "I often fancy the pleasure of being in Washington,"[46] and she was now visiting for longer periods as often as she could, even without her mother. Unlike Frances, for whom the South Street home in Auburn served as a cocoon,[47] Fanny seemed to be emerging from that cocoon, embracing, in her own quiet way, some different life choices.

Thus, despite the losses that devastated the lives of thousands of young people growing up during a time of war, the wartime experience was often mitigated by consolations, consolations that in Fanny Seward's case took the form of friendship, reading, the photography studio, the theater, and the activity of keeping a diary. Fortunately, the diaries that have come down to us have provided a unique kind of consolation for the losses of war. Forged in the cauldron of conflict whose final product was often death, Fanny's diaries managed to leave behind a life-affirming record of an emerging young life.

# 11

# "The Work I Cannot Choose But Take"

Although Fanny Seward understood the consolations of running words like stitches across the tapestry of loss that was the American Civil War, the most important reason why she kept a diary was a personally meaningful one. Fanny was cultivating a quiet dream of her own, a dream more consoling than reading or friendship, a dream that enabled her to imagine a better future, a future beyond the turmoil of war. In the midst of an historical era destined to destroy the dreams of many, Fanny Seward held on to a dream of her own: she dreamed of becoming a writer.

That dream had been evident from a very early age, and, as a young adult, Fanny continued her fascination with "things written."[1] As a young girl who had delighted in a paper theater, she now was displaying a continued fascination with drama, and critiques of the plays she saw appeared with frequency in her diary. She had tried her hand at writing several dramatic pieces that remained incomplete, yet in May of 1862 she was beginning another dramatic scene that she hoped to finish.[2] In addition, Fanny's ability to write was being developed alongside her developing skill as a critical reader, and her diary entries confirm this significant development.

Fanny's diary during the wartime Washington years confirmed that her palette was expanding. Despite the anxieties the war had spawned, it had also provided Fanny with something every writer needs: experience. Although still the shy observer of the scene and not its lively actor, Fanny now had a great deal of experience behind her, experience on the campaign trail, experience among the political elite, and experience with a culture at war. She had developed acquaintances with ambassadors and ministers, dined often with notables in the arts and politics, watched her father handle crises both domestic and international, and engaged with soldiers and generals in their camps and forts. She had not only participated vicariously but had witnessed directly many monumental historical events: a political campaign unprecedented in history, the departure of a beloved brother into the arms of war, a series of political crises impacting the members of her family, and the erection of a ring of armed fortifications around embattled Washington that changed a familiar city into an unfamiliar fortress. Attuned to these experiences, Fanny Seward had now acquired something to say. The longer and more expansive diary entries she composed during the war years confirmed the growing catalog of her experiences, her awareness of their importance, and her determination to take good notes.

In fact, the war period was a time of expanding productivity for this blossoming young writer, and her palette owed much to her experience of the war itself. The dramatic scene she began in May of 1862 was likely the beginnings of *Laura*, a 115-page play she commenced in the summer of 1862 and likely finished that year.[3] Set against the backdrop of war, this "sentimental and patriotic"[4] play drew heavily from Fanny's own life experiences.

The drama takes place in 1862 in New York State, and it involves young Robert who has enlisted for the Union, leaving behind his sweetheart, Laura. One scene features Robert's widowed mother resigning herself, like Frances Seward, to her son's enlistment. There are scenes in camp, complete with campfire singing, that clearly reprise some of Fanny's own experiences. Naturally, like the Auburn soldiers of her acquaintance, Robert accompanies General Burnside's amphibious campaign along the North Carolina coast and is reputedly killed in the battle of New Bern. After the news of Robert's death, heartbroken Laura devotes herself to serving others by working at a contraband camp. There she teaches an African American woman to read the Bible; the character Tamar is eerily similar to the real-life Aunt

Margaret. The play ends happily, with Robert found to be alive, having been nursed back to health by the slaves who saved his life. *Laura* is only one example of the way in which Fanny Seward was turning her experiences into literature.

Although the outlines were sometimes indistinct, a silhouette was emerging from the ink-stained pages of her diaries: Fanny Seward was becoming a writer. Still, questions remained: As a writer, what were her skills? Did she have a penchant or a gift? What modes of writing attracted her? What genres held her interest? Was writing a vocation she could hope to pursue with any success?

Fanny Seward clearly possessed what every writer needs: an observant eye. Fanny's keen powers of observation were turned into a flair for description. Some of Fanny's descriptions were short and pithy. For instance, the wooden decks of the *U.S.S. Minnesota* were "as smooth & bright" as a "waxed dancing room." On a wintry walk to church, "the wind shook off the melting icicles in showers from the trees." A storm at sunset looked like "sky curtains."[5]

Other descriptions were longer and more discursive. For example, in Fanny's day the disagreeable nature of the streets of unpaved Washington, DC, was much remarked. In dry seasons, Washingtonians choked and coughed on the powdery clods ground under the hooves of passing horses. In wet seasons, the mud stained ladies' skirts and fancy slippers. Fanny, too, turned her pen to the subject of muddy Washington, providing a memorable description, circa 1863:

> [T]he mud was perfectly astonishing—thin as water—it stood like a pond where the road should be; & the gutters were flowing rivers. Army horses were wading along, knee-deep, splashing drops . . . before them, as children skip stones, breaking the surface of a sheet of water.[6]

Gazing out her windows at night, Fanny created another memorable scene:

> [T]here was a man holding a horse by the bridle, a tall soldier stepping from the door to the curb stone, the road clear, the park for a

> background, the clear, calm moon-light beautifying the scene. The handsome soldier mounted the graceful horse, & rode away over—the broad road with the moon for a lamp.[7]

Still, Fanny's best descriptions were miniature portraits of the people she was privileged to meet, people she observed at the dinner table or from the seat of a carriage, people she then described pertly and perceptively in the pages of her diary. The merry kindness of Charles King, a portrait painter who loved children, came alive in Fanny's diary, for he kept "like Santa Claus a store of pretty things" for young Fanny, pulling from his pockets the gifts of little trinkets like needle cases and perfume bottles.[8] A hostess on Fanny's visit to Fort McHenry was sketched as a "sharp featured, vinegar looking woman."[9] Kate Chase's classic beauty was underscored by its simplicity. The "only ornament" in the front of Miss Chase's chestnut hair, wrote Fanny, was "its own graceful wave."[10]

Fanny's best character portraits displayed a tone that was arch, biting, and piquant. For instance, Fanny described a Republican representative from Pennsylvania whom she "should have called handsome had he not had a satanic sort of moustache, short & curled up on each side." This devilish-looking figure was Galusha Grow, soon to be Speaker of the House. Fanny's description of the odd looking General Benjamin Butler suggested that he "would be well looking were he not *very very very* cross eyed—and his best eye half shut." When Anthony Trollope, the heralded British author, sat at the opposite end of the dinner table from Fanny, he was memorialized as merely "a great homely, red, stupid faced Englishman, with a disgusting beard of iron grey."[11] In these impious portraits, Fanny is like the quiet but observant Austen heroine on whom nothing is lost.

Sensitivity, that fine-tuned alertness to the undercurrents churning beneath the surface of life, is something else a writer needs, and Fanny's natural sensitivities, heightened in the cauldron of Civil War America, found a voice in her writing. For instance, the symbolism of war-ravaged regimental flags was apparent to Fanny Seward. She recognized that these banners, "stained, torn to ribbons, hanging in fragments," were often as wounded as the men who carried them. "One blue state banner," Fanny observed, "was now only a pole with a ragged and notched blue edge of silk."[12] Leaving Hooker's army in April of 1863, Fanny was moved by the sight of the wreck of the *Cumberland*, which had been sunk by the *Merrimac.* Paying silent tribute to those who lay buried beneath the waves, Fanny was stirred to contemplate the irony of naval battles in which the only tombstones were the sun, the waves, the quiet shores, and the blue sky.[13]

One of the most affecting passages in all of Fanny's diaries was her account of the Auburn funeral of young Hugh McNeil, which coincided with her brother Will's departure for war on September 22, 1862. This reflection combined her heightened experience of war with her gift for description and her natural sensitivity.

Colonel Hugh McNeil, a thirty-two-year-old lawyer and Yale graduate, was described by Fanny as "young, handsome, brave, and daring."[14] McNeil, a favorite cousin of Jenny's, was a member of the famed Pennsylvania unit known as the "Bucktail Wildcats," and his battlefield death was filled with heroic and patriotic drama.

In the pages of her diary, Fanny described the report of McNeil's death on the night before the battle of Antietam, which began in full on September 17, 1862. "He had just taken a piece of ground from the rebels. He had dismounted, tied his horse to a tree, and rushed foward [sic], cheering on his men; his drawn sword in his hand, his arm raised; a bullet struck him, passing through his chest from side to side." The young colonel lived only half an hour, unconscious and unable to speak.[15]

Such dying in defense of one's country was evidence of a patriotism which had become as sacred as religion to Civil War Americans: such deaths required veneration.[16] In recording the details of his funeral and burial, Fanny provided a literary veneration for young Hugh McNeil.

As Fanny wrote, the hearse and the impressive military escort waited before the gate of Jenny's family home. Inside the house, where the funeral service took place, the young man's sword, "draped with crape," stood silently in the hall. Reverend Samuel Boardman of the Second Presbyterian Church read from a scrap of paper found on the young officer before he died. "Neither mourn," it said, "nor cry," but the mourners at the service failed to heed young Colonel McNeil's unsettling directive from the grave.[17] Coming so close to her brother Will's departure for war, this memorial unleashed powerful and heartfelt words from Fanny Seward.

Fanny described the long procession to Fort Hill Cemetery accompanied by martial music; behind the hearse walked a horse left on the field of battle and draped with the young officer's overcoat as well as the haversack filled with provisions exactly as it was found on the day of the young colonel's death.[18] Fanny and those of her Civil War generation understood that such soldiers' personal possessions were *memento mori*, relics that comforted the living.[19]

At the gravesite, atop a hill, Fanny described the scene:

> The coffin, with the flag laid over it was carried to the grave and lowered. It was just sunset, a gorgeous sunset, the light tempered by falling through rich green leaves, fell like a blessing on the scene. Such brightness &, such radiance seemed to forbid the presence of grief . . . and . . . to pour upon our minds the realization of the completeness of that early finished life.[20]

The Fanny Seward who recorded the moving details of this soldier's funeral, the girl who had always loved "things written," was herself beginning to produce some written things of note.

In fact, Fanny's powers of observation and her gift for description signaled the possibility of a journalistic career; furthermore, she possessed the curiosity about the world around her that journalism required. As early as twelve years of age, she was eagerly describing the bureaus, the rocking chair, the looking glass, even the tin slop pan of the family's seaside boarding house.[21] Fanny was also plucky, unafraid to sleep in an army tent or climb a rampart. Even the gifted Anne Frank wrote in May of 1944 that she first wanted to be a journalist before she became a writer. "Whether I shall succeed or not, I cannot say, but my diary will be a great help."[22]

Without a doubt, a diary, a legitimate ledger for learning the business of journalism, was a great help to Fanny Seward, as well. But Anne Frank, unlike Fanny, lived in a time when a girl could imagine a career in journalism. In Fanny's day, such a career was almost unthinkable. There were a few female journalists, to be sure. In the 1850s, Jane Grey Swisshelm, who worked for the *New York Herald*, covered the Senate from the press gallery, becoming the first female Washington correspondent. Laura Redden, despite her deafness, made a name for herself as a journalist, but writing under a man's name. However, not until 1971 would women be permitted to join the National Press Club.[23]

Furthermore, even had such an opportunity been available, Fanny's poor health would have made it impossible for her to pursue such a career with regularity.

However, even if journalism had been available as a profession for women, Fanny lacked the necessary objectivity to become a journalist of note, even given that objectivity might not have been held out as a standard for journalists in the nineteenth century as it is today. For one thing, Fanny characteristically demonstrated a willingness to confirm her own prejudices rather than confront them. Many of those prejudices were political. An impassioned Northern patriot, Fanny never appraised the war and its participants from any side other than that of the partisan Yankee. General McClellan, the object of justifiable criticism for his reluctance to fight, was fiercely defended by Fanny. She railed about the "shameful . . . attacks upon him by the Tribune," ranting that "those who [were] so anxious for slaughter" should instead be "placed in the front ranks" to "receive the fire instead."

She failed to question the proposition that Southern ladies were shallow, obsessed with their dresses and jewels, conveniently ignoring the fact that Northern ladies, many of whose dinners, balls, and receptions she had attended, were just as addicted to elaborate finery. She took at face value the "harrowing" reports of the mistreatment of Northern soldiers that included reports of the wrenching off of limbs.[24] Thoughts of similar atrocities on the part of Union soldiers were not indulged.

Possessing a talent for observation and description but lacking the opportunity for a journalistic career and the objectivity needed to succeed in it, to what use could Fanny Seward hope to put her writing skills?

Imaginative fiction was always a possibility. After all, the nineteenth century swarmed with outstanding novelists like Hawthorne and Cooper, Dickens and Thackeray, and Fanny read many of the best writers with eagerness. Unfortunately, however, despite the scores of passages in her diary showing promise, a genuinely creative talent did not lie beneath Fanny's flair for language. The best examples of this limitation can be found in her poetry. Although memorable poetry unites creative thought with inventive language, Fanny's poetry was remarkably prosaic. Most of it was not inspired by flights of imagination but by earth-bound experience. For instance, "The Cloud Eagle" was inspired by a cloud formation suggesting the shape of an eagle. She had observed this cloud picture on a drive to and from Owasco Lake in July of 1861, soon after the Civil War had begun. In this poem, Fanny took the eagle's outspread and protective wings as an omen of success for the Union cause.[25] Another patriotic poem was Fanny's worried farewell "To the 3rd 'Seward' Artillery N.Y.S.V." Written almost a year after the war began, when the reality of a long and bloody conflict had settled in, the poem offered little more than predictable sentiments and soothing rhymes.[26]

Two poems about friendship were written during Fanny's stay in Philadelphia in the winter of 1862. "Together" was a conventional poem on friendship with syrupy sentiments and cloying rhymes,[27] but "To an Ideal Girl" was a stronger poem that showed a bit more originality. In it, young Fanny was dabbling in a different kind of non-rhyming expression and evoking a more difficult exploration on friendship.[28]

Significantly, however, during the late war period a maturing Fanny began experimenting with a more literary and imaginative form in a remarkable poem called "Kate's Thoughts." Divided into three sections or "thinkings," this extended poem, written in classic iambic pentameter, was a soliloquy in which seventeen-year-old Kate mused about her future. Although Kate's "thoughts" often involved conventional speculations about marriage and hinted that young Kate may have fallen for a considerably older man, Fanny's frank experimentation with a new form and her heightened willingness to explore a character's inner thoughts were clearly significant.[29]

Significant, too, was that Fanny's expanding interest in writing was pursued against a restrictive cultural backdrop. Fanny lived in a time when sentimentality was revered, when romanticism was flourishing, when regard for the conventions was admired, and when women were not considered to be capable of independent thinking. Given those limitations, it was plainly remarkable that a girl so young would exhibit such persistence and determination about her writing across so many years. In addition to the stories and poems she was producing, her habit of jotting daily notes in her pocket diary as a spur to memory when she had the leisure to expand on them in her diary proper suggested that Fanny was committed to devoting the necessary writerly attention to her accounts of her experiences, preferring careful exposition to careless scribbling.

Despite the restrictions imposed on women of her time and the conventions that circumscribed her opportunities, Fanny Seward persistently pursued her own development as a writer. The descriptions, the conversations, the piquant observations, the reflections on her reading and theater-going, and the strike-outs and corrections in the pages of her diary confirmed the perseverance required of any writer in any age who can ever hope to thrive. So, too, did the stories, sketches, poems, and plays that supplemented her diary as evidence of her allegiance to her craft. Although her early pieces do not mark Fanny as a writer of exceptional talent, they do affirm that she was a young woman serious about writing who, given time, was likely to grow in competence.

Perhaps, however, the real stumbling block to her potential as a writer might prove to have been Fanny's own sweet temperament. She was inveterately guileless and naïve. She was trusting and openhearted. She preferred believing in the best, not the worst, about others. Fanny's father frankly declared that his daughter was "wise beyond [her] years, and good beyond [her] sex." When she brought the ailing Mr. Ethan Warden the flowers that she knew he loved, he summed up her character: "You're a good girl Fanny as good as all the rest." Nathaniel Hawthorne, usually critical of women writers, praised the writing of Sara Payson Willis by recognizing that her *Ruth Hall* had "the Devil in it . . . the only condition under which a woman ever writes anything worth reading."[30] Whether a good girl like Fanny Seward, lacking a devilish spirit, could transcend the conventions of her age and the disposition of her nature to become a writer, a profession not always dominated by the sweet-spirited, remained to be seen.

Even so, although unlikely to achieve distinction as a novelist or playwright or poet of the first order, it is not out of the question to imagine Fanny with some kind of a writing career, for a great deal of the literature produced during the nineteenth century was written for, by, and about women. From 1850 onward, publishers laid out a smorgasbord of fiction by women on which the reading public, largely women themselves, greedily gorged.[31] While their men marched off to their factories and offices to build a new industrial society, women, chained to the home, embraced reading as a welcome escape.[32]

These women readers did not confine themselves to *Jane Eyre* and *Wuthering Heights*. They devoured shelves of domestic novels, novels by a legion of women authors with names like Alice and Phoebe Cary, Caroline Lee Hentz, Ann S. Stephens, Sarah Josepha Hale, Mary Jane Holmes, and those recognized by their pseudonyms like "Grace Greenwood" (Sara Jane Clarke) or "Fanny Fern" (Sara Payson Willis).[33] Ironically, these books were simultaneously published by men and dismissed by them as "sentimental, narcissistic, domestic, diffusely religious and female chauvinistic."[34]

Despite such dismissals, these women writers achieved enormous success, opening first a crack and then a hole in the dike that had been holding women back from literary careers for centuries. Only two years after its publication in 1850, Susan Warner's *The Wide, Wide World* was in its fourteenth edition, earning laurels as the first American best seller. Perhaps it was professional jealousy that prompted Nathaniel Hawthorne to grouse about "that d-----d mob of scribbling women." Admittedly, the subject matter of these novels confounded men. In the tradition of the modern soap opera, these books offered convoluted plots and bleak conditions that featured a female character, often a girl, struggling to mature in the face of dismal circumstances. Predictably, these novels fed on plots that prompted wellsprings of emotion in their readers: "When mother dies, and little children die, and hardships come to young dreamers, then all will wipe a tear." Cultural historian Fred Pattee noted that humorist Artemus Ward, also a successful product of the age and a favorite of Lincoln, acknowledged the male bafflement with a joke, asking, "Why these weeps?"[35]

The literary establishment, made up of men, often dismissed this fiction for its emotional sentimentalism. Somehow, the pejorative "domestic novel" came both to describe and to dismiss these works by women, for men did not yet understand the domestic world from which they sprang. "In the same way that Melville explored life's complexities in the world of a whaling vessel," noted the scholar Ann R. Shapiro, who has studied the genre, "women novelists often viewed life's conflicts among the pots and pans and bric-a-brac of a world familiar to them. Nevertheless, the subject of the novels is not domestic detail any more than Melville's real subject is whales."[36]

It was this world, the world of women's popular fiction, in which Fanny Seward would have been most likely to shine. She understood the "pots and pans and bric-a-brac" that made up the texture of a woman's life. She had a keen eye for everything from the draperies at a window to the desserts on the sideboard. She had an ability to express herself through descriptive prose. She was familiar with the theater arts, built on a foundation of dialogue and scene. She understood the world of the privileged class, which might translate into the world of a kind of novel that did not require incisive thinking or impassive objectivity. She had the practiced habit and the perseverance of a professional writer. She could ply this trade without leaving her home, observing the conventions about the conventionally homebound woman while at the same time challenging their restrictions. She could achieve some recognition in the world without stepping outside the proscribed boundaries. She could practice her hoped-for profession at times of her own choosing, picking up her pen when she was well, putting it down when she was ill.

In the novel she began on November 28, 1862 and completed on June 28, 1864, there is evidence that Fanny might have become one of those scribbling women successfully creating domestic fiction. *Tried and True* covered 225 pages and twenty-nine chapters.[37] The plot involves two sets of siblings, Ernest and Emma Keen and Marion and Claude Lemmore. It is played out against a background of the theater, artistic pursuits, New York and Europe, and a mysterious search for the identity of an unknown woman in a picture. Drawing on her own personal experience with the theater and her own artistic ambition, Fanny produced a work that, like most domestic novels, had its share of contrived coincidences that tied "everything into a nice bow."[38] Without a doubt, the creation of that completed work contributed to Fanny's knowledge of the novel as a literary form and provided experience with its demands. Astonishingly, when she completed *Tried and True*, Fanny was only nineteen years old.

To her mother, Fanny confessed that writing was "the work I cannot choose but take."[39] Whether she would become a writer could not yet be known. That she was able to do so was certain. In the final analysis, in the daily practice pages of her diary and other writings Fanny was watering and nurturing a root system that might one day flower.

# 12

# The Marriage Option

Fanny Seward was present at an unusual dinner-table conversation that took place at the family table in late January of 1863. Occurring soon after Fanny's coming out and her formal initiation into the adult world, the timing may have been fitting, but the subject matter must have shocked Fanny Seward: over dinner, Fanny's father launched the topic of Fanny's future.

Invited to the family supper was Senator Orville Browning, an Illinois politician who was a longtime friend of Abraham Lincoln. Handsome, wealthy, and a bit of a dandy, he had arrived in Washington to serve out the term of Stephen A. Douglas, who had died in June 1861.[1]

Fanny Seward was a properly conventional girl, a girl of her age and class. She understood that there were boundary lines over which a young lady never stepped. Outside the pages of her diary, conventional Fanny rarely offered an opinion that could offend; even inside the pages, she was remarkably discreet. She was more likely than most to mirror the social, political, and cultural positions laid down by her parents. She never displayed the slightest peep of rebelliousness. She was fiercely loyal to her family and happiest within its circle. She was shy by temperament and reluctant to be noticed. She dressed modestly and in a style unlikely to attract attention. She was as well-mannered in the pages of her diary as she would have been with a visitor in the parlor.

Naturally, for such a conventional girl, a conventional future was to be expected, and that future was likely to involve marriage.

But during this unusual dinner table conversation, Fanny's father revealed that when his daughter was born, he had taken out a life insurance policy to provide for her after she had grown up. The policy was intended to insure Fanny's "future comfort" completely "independent of any consideration of marriage."[2] In other words, Fanny's father intended for his daughter to be financially secure, whether she chose to marry or not.

According to Fanny's diary recollection of the conversation, Senator Browning harrumphed, putting forth a more conventional point of view. He dismissed the possibility that Fanny might remain unmarried and in need of such paternal financial protection. Browning argued that it was "best for young ladies to be married and not be left alone" because their siblings were likely to "marry & leave" them. At this remark, Fanny's father gave a knowing look to his son Augustus, his fully adult and entirely unmarried eldest son: "Some of them will," Seward mused aloud, likely winking at Fanny, "and some of them *won't*."[3]

Although the two men were discussing her future in her very presence, Fanny Seward said nothing. She "kept still," admitting to her diary that she thought it "best to be silent."[4] That Fanny kept her lips shut tight perhaps says as much about Fanny Seward's age as about Fanny Seward herself. After all, in mid-nineteenth-century America, silence was expected from a well-bred young woman, and Fanny Seward knew how to be a good girl. Yet perhaps during that silence, even Fanny dared to contemplate her future. Would it include marriage? A single life under the protection of her family? A more independent spinsterhood? A vocation as a writer?

Naturally, marriage was the most likely option for any young woman in Civil War America. Despite her father's protective insurance policy, the social world Fanny entered after January 1, 1863 offered many opportunities for contacts with potential husbands. Yet those opportunities held challenges for shy Fanny Seward. If she wished to marry, Fanny would have to become familiar with an unfamiliar and somewhat foreign species: eligible young men.

Whether she wished to marry or not, her father's political position and the social world that supported it required that Fanny learn to socialize with the opposite sex. It was not an easy requirement for her. A reception that took place soon after her debut underscored her dilemma. At that gathering, Fanny was introduced to some "flat young gentlemen" at "a loss for conversation." Naturally, the well-bred but unimpressed Fanny Seward eased the awkwardness by introducing the "inevitable" conversation about the weather. Promptly, the single young man who "agreed that it was warm" saw an opening, asking Fanny to accompany him in to supper. Firmly, she declined.[5] Perhaps solitude seemed preferable to boredom, and being alone offered a brighter prospect than indulging a bore.

More and more, however, Fanny's diaries recorded her observations and opinions about young men. A younger Fanny had early noticed that her friend Fanny Bailey had "two handsome brothers," especially Fred, the "handsome intelligent" sixteen-year-old.[6] Aboard a vessel, the pre-debut Fanny noticed the handsome steward serving lunch, "his fine figure set off by his loose, dark blue clothing."[7]

But after her coming out, Fanny was observing the opposite sex more intently, making distinctions between a man who was "well looking," her synonym for "attractive," and a man who was downright "handsome." A Captain Parker, for instance, with his "striking face," was "well-looking rather than handsome," but a young Lieutenant Colonel of Cavalry was "quite handsome," even more handsome than the good-looking General McClellan. However, a young Captain Montgomery was "one of the handsomest men I ever saw," exclaimed Fanny, noting his "dark eyes, hair & moustache, tall & graceful figure, easy yet dignified address."[8] These and other observations suggested that Fanny was not uninterested in the opposite sex, just that she had not yet learned how to negotiate a relationship with a man.

In fact, not just her diaries but her imaginative works testify to her interest in men and marriage. Her completed play *Laura* involved two lovers, Laura and Robert, who are separated by the struggles of war. Their love, intensified in the cauldron of conflict, ultimately triumphs. *Tried and True*, her completed novel about star-crossed pairs of siblings, displays a longing for love and a denouement that satisfies such yearning. Her three-part poem, "Kate's Thoughts," is an exploration of the complexities that attend romantic desire.

Increasingly, in fact, this youngest girl in a family of boys was learning to converse with young men who were not simply brothers: Fanny's tongue was becoming more pliable around young gentlemen. One case in point was a conversation she had at a party with a lieutenant colonel of the cavalry named Breton. In her diary Fanny related her conversation with him, a conversation marked by uncharacteristic ease.[9] At that same event, Fanny engaged in witty repartee with General Silas Casey, who hinted that a member of the diplomatic corps might "run away with me." Briskly Fanny replied that "I liked foreigners very well but Americans better."[10]

Two encounters with a Lieutenant Edward Walter West were recorded with care by Fanny in her diary, and they suggested not only her evolving ease in conversing with young men but also her growing interest in them. At a party at the Brazilian minister's home, Fanny wore a white embroidered muslin dress, and one of her sisters-in-law had tied Fanny's blue sash, adding the touch of blue forget-me-nots to Fanny's hair.[11] The young Lieutenant West, a member of General Casey's staff who had enlisted as a private in New York's "silk stocking" regiment when the war broke out,[12] struck up a conversation with Fanny by inquiring about her health.

In great detail, Fanny recorded their conversation in the pages of her diary. Although she confessed that she had been ill since the last party at which they had met, Fanny quipped that she had "tried the typhoid fever, like every body [sic] else." In response, Lieutenant West shared a touching story about his own experiences with typhoid in which a young slave boy saved his life by cooking chickens for him and ministering to him in his freezing tent.[13]

Fanny recorded many specifics about this lengthy conversation with Lieutenant West. The young officer offered that he had seen Fanny at the opera recently and discussed his admiration for Fanny's father. He asked if she rode horseback, and if so, he hoped to "have the . . . pleasure of inviting me to ride," gallantly offering to send a "horse & saddle." Once the music started, Lieutenant West invited Fanny to dance, and while they danced, both young people spoke of their admiration for soldiers. After confessing how much she enjoyed the conversation to her diary, Fanny revealed that the young man was engaged to Miss Casey, presumably the general's daughter. Fanny confessed that she had been "quite talkative" because it was easier to "converse with an *engaged* gentleman."[14] The implication was not that Fanny was uninterested in young men but that an eligible young man would be more likely to tie Fanny's shy tongue up in knots.

A few days later, however, as she was departing from her visit to General Joseph Hooker's camp, she saw "a young officer, in a long military overcoat hastening towards us—he smiled as if he knew us . . . ," and Fanny recognized Lieutenant West. Shaking hands, inquiring about their visit, offering that he had come to volunteer for the battle, and asking if Fanny had arrived home safely after the party at the Brazilian minister's house, the young officer—and Fanny—seemed disappointed to have their conversation cut short by Judge Goodrich, impatient to depart.[15]

This young man made no further appearances in Fanny's diary, but her records of their conversations evidenced Fanny's evolving ease in conversing with young men. Having observed the two young people, one of the women in Fanny's party at Hooker's camp even winked that "the only unmarried one among us"—meaning Fanny—"would choose a soldier for a husband."[16]

That Fanny admired young men in uniform was undeniable. There can be no doubt that soldiers, marching in the uniforms of their regiments, captured young ladies' attentions during the Civil War. Their uniforms were often as variegated as the communities they hailed from: Glengarry caps for the Highland Lads of the 17th New York Regiment or green facings for Vermont's Green Mountain Boys. There was romance in the colorful uniforms of the Zouave regiments with their exotic fezzes and pantaloons and leggings, even though commentators ridiculed the varied outfits of the early Union forces as "a circus on parade." Although both men and uniforms grew seedy and ragged as the campaigns continued, the hearts of young women could still flutter at the appearance of the dark-blue jacket and sky-blue trousers of a Northern soldier in uniform.[17]

That soldiers were honoring their duty to their country was another reason for admiring them. When Lieutenant West attested to the "quiet & satisfaction a man feels when in the army—doing all he can," Fanny agreed, acknowledging her reciprocal respect for such dutiful soldiers. After all, shirking one's duty was a moral offence. Besides, enlisting offered several benefits. It enabled young men to earn respect, to validate their worth, to gain the honor of their communities, and to make family members, especially their fathers, proud of them. Even better was the fact that they could demonstrate their manliness before wives or fiancées. "If a fellow wants to go with a girl now," one young Indiana recruit wrote in his diary, "he had better enlist." Fanny agreed. "How admirably," Fanny gushed, "the Army develops all the best part of a man!"[18]

Conversely, refusing to enlist garnered only shame. One young man who was reluctant to fight was sent a package. It contained a skirt, a petticoat, and a note. Enclosed was a blunt message from his fiancée, suggesting he had better enlist unless he wished to dress in petticoats. Fanny Seward concurred with these sentiments. To Lieutenant West Fanny confessed that, had she been "a man and able to go," she "could not live and not go to the war." For young men who refused to fight for their country, there was "shame" in "having stayed at home." Fanny even questioned the patriotism of the lively and engaging John Hay. Even though the young man was serving in tandem with John Nicolay as one of Lincoln's secretaries, Fanny wondered why he wasn't serving in the field. After all, "a man of true nobility" would have enlisted.[19]

There was also something romantic about soldiering. After all, it involved the heroic gesture of giving one's life to a cause. Acknowledging that it seemed splendidly patriotic to offer to die for one's country, young women treated soldiers as heroes, and hero-worship was a tendency lodged deep in the character of Fanny Seward. Recognizing the dangers of the battlefield, girls regularly swarmed the local train station to give the troops a patriotic send-off. Often the young ladies would exchange flowers for the souvenir of a button from a soldier's coat.[20] The wounded also collected female sympathies. For instance, Admiral Dahlgren's young son Ulric, formerly a graceful dancer, lost his leg at Gettysburg. Even so, he proudly appeared at a Washington party on crutches and in his cavalry uniform, the pretty girls swarming around "the hero who could not dance."[21]

That Fanny was sympathetic to the plight of soldiers and responsive to their needs was evidenced in a letter she wrote to her father in the fall of 1862: "This afternoon six or eight nice looking soldiers came to the door to ask for apples; their request was very readily granted, and they expressed themselves glad that this was 'Mr. Seward's residence.' Every day there are more or less of them here. The regiment is expected to leave in a day or two; how much we shall miss their blue coats in the streets!"[22]

In addition, women also served the country and showed respect for its soldiers by nursing the wounded that were sent home to recuperate. Noah Brooks, a journalist and friend of Lincoln, described the wounded as "bandaged and limping, ragged and disheveled, blackened with smoke and powder, and drooping with weakness. They came groping, hobbling, and faltering, so faint and so longing for rest that one's heart bled at the piteous sight."[23] In Washington, they arrived in the over thirty-five makeshift hospitals, cobbled together from schools and churches and government buildings, some housing over a thousand patients.[24]

The ministrations of one the era's most famous nurses, poet Walt Whitman, catalogued the wide variety of needs: some needed a few cents or some crackers; others needed writing paper and stamps; some wanted to be read to or held; others needed a laugh or a joke; some needed drink; others were heartened by a taste of figs or peaches or raspberry jam.[25] Few could resist sympathizing with the plight of these wounded men.

Fanny herself, like many women and girls during the Civil War, understood what it was to have an injured family member-turned-soldier in her midst. Her diary recorded the toll taken by the war on the physical condition of her brother Will. He fell ill with the common camp fever or typhoid fever soon after he began his service and was sent to Washington to recover in 1862.[26] In the fall of 1864, Fanny described the family home in Auburn as "a hospital." Aunt Lazette was sick, and her mother was suffering from a cough and facial pain.

Intensifying the anxiety was the presence of Will, recovering from the battle injuries. In her diary, Fanny described her anxiety at the pitiful sight of Will's hobbling around on a crutch and cane with his still-feeble friend Clinton MacDougall in tow.[27]

In September of 1864, however, Fanny stepped outside of her family circle to minister personally to soldiers recuperating in Auburn. In letters, she recounted her visits with these soldiers to her father. "We have a great many soldiers at the barracks," she wrote, "and of course more or less of them are sick." In the company of Mrs. Perry and her daughters, Fanny found "much happiness" in being able to help them. Carrying "fruit & flowers, papers and magazines—& such sick fare as the doctor allows," Fanny's visits undoubtedly cheered these young men who were "longing to see their own state again."[28]

In fact, Fanny's letters confirmed that she had begun to know and enjoy some of these young men as individuals.

> One sturdy old Methodist we called 'John Brown,' & he seemed quite pleased with the title. Another veteran, who wore a badge of honor, inscribed with the names of many battles, we at first feared might never recover; and it was such a pleasure to see him better! Some have served their time out, & will soon go home, others have six months or a year of service before them. How I should like to know what becomes of them all! One of the new recruits is very ill—consumptive. Saturday Mr Alward brought him in our wagon to his own room, & placed him in his own bed, to take care of him till his relatives come. Mr A. lives opposite Mrs Perry & she assists in nursing the patient—carrying him his meals, three times a day. So the poor fellow is sure to fare well, with two such kind nurses."[29]

A poem Fanny wrote in October of 1864 suggested that she had been deeply affected at this time by the death, either real or imagined, of a young soldier. Because Fanny's poetry was almost always grounded in real-life experiences, the poem, called "Dead! Dead?," raised some intriguing questions about Fanny's relationship to the poem's subject. Clearly, the young soldier who was being mourned throughout the poem has been killed on a battlefield, yet it was also clear that the author of the poem had been involved in a romantic relationship with him. The outpouring of grief expressed in the poem seemed both genuine and intense, as noted from some of the verses below.

**Dead! Dead?**

I

Dead, dead, did your white lips say "dead"?
Unsay the words ye dare not say again.
What means this sudden sense of shooting pain
With fiery track accross [sic] my reeling brain?
Why stand ye silent all as if in dread?
Dead! Dead?

III

Who's dead? Answer me: quickly say—
Ye shall not tell me of one cherished name—
Utter not that—it cannot be the same.
His life was—is—a flame an ever bright'ning
flame
That God gave me, to light my whole life's way.
*Dead*, dead?

IV

Still, still your lips repeat his name:
It conjures up before my waiting soul
Beautiful visions, which unfolding roll
Far back into the time when to the goal
Girls look to, panting with delight I came.
Dead, dead?

V

~~I was not yet a woman—till he smiled!~~
Not made a woman till he smiled!
He came, I strain my eyes to see him now,

I hear his voice his low-breathed lover's vow,
I feel his tender lips upon my brow.
That kiss through which I ceased to be a child.
Dead! dead!

VI

You speak his name. I see him stand
So tall, and brave, and handsome, and so strong!
The hours I pass without him are so long!
But I forget them when he comes. From wrong
He shields me, and in his I lay my hand.
Dead, dead!

IX

O Heaven! He is dead! I know at last
Why all who look on me do weep
And with such sad eyes watchful gazing keep
On me—me, almost crazed, I think. Yes, weep,
I cannot weep, you see, I loved him so.
Dead—dead.

X

He will not come to see me ~~my~~ more!
His fair face with its clear and steadfast eyes
Upon that dreadful field of battle lies,
Up-gazing at the everlasting skies,
Where God has drawn his spirit. All is o'er,
*Dead! Dead!*

XII

"God took him," say you? Will he take
Me too, do you think, God ever just,
In whom his scriptures tell us all to trust,
Who know my poor, weak heart is only dust,
And so—with such a weight of grief must break?
Dead—Dead.

XVI

God! Let some angel touch my brow
Lest I go mad! Let my beloved one fly
A moment back from that far home on high,
And kiss me, lay cool palm on eyelids dry.
Thanks, Father Merciful, I feel it now.

Dead. Dead.

XXI

Live dear one, I below will toil to rise
To thy sublime, & the dear God will let
Thee sometimes come to whisper to me yet,
And know thou'rt near me when my eyes are wet
With blessed tears. Till both, met [sic] in the
skies

Live. Live![30]

It is difficult to know what inspired Fanny to write this poem. Perhaps a young Auburn man had perished on a battlefield somewhere. Perhaps one of the ailing soldiers she had visited with the Perry sisters had died. This seems a possibility, as the poem was composed in October, 1864, a period that coincided with the girls' convalescent visits with these young men. Whether the dead soldier of the poem was someone Fanny knew or simply imagined, the intense emotion of this poem suggested such overwhelming grief that a romantic attachment between Fanny and a young soldier seemed entirely possible. Clearly the dead soldier of the poem was someone "cherished" by its author, and the mention of tender kisses more than hinted at a lover. What is even more intriguing was Fanny's declaration in this poem that this relationship transformed the narrator from a girl to a woman, a transformation in which she admittedly "ceased to be a child." Furthermore, the possibility of marriage with this soldier was underscored, as Fanny articulated that "panting with delight" in which the author of the poem confessed a movement toward marriage, "the goal / Girls look to." Still more intriguing was that Fanny gave copies of this poem to her friends Ellen Perry and Sallie Linnard, suggesting that these young women might have understood and empathized with the provenance of this poem.[31]

Clearly, Fanny's diaries established her admiration for soldiers, and her poem suggested that a desire for marriage was not out of the question. But admiration for soldiers was not unusual among young girls of the Civil War generation, and the existence of this poem did not necessarily imply an interest in marrying a soldier or anyone else. In fact, the possibility of her own marriage, only hinted at through a poem whose origin was unclear, was never mentioned by Fanny in her diaries. If it was a goal she imagined as she contemplated her future after the Civil War, she never overtly confessed to it. Yet she never denied the possibility of marriage, either.

Sensitive Fanny was also acutely aware that her marriage prospects were not especially bright. After all, she was a shy woman who was also not beautiful. Her three-part poem "Kate's Thoughts" recognizes these deficiencies as it assesses a young girl's prospects for romance. Examining herself in the mirror, Kate concludes that there is "Nought there To make / one vain!" However, in the course of the poem a Mr. Hasting or Hastings, an older man with a "king / ly man / ner" who is at least forty-nine, expresses an interest in Kate. She is touched that here is a man who "must like timid girls" such as she. Kate falls deeply in love, rhapsodizing about her new-found but unexpected "love-love-love."[32]

Even had Fanny Seward secretly nurtured a desire for marriage, her standard for an eligible marriage partner would have been an impossibly high one. After all, her ideal man was her father, and many of the young men she met seemed "flimsy and foppish."[33] On the issue of marriage, Kate Chase, the intelligent and beautiful daughter of Lincoln's secretary of the treasury, shared a mutual dilemma with Fanny Seward. In Kate's eyes, "all other men sank into insignificance when compared with her father."[34] Fanny faced the same predicament. To Fanny's way of thinking, "ordinary" men lacked advantages of "intellect, heart, and morals." Among "the men of our day," Fanny confessed that she usually found one of these qualities lacking, "excepting," of course, within "our own family."[35] It is not surprising, therefore, that the love interest in Fanny's "Kate's Thoughts" was an older man. Even if Fanny desired to be married, her search for a fitting partner was likely to prove difficult.

# 13
# The Sewards on Women

The dinner table conversation between Senator Browning and Fanny's father, to which silent Fanny listened intently and recorded in detail, revealed much about the Seward family's attitudes about marriage, the status of women, and the shape of the future for Fanny Seward.

As Fanny's father continued to explore the topic of marriage for his daughter, he openly described his own ideas about marriage to Senator Browning. Fanny captured his commentary in her diary:

> Father . . . did not want me to marry some scamp & be ill-treated. Mr. Browning thought young ladies . . . ought to look forward to marriage as a desirable event. Father thought it was a great risk & chance; that even marriage for love was as likely to prove unhappy as not, for at my age I would not be capable to [sic] understanding the character of any man.[1]

Fanny continued to sit wordlessly as this conversation unfolded. To her diary, however, Fanny revealed the real reasons for her silence.

> It was on the end of my tounge [sic] to say that in case of necessity I thought I would be able to support myself—but as he might have asked *how?* and I should have had to say something of my hopes of writing, I thought [it] best to be silent, I have a horror of appearing to class myself with the blue-stocking number. So I kept still.[2]

That confession confirmed Fanny as a conventional girl of her time, a girl who harbored, perhaps, hopes for a future vocation, yet who was afraid to assert herself as a "blue stocking," the pejorative term used to refer to literary, intellectual women,[3] distinguishing them from the "ultras," those extremists who were radical out-and-out feminists. After all, girls in the nineteenth century were expected to display merely artificial accomplishments, not genuine knowledge.[4] Although her own ambition to become a writer was a powerful one, Fanny still quivered before the prospect of becoming one of those horrid blue stockings.

An evolution into something other than a conventionally married young lady might be hard for most nineteenth century females to imagine, for few role models with self-assured voices were available to young women of Fanny's era. But Fanny was lucky. She had been born into the Seward family, a family open to unconventional ideas about women's place in the world.

Both of Fanny's parents shared a progressive outlook on the status of women. William Seward valued his wife's intelligence and always treated Frances as an equal. With spirit, William and Frances debated the grand issues of their day, and neither one withheld an opinion or diminished the other on the grounds of gender. Unlike the majority of men in his time, Fanny's father not only liked women: he genuinely respected them.

In recording her father's unconventional responses to Senator Browning's conventional views on the role of women, Fanny made clear her own attitudes in the pages of her diary. "Father maintained the woman side better than I could have done," she admitted. In fact, she concluded with satisfaction that "my dear Father is always one who takes the woman's side of the question without identifying himself with the absurd & ultra woman's [sic] rights theorists." For Senator Browning's opinion the eighteen-year-old Fanny had no use. He "quite provoked me," she insisted. The senator had "wornout notions of man, the chief end of woman." Naturally, Fanny preferred her father's "generous and manly sentiments" to the "conceited old, notions of Mr. B."[5] Such a bold declaration from a scrupulously shy young woman was telling.

Increasingly, and with some success, women had been challenging the notions of men like "Mr. B." In the early decades of the nineteenth century, a married woman was considered the property of her husband, an unmarried woman the ward of relatives. A wife could not write a will or sign a contract without her husband's consent. The professions were closed to women, and women could not hold office or vote.[6] In the two decades prior to the Civil War, when Fanny Seward was growing up, some modest changes in the laws about property rights had been made, but custom still considered a woman her husband's property, and custom also dictated that a woman not leave her house without a male escort or speak in public, especially before mixed audiences. In addition, a woman's opinions were expected to echo those of her husband, reinforcing one of the highest female virtues: submissiveness.[7]

Still, things had been changing, and a few brave women were unsubmissively stepping forward. At the time of Fanny's birth, Margaret Fuller had been holding public "conversations" in Boston to educate and empower women. Annually, Harriot K. Hunt protested to the treasurer of Boston about being forced to pay taxes without representation.[8] In 1847, Lucy Stone gave the first public women's rights address. Most notable was the 1848 Seneca Falls Convention, held not far from the Seward home. There, Elizabeth Cady Stanton and sisters Lucretia Mott and Martha Wright declared that women's rights had been too long ignored.

Women in general had gathered strength from their associations in the countless charity movements that proliferated during the 1830s and 1840s. In this age of reformist zeal, called "the heyday of crusades,"[9] women led the benevolent societies that sprang up to help the poor, the blind, the orphaned, the insane, the intemperate, the irreligious, and the illiterate. Above all, women served in the forefront of the Northern abolitionist movement, acquiring organizational and communication skills for themselves as they garnered mounting sympathy for the plight of the slave. Gradually, advocacy on behalf of the slave enlightened women to their own plight as second-class citizens.

In fact, as these activist women were discovering, there were parallels between the slaves and themselves. Few have written more dramatically about those similarities than Mary Chesnut, the daughter of a governor of South Carolina and the wife of a senator and war aide to Jefferson Davis. As the mistress of a large plantation, Chesnut, who kept a diary during the Civil War, boldly declared, "I hate slavery"[10] because it was an out-and-out "misuse of power."[11] From there, it was an easy stretch for Chesnut to outline the similarities between a slave and a wife. After all, both slaves and wives understood that their liberty was restricted, their property was not their own, their civil rights were ignored, and their dependence was complete.

Although Fanny Seward did not share the heretical views of Mary Chesnut that equated wifedom with slavery, the fact remained that Fanny was aware that ever since the decade of her birth, heated debates had swirled around women's agitation for property rights, higher education, dress reform, more liberal divorce, and their own suffrage. Fanny felt such injustices most keenly. When she attended a lecture by Thomas Wentworth Higginson, a keen advocate of rights for women as well as a thoroughgoing abolitionist, Fanny praised him for his habit of refusing to refer to "the human race as '*men*'—but always '*men* & *women*' as was right."[12]

A dinner party in December 1861 provided another example of Fanny's embryonic feminism. Kentucky senator John Crittenden, examining Florence Nightingale's picture, expressed disgust that such "a gentle lady" would enter a hospital of wounded men. After Crittenden had deplored Nightingale's actions as "a very unwomanly thing," Fanny declared to her diary that "that was enough of you, Mr. C," recording for posterity that the senator then rudely turned his head from the dinner table to "spit on the floor cloth."[13]

Ironically, Civil War women like Florence Nightingale, Clara Barton, and others were hastening the day in which women could challenge the Senator Crittendens of the world by imagining a different future for themselves. In fact, the work women had undertaken on behalf of soldiers would come to benefit themselves. Working for worthy causes like the United States Sanitary Commission became an exercise in confidence-building for women. Running relief societies required organization and leadership. Such efforts not only drew on women's previous volunteer leadership experiences on behalf of education, abolition, and temperance,[14] but they expanded and broadened that experience base for hundreds of ordinary women. During the Civil War, as women sewed, stitched, and rolled bandages, these mothers, wives, sisters, and aunts shared their collective anxieties and fears, creating a sisterhood of shared support that would serve them well in the post-war years.

The most liberating work, however, involved the services women performed in hospitals. Such services were essential, for the nation itself had become a veritable hospital. A few of the volunteers—like Clara Barton and Louisa May Alcott—were famous.[15] Most of them, however, were simply committed, compassionate female volunteers who desired to serve the war effort. That their contributions were extraordinary is indisputable. In an age in which there were no nursing schools, the achievements, for instance, of the nurses on hospital ships were impressive. Because of their skills, a July 1862 directive required that women must make up a minimum of one-third of the army nurses in general hospitals. Clara Barton, one of the most famous of the North's nursing volunteers, recognized that the prejudices against women in hospitals were dissolving. Americans were beginning to recognize that caring for the hurting and dying was no more improper for women than killing and dying was improper for men.[16]

In imagining a future for herself that might not include marriage, Fanny was aided by a number of factors: her own interest in writing, the progressive attitudes of her family, the national debate over the status of women, and the brave work of scores of individual women during the war displaying their talents at organizing relief efforts, managing the farms and businesses of absent husbands, or nursing the wounded on battlefields or in hospitals.

Fanny's emerging feminism was strongly influenced by her mother, who quietly embraced a number a progressive issues. Frances Seward was acquainted with Elizabeth Cady Stanton and had visited Locust Hill, Stanton's home, which Mrs. Stanton hailed as the "center of the rebellion."[17] In her book, *Eighty Years and More*, Elizabeth Cady

Stanton described Frances and her sister Lazette as women with "independence of character" and "great simplicity of manner."[18]

In fact, ever since the 1830s Fanny's mother had been interested in the issue of married women's property rights; after all, she and her sister Lazette would inherit a large estate from the wealthy Judge Miller at his death. In the collection at Seward House is a little booklet from 1837 about the political rights of women; in it are many highlighted sections, including text describing "the need for women to control their own estates."[19]

Naturally influenced by her mother, Fanny's sympathy with women's causes was real. In fact, in imagining a future for herself, during the war Fanny began to consider the lives of a number of single women who offered themselves as role models to a young girl still unsure of her destiny. "Washington," Fanny noted in her diary, seemed "particularly favored" with women who were able to maintain their dignity in conjunction with their unmarried state. She cited a Miss Dahlgren, sister of Captain John Dahlgren, as "a charming maiden lady" who, although "not young," was nevertheless "not old-maidish," either. Fanny confessed to admiring "these single ladies whose presence defies the term of 'old maid.'"[20]

Fanny recognized that those single but unmarried women still lived useful lives. Perhaps Fanny's idea of a "useful unmarried woman" was imparted by her mother, Frances. After reading a book called *Women of the Revolution*, Fanny's mother observed that its example served to "convert the many idle, unrefined & useless" into "persons more respectable and self reliant." After all, Frances deplored nothing more than "a young lady who has 20 new dresses made every year." Such preoccupation with "bonnets" and "cloaks" provided a young lady with little time "to devote to the comfort of others." Perhaps that is why Frances told a friend that she was raising Fanny, twelve years old at the time, "not to be married."[21] It was likely that Frances thought it more important for a woman to lead a useful life than a married one.

Fanny herself recognized the virtues of such "useful" single women. "[H]ow much good they do," acknowledged Fanny, "& how many hearts they gladden!"[22] She confessed to her mother that she was "full of hope that I may yet make my life worth the living and be of some use in the world."[23] Gradually, Fanny acknowledged that such "useful" women might become role models "in the maiden life I am perhaps to lead."[24]

Increasingly, Fanny began to mull over the possibility of leading that kind of maiden life, and she was keenly observant of those women who might serve as examples to her. Fanny's privileged position as the daughter of the secretary of state gave her the opportunity to observe several of these women up close. One of these outstanding women was Dorothea Dix.

Dorothea Dix, born in 1802, spent a miserable childhood as the daughter of an alcoholic father and a semi-invalid mother. This experience enabled her to empathize most keenly with anyone who suffered. Teaching a Sunday School class for women in a freezing jail, Dix was shocked to learn that those who were insane were housed along with drunkards and prostitutes at the hands of jailers who believed that the mentally ill had no sense of cold. Arranging heat for these suffering women, Dix went on to champion the cause of the insane, undertaking a painstaking examination of the treatment of the mentally ill in the state of Massachusetts, an examination that resulted in funds to expand the mental asylum in Worcester. Dix's crusade for better treatment for the insane earned her a well-deserved reputation as a woman with both a compassionate spirit and an iron will.[25]

When the Civil War broke out, Dix, renowned for her tenacity, was appointed superintendent of women nurses for the Union Army. At the beginning of the war, Washington had only one hospital; by war's end, there were over fifty. By the time General Jubal Early's troops arrived outside Washington in the summer of 1864, the city overflowed with wounded soldiers. Public buildings like the Patent Office and City Hall housed the wounded. Classrooms at Georgetown University had been turned into hospital wards. Even hotels and churches and private homes had become medical facilities. "A great battle like Gettysburg," wrote Fanny's brother Fred, "pour[ed] out blood like water." By 1863, Dorothea Dix had appointed more than three thousand nurses to stanch the bloody flow.[26]

But Dix, in her role as superintendent of nurses for the army, was aware of the prejudice against women working in hospitals. She knew such work was considered beneath the dignity of ladies. Most people were more comfortable seeing a woman nursing the sick and injured at home; after all, in the environment of an army hospital, women were exposed to bodily fluids, bloody discharges, and naked bodies, images fine ladies had best avoid. Better that they sit home knitting socks and rolling bandages. To combat such prejudice and to establish nursing as a serious profession, Dix set up stringent standards for her nurses. At first, she demanded that they be above thirty-five, ordinary in appearance, and exemplary in morals. These standards earned her ridicule, and, despite her impressive efforts, detractors minimized her abrasive compassion.[27]

But it was the good work of the hundreds of women themselves that defeated the prejudices against them. In looking for examples of a useful life that might not include marriage, Fanny Seward found in Dorothea Dix a worthy role model.

Fanny first met Miss Dix on the morning of March 30, 1862. Previously, Dix had been known to Fanny only by reputation. Now she met her in the flesh:

> This morning we were all sitting in the library when *Miss Dix* was shown in. She apologised [sic] for coming at such a time—but having heard that Father had been to Winchester, came to enquire what was the state of the wounded, what they needed, and to make arrangements for going there herself, with four or five nurses tomorrow—The name of Miss Dix is dear to humanity as that of one whose life his [sic] been devoted to succoring the distressed. I never saw her before—She is tall, about fifty, with oval face, and small features—does not look strong—She had a low voice—such as the watcher of sick beds should have. Her whole mind seemed filled with the sufferings of others."[28]

7. Dorothea Dix was an important humanitarian, and a role model for Fanny Seward. Library of Congress.

Those sufferings had been acute. All that spring, Stonewall Jackson had been outgeneraling the Union commanders in the Shenandoah Valley. However, at the Battle of Kernstown, Virginia, which took place on March 23, 1862, the Confederate forces had been served a rare defeat by Union troops, having been outnumbered by eleven thousand to twenty-seven hundred.[29] The Union wounded had been sent to nearby Winchester to recover.

In her diary, Fanny recorded the reports from Winchester. Although Fanny herself could not travel because she was ill, her father and others had rushed from nearby Washington to help out, and Fanny wrote down their eyewitness accounts. Fanny was appalled by the first-hand reports of the wretched conditions of the wounded soldiers. She was told that the soldiers had only strewn straw for beds and only salt pork for food. Even worse, the surgeons were "inefficient" and the wounded "not properly cared for."[30]

Unfortunately, the situation at Winchester was not unusual. Facilities for nursing the wounded from a battlefield were often makeshift and squalid. Homes or farms were routinely turned into infirmaries. One Northern soldier described a farm building turned into a field hospital. There, the farmer's hogs ate amputated arms and legs disposed of after surgery.[31]

Fanny's diary supported what Dorothea Dix knew from direct experience: that soldiers who survived the battlefield faced the additional peril of dying from their injuries or disease. As Miss Dix understood, hospital conditions were typically grim. Medical and surgical practices were still primitive. The science of bacteriology had yet to be established; antibiotics were unheard of. As a result, poor sanitary practices coupled with medical ignorance drove the death counts from dysentery, diarrhea, typhoid, and pneumonia ever higher. As one soldier put it, "Tiford fever is Rageing here verry much . . . their has been several deaths of it . . . they hardley ever get over it."[32]

Compassion for such conditions was why Dorothea Dix, in March of 1862, was gathering information at the Seward home and arranging to rush herself and her nurses to Winchester. Fanny was probably unaware of Dix's lack of administrative ability and her frequent wrangling with doctors who then became her enemies.[33] But of Miss Dix's ability to minister as a solitary crusader to an individual in need of help there was no doubt. Thus, Dorothea Dix was one of several single women who served as exemplars to Fanny Seward of their "useful" unmarried life.

The most prominent of these role models, however, was friend and actress Charlotte Cushman. Not only was Cushman the most famous actress of her day, she was also an intimate family friend of the Sewards. A confidante of Fanny's father, Cushman stayed with the Sewards when she visited Washington. In fact, while Cushman was a Seward houseguest, even President Lincoln, a theater devotee, arranged visits to the famous actress there.[34] Fanny, too, was a devoted admirer of Miss Cushman, corresponding with her when away and cultivating her friendship when nearby. Fanny's admiration was well-founded, for Charlotte Cushman was not only an extraordinary actress but an extraordinary role model for this shy young woman.

According to nineteenth-century theater scholar Faye E. Dudden, Cushman first achieved fame on the London stage in the mid-1840s, becoming a star almost overnight and eclipsing the flamboyant Edwin Forrest. She quickly flourished, achieving first admiration, then affluence, and finally adulation. By the time her friendship with Fanny was developing, however, Cushman was wealthy and retired. After 1852 she moved between a villa in Rome and a residence in London, but, a trooper to the last, she vacillated between triumphant returns to the stage and modest semi-retirements that proved how difficult it was for her to leave the limelight. During the Civil War, she held benefits, using her fame to raise money on behalf of Union soldiers. Playing Lady Macbeth on October 17, 1863, she earned over $2000 for the United States Sanitary Commission.[35]

The arrival of Miss Cushman at the Seward house was always an anticipated event, and Fanny Seward provided a physical portrait of her arrival in the fall of 1863 in her diary:

> She wore a drab travelling 'duster,' and black neapolitan bonnet, trimmed with purple—She is very stout, but also very tall—a good deal taller than myself I believe—Her hair, gray & inclined to wave a little, she wore drawn back from the sides of her face . . . On any other face than hers, hair so drawn back, at her age, would be very unbecoming, but her temples still retain a fullness, akin to that of youth. She has a massive brow, over hanging expressive eyes of blue

8. Acclaimed actress Charlotte Cushman was a close friend and role model to young Fanny Seward. Library of Congress.

or gray, a small peculiar & somewhat retroussé nose, lips firm but not prominent, a chin prominent & full both of energy & firmness—I do not know her age. Between 50 & 60. At times her face is girlish, from color & animation—again it is so full of grandeur that it cannot fail to be impressive. It is *full* of soul.[36]

Fanny's description confirmed much of what had been said about the actress's large physique, her owl-like face with its overhanging brow, and her strong chin, sometimes decried as even manly. Cushman was not beautiful, and some unkindly ridiculed her looks. For example, in an undated letter, John Nicolay, never himself admired for his manly physique, described Cushman as "the most masculine woman I ever saw" and noted that she was "getting old and ugly."[37]

But Fanny understood that the actress's expressive face possessed a unique kind of beauty. To Fanny, Cushman's face was so powerfully expressive that "each irregularity" somehow created "a beauty."[38] The fact is that Cushman's plain appearance marked her triumphs on the stage as even more remarkable.

Also remarkable was the actress's tremendous energy, despite her advancing age. Fanny Seward took note:

> Few at sixteen possess the wonderful vivacity which animates Miss Cushman—it is a lesson to young people to see in one who has had, however successful she may have become, her share of troubles—that there is no lassitude, no discontent or fatigue apparent: she seems to live as God intended life—filling each moment—and ever 'a cheerful giver.'[39]

The public's admiration for Charlotte Cushman began with a recognition of the actress's talent. Without question, Cushman's virtuosity was unparalleled. She excelled at historical roles. She played Lady Macbeth with a physicality that compared her to "a pantheress let loose." While Cushman was visiting the Seward family, Fanny was not only able to attend a rehearsal of *Macbeth* at the invitation of her friend, but she attended an evening performance from a box in the company of Lord Lyons and President and Mrs. Lincoln. Fanny praised Cushman's portrayal of Lady Macbeth, noting the way she infused her "dauntless mettle" into her "cowardly husband," suffering "everything in assuming strength." Another historical play in which Cushman excelled was *Henry VIII.* Although she played Queen Katherine as the embodiment of woman's passive suffering, a scene in which Katherine unleashed her anger against husband Henry and Cardinal Wolsey allowed her to employ her feminist indignation.[40]

That feminist indignation was part of her power. As an actress, Cushman was known for her portrayals of strong women, and, without question, the admiration of women accounted for much of Cushman's popularity. Because she was not beautiful, she entranced audiences by sheer force of talent and determination. Women instinctively understood that her body achieved on stage a recognition that was not based on appealing to the men in the audience.[41] In fact, Cushman often gave women their first glimpse of what an emancipated, independent woman looked like. Impressionable young Fanny Seward was given more than a glimpse of this model of independence.

In her diary, Fanny left an explicit record of her admiration for Charlotte Cushman. With each family visit, the friendship between Cushman and Fanny continued to grow. Fanny admired the way Miss Cushman talked politics with her father, expressing her views clearly and, unlike other women, "not crotchety or headstrong." Their evolving comfort with each other was based on trust and understanding; at Lord Lyons's dinner party, Miss Cushman, aware of the dullness of Fanny's dinner partner, gave the young woman a knowing wink across the table. When Fanny expressed an interest in one of James Russell Lowell's poems, Cushman ordered the gift of two volumes of his poetry for her.[42]

The two women enjoyed long walks and long talks together, sharing intimate details about their lives and families that cemented their friendship. Fanny declared that their time together was "among the most delightful memories I possess." During one conversation, Cushman expressed curiosity about Gus's silences and later learned of his similarity to his grandfather, Judge Miller, a man known for his "remarkable diffidence." Fanny confessed that "I can put my hand in hers or take that strong arm, and feel so confident. . . . That great heart of hers is full of warm affection & tenderness."[43]

Innocent Fanny, however, probably did not know that Cushman was deeply attracted to other women. Cushman had shared a twenty-year relationship with sculptor Emma Stebbins. Had Fanny ever gone to Rome to visit her idol, she might have learned of Cushman's other well-known affair with the American sculptor Harriet Hosmer, which took place between 1858 and 1865. Thumbing her nose at the Victorian conventions, Hosmer openly drove her own carriage, dressed in men's garments, and even rented her own space where uncovered models could pose.[44]

However, during the Civil War years, a close relationship between women was usually considered an intense friendship rather than a same-sex "perversion." Homophobia about such relationships that labeled them as "congenital inversions" or "Boston marriages" did not appear until the 1880s or 1890s, and the word "homosexual" did not appear in the language until 1892. In any event, Cushman was "discreet" about these female friendships.[45]

At a time when Fanny Seward's personality was maturing, Charlotte Cushman served as an especially fine role model of the independent woman. Unlike Fanny, Cushman was no shrinking violet. She was ambitious and proud of her fame. She knew what she wanted and how to get it. She possessed a savvy suspicion of grasping theatre managers and egotistical actors. She could be as manipulative as the men with and for whom she worked. She learned how to appeal to the respectable middle classes, especially its women. She rubbed shoulders with the Brownings and the Carlyles in England and the Longfellows in America. She was a success not only in the box office but in the world at large. She achieved success, to be sure, but she kept her selfishness and her tough side from the public, carefully carving out a persona that made her name synonymous with greatness.[46]

From her family, Fanny Seward learned to respect an independent woman; from Charlotte Cushman, she was privileged to share an intimate friendship with one in the flesh.

# 14

# Connections to Catastrophe

As the war moved toward its final curtain, few could have predicted that the conclusion of the Civil War would end in tragedy, a tragedy that would touch even gentle Fanny Seward. Yet chilling connections to the catastrophe to come abounded in the final period of the war. Viewed from history's perspective, there were tantalizing connections among those who would be assassins, victims, and participants in the events of April 14, 1865. One of these involved Fanny Seward's personal introduction to Ford's Theatre.[1]

After the Athenaeum, Ford's original Washington theater, was gutted by fire, John Ford was determined to rebuild it. When the new 2,400-seat Ford's Theatre was reopened in August of 1863, it was proclaimed to be a "magnificent new Thespian temple."[2] In an eerie premonition of things to come, Charlotte Cushman brought Fanny and Anna along on a tour of Ford's new theatrical temple on October 10, 1863, a tour thoroughly described by Fanny in her diary.[3]

Warmly welcomed by John Ford and his brother Harry, the group made a lengthy tour that allowed Fanny to make note of improvements like the chairs replacing the "long, cushioned seats" and the lighting that came from the "windows all around." Taking a "door-way back of the lower boxes," the group finally reached the stage, where Fanny looked up to marvel at "[s]tory upon story" of "complicated pulley work—all connected with stage machinery."[4]

At stage right, Fanny and the others saw the prompter's box and directions to the carpenters about scene changes. At stage left, they saw the "green room" where "the actors are expected to be in readiness when the call boy is sent, about a page & a half before their cues."

After visiting the green room, where Fanny was puzzled to have seen "nothing green," she was taken to the "star dressing room, a pretty little room conveniently furnished with bureau, wash-stand, . . . chairs, sofa, carpet & lights." When the group was finished with the tour, Mr. Ford invited Miss Cushman to bring a party to a play, offering to give her a double box.[5]

Ironically, prior to the fateful night of April 14, 1865, throngs of Washingtonians would also traverse this new theater, becoming innocently familiar with the place where a president might alight from his carriage or the path he might take to get to his seat. But John Wilkes Booth was familiar with other parts of this thespian temple, parts only known by an actor who worked there, parts that would figure into his plan: the secret pathway underneath the stage that would enable an assassin to move undetected from one part of the theater to another, or to the box overhanging the stage, from which an assassin might leap after murdering a president.[6]

Chillingly, Fanny Seward was now acquainted with many of those places, too. In fact, she had taken special note in her diary of a "doorway opening on an alley."[7] That doorway would become the fated passageway through which Booth would escape, galloping away on a waiting horse after his murder of President Lincoln. In a twist of irony, in that same theater less than a month after Fanny's visit, John Wilkes Booth would play the part of a young sculptor in *The Marble Heart*, and Abraham Lincoln would be in the audience.[8]

In that not-too-distant future, Ford's Theatre would become the site of the first presidential assassination in American history. From the theater, which Fanny Seward loved, would be launched the drama of her lifetime.

Fanny's tour of Ford's Theatre was not the only eerie premonition of things to come. There had been other connections with the Booth family prior to the night of April 14, 1865. Miss Lucy Hale had been a guest at a dinner party at the Seward home in the winter of 1860. Lucy was the beautiful daughter of New Hampshire senator John P. Hale.

Although Senator Hale was a supporter of Lincoln and an abolitionist as well, by the time of the Lincoln assassination his daughter Lucy would be romantically linked with and reputedly engaged to the Confederacy-loyal John Wilkes Booth. In another instance of foreboding, Fanny and her sister-in-law Anna had sat beside Miss Clara Harris at church on an April Sunday. On the walk home from church that day, Fanny's father, musing on a diplomatic crisis, remarked that people who had been unacquainted with each other might still have "a very strong influence on each other's destiny."[9] Three years later, on a more fateful April date, Miss Harris and her fiancé Major Henry Rathbone would accompany President and Mrs. Lincoln to Ford's Theatre.

However, the most eerie coincidence foreshadowing the tragic events to come occurred when Edwin Booth dined with the Seward family in March of 1864.[10] Without a doubt, he was the most famous Shakespearean actor of the Civil War era. Ironically, he was also the elder brother of John Wilkes Booth, whose assassination conspiracy would encompass not only President Lincoln but his secretary of state.

Edwin's birth in 1833 signaled an auspicious beginning befitting a Shakespearean hero, for a meteor shower attended his birth, and he was born with a caul. His father, the brilliant but eccentric actor Junius Brutus Booth, introduced Edwin to the theater in a backhanded way. Junius drank too much, and several instances suggest he was teetering on the edge of madness. Once, shoeless and clothed only in his underwear, Junius took off for Providence, Rhode Island, reciting poetry beside the road. To Edwin fell the role of his father's babysitter, keeping his parent sober and sane enough to perform.[11]

As he watched his father on stage, young Edwin naturally absorbed the roles Junius played. Edwin first went on stage in a bit part in 1849, but gradually he began to take on roles like Othello or King Lear.[12] But Edwin Booth would become an actor different from both his father and his brother. His flamboyant father Junius was given to the showy style of Edwin Forrest, and his handsome brother John played romantic roles like Romeo. Edwin, of a dark and brooding nature himself, was most closely identified with the role of Hamlet.

In fact, from 1853 to 1893, Edwin Booth's portrayal of Hamlet represented a pinnacle of achievement in the American theater at the time. Edwin Booth's interpretation of the role stood in stark contrast to Edwin Forrest's. Booth's Hamlet was neither bombastic nor flamboyant; instead, he was complex, tortured, elusive. Hamlet seemed a role sculpted for Booth; after all, Hamlet, like the man who played him to such acclaim, was melancholy, soulful, and burdened with an obsession to understand and come to terms with the sins of his father.[13]

The personal and professional differences between Edwin and John, however, were especially striking. Like Fanny, Edwin was socially shy. He had trouble expressing emotion. While the passionate, confident John, his mother's darling, flirted and romanced young women with ease, Edwin often sat alone, speaking to no one.[14] A *Boston Post* critic of the time, in comparing the two brothers' professional acting styles, suggested that John was more lively, Edwin more lyrical; John more animated, Edwin more graceful; John more histrionic, Edwin more classic; John more appropriately cast for Richard III, Edwin for Hamlet.[15]

Most striking for the fate of the Seward family were the political differences between the two brothers. Edwin appeared to have inherited the political instincts of his father. Junius Booth, Senior, refused to own slaves, even though such ownership was common practice in the border state of Maryland, where the family lived. Junius even hired free blacks to help farm his land. His youngest son John, however, felt differently. A Southern loyalist through and through, John Wilkes Booth impulsively abandoned a theater engagement to witness the hanging of abolitionist John Brown. When the firing on Fort Sumter launched the war, John was making "treasonable statements" in Albany, and some of the Northern partisans wanted him banished from the stage there. After the draft riots of 1863, John Booth declared to his sister that "so help me holy God! My soul, life, and possessions are for the South!"[16]

However, when Edwin Booth, a Republican sympathizer, dined with the Seward family in March of 1864, a total rift with his younger

9. Actor John Wilkes Booth assassinated President Abraham Lincoln on April 14, 1865. Library of Congress.

10. Edwin Booth, acclaimed actor, shared a dinner with Fanny's family. His brother John would target Fanny's father for assassination a year later. Library of Congress.

brother over politics was still in the future. Lincoln would be nominated for a second term that June, and after Lincoln's November reelection, Edwin and John were acting in a production of *Julius Caesar* to raise money for a Central Park statue of William Shakespeare.[17] Their roles matched their personalities, Edwin playing the brooding Brutus, and John the good-looking Marc Antony.

Off-stage, however, the brothers' political differences came to a head. Over breakfast on November 26, 1864, after the successful benefit of the night before, Edwin confessed that he had voted for Lincoln, and John flew into a rage. Raving that Lincoln would establish a monarchy with himself as king, John grew so explosive that Edwin forbade him to make any more volatile statements in his house. Banishing him then and there, Edwin Booth could not have known that he would never see his brother alive again.[18]

At the Seward table in March of 1864, neither Edwin Booth or the Seward family could have imagined the tragedy that would befall themselves and their nation when, only a year later, their dinner companion's brother became the first successful assassin of an American president. At the time, the tragedy that Edwin was attempting to recover from was his own personal tragedy, an episode that marred his happiness for life. For a while, Edwin seemed to have found contentment with actress Mary Devlin and their baby daughter, but he had inherited his father's propensity for alcohol, and his bouts of drinking caused problems between them. When Mary became fatally ill with pneumonia in Boston in 1863, Edwin was performing at the Winter Garden in New York. Rushing through the night to reach his wife's bedside, he just missed saying his final good-byes. He had been too drunk to arrive in time. Edwin Booth, whose life had been and would be so often marked by tragedy, was devastated.[19]

While Edwin Booth was performing a three-week engagement at Grover's Theatre in March of 1864, Lincoln and Seward, faithful attendees, showed up night after night to watch. During this engagement, Fanny herself saw him as Richelieu, as Richard III, as Hamlet, as Don Caesar De Bazan in a French drama, and twice as Shylock.

Finding each performance "intensely interesting," she observed that Booth always "seems to *be* the character."[20]

When the actor joined the Seward family for dinner on March 11, 1864, Fanny carefully recorded her impressions of him in her diary:

> As I entered the parlor I saw across the room a small, slight gentleman, with the face we had seen before on the stage . . . a melancholy face betraying an intensely sensitive nature, and such a quick apprehension . . . ! He has dark, long, silky hair and magnificent dark eyes—wears neither beard nor moustache—His face is very thin and handsome more from its intellect than features.[21]

Fanny's garrulous father offered some armchair criticism of the actor, suggesting that Booth played Richelieu "too old and infirm"; Booth himself confessed that he was not satisfied with his playing of Shylock, having "a painful sense of something wanting—could compare it to nothing else but the want of body in wine." Booth also lamented the fact that actors were not content to remain in roles that were most reflective of their talents, spurning the minor parts in which they excelled. According to Booth, they longed for the chance to "go out West & there play Hamlet," playing such major roles, presumably, less skillfully.[22]

Throughout his career, much would be written about the eyes of Edwin Booth, and Fanny confirmed their powers of expression in her diary.

> Those wonderful eyes—how can they be the same, they are black *points* in Shylock, in Richelieu they read the characters of all about . . . —in Richard they hate—in Don Caesar they flash & dance, & sparkle & smile, & kill with there [sic] brilliant beauty—In Hamlet they are so full of tenderness, & sadness, that one's heart aches at the sight—and Booth's eyes are Hamlet's eyes, in their sad expression.[23]

But Fanny and her family were likely not aware as they dined with Edwin Booth that his brother John Wilkes had mesmerizing eyes, too. Like his brother's, John's eyes were intense and dark, and Sir Charles

Wyndham, a fellow actor, understood that "[a]t all times his eyes were his striking features." This player, too, noted that when John became emotional, which was frequently, his eyes became "like living jewels," and "flames shot from them."[24] Sitting at the family dinner table in the company of John's brother Edwin, the Seward family could never have imagined that John Wilkes Booth would, in little over a year, turn those glittering eyes to a plan that would play itself out in that very house, devastating Fanny, her family, and the nation itself. The curtain on that act was yet to be raised.

Ironically, Fanny's reflections on the visit of Edwin Booth to her family home in March of 1864 made up the final entry in her diary for an entire year. Fanny would abandon her diary until April of 1865, when she picked it up in time to record the details of her father's tragic carriage accident on April 5. We cannot be sure why Fanny abandoned her diary during this period. Often she abandoned her diary for periods of time when she was living in predictable Auburn, where she was for some of this period. In addition, when events were accelerating, she was sometimes too preoccupied to write, waiting for more leisure to explore these events when time permitted.

One plausible explanation was that Fanny was devoting herself more intensely to her writing during this year; those efforts probably left little time for diary-writing. Still, her most ambitious work, *Tried and True*, the novel with the theatrical background, was finished in June of 1864, its completion likely inspired by the intimate connections forged with Charlotte Cushman the previous fall and the frequent theater-going in which she participated during this period. With that major work behind her, surely she had the freedom to devote to her diary.

Perhaps Fanny's move to Washington in October of 1864 preoccupied her. She seemed eager to settle there for an extended period, and it was certainly a more exciting place for a young woman than Auburn. Fanny's creative writing during this period, however, suggested that young Fanny was focused almost exclusively on the topic of love. Perhaps Fanny had fallen in love with someone, at least from afar. Perhaps it was someone in Washington, someone whose presence would explain why the Washington scene during this period was so inviting. "Kate's Thoughts," penned in the first three months of 1865, hinted of an older man as a love interest, and her "Mable Gray/Story of Love" tale, finished in 1865, had love at its heart, as well.

We simply do not know exactly what was on Fanny's mind between March of 1864 and April of 1865. Letters from this period are few, but they reveal that her focus from July to October of 1864 was on the fate of young soldiers. Clearly, the young soldier who was always the object of Fanny's greatest concern was Will, the dear brother who, like thousands of other young men during this most gruesome period of the war, was facing danger on the battlefield. Those anxieties were enough to distract even the most devoted of diarists.

# 15
# When This Cruel War Is Over

The spring of 1864 marked the beginning of the end of the war. Gradually, victory for the North seemed more and more likely. Still, the South remained a determined foe, resolute in its effort to preserve its way of life. That determination, however, was thwarted by the elevation of Ulysses S. Grant as commander-in-chief of all federal forces in March of 1864. His "gritty pugnacity" was what the North had required for so long.[1]

The killing that was unleashed during 1864 can only be described as carnage, and it sent shivers through both North and South. In early May, General William T. Sherman began his punishing drive to Atlanta. At the same time, Grant launched his Overland Campaign, a forty-day onslaught at the Wilderness, Spotsylvania Court House, and Cold Harbor. It was a gruesome campaign that resulted in eighty-six thousand Union and Confederate casualties: dead, wounded, and missing.[2] From Auburn, Fanny wrote her father about "the details of suffering and slaughter" that were "heart-sickening," acknowledging that such details must be "worse to you, so near the scene of the action, and with the wounded coming to the city."[3]

Fanny was right. The suffering and slaughter sickened both Lincoln and Seward, who witnessed daily the deluge of dead and wounded flooding Washington by the thousands. Throughout May and June of 1864, "day and night, night and day," during the course of seven bloody weeks, death hung in the air."[4]

And death hovered over the Seward family, as well. William Henry Seward, Junior, Fanny's beloved brother Will, was commissioned as a colonel right before he went into the Battle of Cold Harbor. From

Auburn, Fanny anxiously scanned the headlines, searching for word of the movements of Burnside's corps, "imagining Will to be there."[5]

But on the evening of June 1, 1864, Will's wife Jenny had an eerie premonition. "Sitting in the twilight," Jenny heard her husband call her name. "I jumped up," she wrote. She cocked her head, listened, and heard again, "'Jenny' so distinctly, that I went into the hall, and again came the voice, 'Jenny,' so plain that I looked over the railing, fully expecting to see [Will] coming up the stairs." Later, Jenny discovered that at that very hour of her eerie premonition, Will was fighting in the Battle of Cold Harbor, coming "very near losing his life."[6]

But the family failed to hear from Will for weeks, an anxiety-producing situation common to families all over the country awaiting news of their loved ones in an age without modern communication. "No word," lamented Jenny, "only news of terrible battles every day." The first news was a few words from Colonel MacDougall scribbled on a piece of brown paper and stating that Will "had a hard fight, in which most of his clothes were torn from him."[7] A letter from a quartermaster, written on June 4, only reached Jenny two weeks later. Another letter, dated June 5, took until June 20 to reach her.[8]

In a letter to her father, Fanny confirmed what the family had finally learned. "[I]n one of the battles of June 1st, 2nd, or 3rd," Will had been one of the first to enter the rifle pits, receiving "a heavy blow on the head from the butt of a rebel musket." Instantly, "the rebel who inflicted the blow was riddled by the bullets of our men." Even though Will had the leg of his boot torn open by a shell, Fanny proudly reported that Will refused to go to the rear "as some would have done." The Seward children did not share this news with their mother,[9] sparing Frances the details about what really happened to Will on the battlefield.

Throughout his military career Will Seward proved himself an exemplary soldier whose family took pride in his service. In 1862, Fanny's father wrote to her about how her brother "grows in his new profession," observing that "[h]e is now in command of a separate battalion, and in charge of Fort Gaines. He drills his men constantly, and they are greatly attached to him."[10] President Lincoln had even tapped

Will for a special mission to Louisiana. In the spring of 1863, the president chose Fanny's brother to deliver a secret dispatch to General Nathaniel Banks, a message so important that it had to be memorized to avoid falling into enemy hands. After Will sailed for New Orleans, he was gone for three weeks, and the family heard nothing from him during that period.[11]

His bravery during the Battle of Cold Harbor was followed by command of an artillery regiment in the VI Corps; more dangers, unfortunately, awaited young Will. During the Civil War, combat on the battlefield confronted young men with the ultimate danger, and those battlefield experiences were known as "seeing the elephant." That phrase referred to the nineteenth century practice of letting boys see the circus for free in exchange for watering the elephants. For "boys transformed into soldiers, zipping bullets and screaming shells replaced the elephants; they became the price one paid for seeing 'the show' of battle." The mementos of war, strewn across battlefields North and South, were grisly reminders that the show was not pretty. One Ohio infantryman, for instance, reminiscing over the Bull Run battlefield, saw that the rains had washed over the shallow graves, revealing "bony knees . . . and grinning skulls." Observing "a man's boot protruding from the grave," this soldier could only hope that "the skeleton's toes" pointed "to a land where there [was] no war."[12]

But the nation had not yet arrived at that land without war, and Fanny's brother would be forced to see the elephant again. With Grant engaging in siege warfare in Virginia and Sherman slogging his way to Atlanta, the Confederacy determined to train its sights on Washington in July of 1864. As scholar Marc Leepson has so aptly pointed out, if victory over the nation's capital could be achieved, the South would reap several rewards. The U.S. Treasury could be plundered. War supplies could be commandeered. Southern prisoners-of-war held at Point Lookout could be freed. The capture of the president, the Capitol, and government buildings would secure Confederate control over the center of the war effort and persuade England and France to support the Confederacy; even better, such a demoralizing victory would likely defeat Lincoln in his fall reelection campaign.[13]

The South's plucky mission was placed in the hands of General Jubal Early, a cantankerous character renowned for being disagreeable and dismissive of both his superiors and underlings.[14] Although a ring of forts surrounded the capital, it became clear that the Union leadership had misunderstood Early's plan and underestimated the strength of his forces. Telegraph wires were cut, and railroads were prevented from leaving or entering the capital. The citizens of Washington were thrown into a panic, and Washington's residents began to engage in frantic preparations for battle. The militia was called up, bureaucrats were issued arms, even soldiers convalescing in hospitals were recruited for the effort as Washingtonians scurried to protect themselves from the irascible Jubal Early.[15]

But before General Early could arrive at Washington's doorstep, he would have to face Union General Lew Wallace and his brave troops, which included Fanny's brother Will. Their mission was to protect the roads and bridges to Washington and Baltimore, and on July 9, 1864, on the east bank of the Monocacy River, the battle was engaged. "Here," at the Battle of Monocacy, Wallace declared, "the fate of Washington was to be determined."[16]

In the Battle of Monocacy, the Union troops were greatly outnumbered.[17] The soldiers that were hurled against Early's advancing forces included the Ninth New York Heavy Artillery led by Colonel William H. Seward, Junior.[18] At Monocacy, Fanny's brother was engaged in a fight-to-the-death struggle in which the Union forces were finally but not easily routed. Despite the Union retreat, the battle could be counted a victory nonetheless. In the conflict that raged from morning until evening, General Wallace gained time for Washington. Because Wallace managed to hold off the Confederate forces for a day, Grant then had time to divert his crack troops from Petersburg to enhance the capital's defenses.[19]

But the news about Will Seward was terrifying. Returning home from the State Department at midnight on July 9, the elder Seward was soon visited by Secretary of War Stanton. Stanton had grim news: Will was wounded and had been taken prisoner. There was little sleep at the Seward home that night. Early in the morning, Fanny's

11. Brigadier General William H. Seward Junior, Fanny's beloved brother "Will." Collections of the Seward House Museum, Auburn, NY.

brother Gus was sent to Baltimore to seek word of Will's status. With relief, Gus had telegraphed by afternoon that Will was not a prisoner; instead, the report was that Will had been wounded.[20]

Hurrying to seek more information about Will's condition, both Fanny's father and her brother Fred took a carriage out Washington's Tennallytown road, hoping soldiers from Will's regiment might know something about Will's injuries. With grateful hearts, they learned that Will had indeed been injured but that his wounds were not fatal.[21]

In Auburn, Fanny was following the news by telegraph like her sister-in-law Jenny, who was desperate to receive word of her husband. What they learned was that Will's horse had been shot from under him. When the wounded animal fell on top of Will, Will's ankle was broken; meanwhile young Colonel Seward had also received a wound in his arm.[22] Because he had been wearing a private's uniform, having lost his own uniform at the Battle of Cold Harbor, Will narrowly escaped being taken prisoner. After the rebel line "passed over him, he crawled on the ground to a piece of woods, where he found a mule, which, with the help of a straggler, he mounted." Improvising a bit and bridle with his red silk pocket handkerchief, Will rode fifteen miles during the night to Ellicott Mills, finally hooking up with his retreating regiment.[23]

The fate of Will's horse and mule were also recounted by Fanny's sister-in-law. Wounded in the neck and thought to be dead, Will's horse was apparently only in shock; once recovered, the animal managed to find its troops. An orderly treated the horse's bloody neck wounds with "the contents of his tobacco pouch," sending the animal on to Washington for proper care. "Jenny," the name of the mule which Will rode to safety, was sent to the farm of a relative near Canandaigua Lake. There, "for bringing her master safely away from the rebels," Jenny was lovingly cared for until she died.[24]

Confederate troops had come close enough to Washington to fire on Union troops at Fort Stevens, just a few miles from the White House. But the petulant General Jubal Early abandoned his plans for an attack on Washington in the face of Grant's rugged reinforcements to the city. That fall, as a result of his valor at the Battle of Monocacy, Will Seward was promoted to brigadier general.[25]

Now, however, Secretary of War Stanton had something else to worry about. Ominous reports had reached him that Lincoln's carriage was being followed by an unidentified horseman. Quickly, in light of that threat, Stanton enlarged the president's cavalry escort.[26] There were worries in addition to those from the battlefield.

# 16

# A Conspiracy Evolves

By 1865, the final turning point of the war had been reached. Only a few months earlier, on September 3, 1864, General Sherman had wired General Halleck that Atlanta had fallen.[1] That military victory also signaled a political victory, for it had brightened prospects for Lincoln's November reelection. Receiving the news of the capture of Atlanta in his library in Auburn, Fanny's father delivered an impromptu speech to a local crowd, praising the valor of the North's military forces and the steadfastness of his colleagues in the cabinet.[2]

With the wreckage of Atlanta behind him, Sherman continued his unrelenting "March to the Sea," presenting the city of Savannah to the president as a Christmas gift at the end of 1864. In February of 1865, the swath of destruction was enlarged as Sherman struck out for Columbia, South Carolina. Combined with the earlier victories represented by Admiral David Farragut's capture of Mobile Bay, Alabama, and General Phil Sheridan's destruction of Confederate forces in the Shenandoah Valley, these military triumphs insured the inevitability of a Northern victory.

The South, however, was in the throes of utter devastation. By 1865, two-thirds of its territory was in Union hands, and a quarter of its soldiering population had died. The war had been fought largely on Southern soil, so citizens of the Confederacy suffered more deeply than their counterparts in the North. With its railroads destroyed, its cities burned, and its farmlands plundered, the Southern landscape was awash with refugees who were hungry, sick, and disoriented.[3] Confederate currency was devalued, and inflation was rampant. By

January 1865, for instance, flour in a city like Richmond cost more than $425 a barrel.[4]

Even sheltered young women like Fanny Seward grew familiar with the stories of suffering in the South, repeating to her diary in late January of 1863 the reports from Northern visitors to the South who declared that, in contrast, "our people know nothing of the hardships of the war." Rumors abounded that Southern women were using Spanish moss to make rope and raspberry leaves to make tea. Fanny had heard that Southern women were giving their "carpets for blankets" and "all but their most necessary bedding to the hospitals." Southern ladies were even donating their silk dresses as cloth for military balloons used to spy on enemy positions. "The least scrap of silk," Fanny noted, "is made to do duty as a face trimming for old bonnets," and Fanny had heard that common shoe coverings or "gaiters" were sold for twenty-five dollars a pair.[5]

Such desperate times led to desperate measures. In Georgia, a wagon was held up by women desperate for a few sacks of flour. In Alabama, women raided a mill to get flour, wielding guns, knives, and pistols to make their mission clear.[6] Southern diarist Mary Chesnut commented archly in March of 1865 on the ironic arrival of Lent. That religious period of fasting struck her as "quite convenient, for we have nothing to eat."[7]

So much had been lost that the South was now awash in the last-ditch efforts of bitter-enders. Indulging in the guerilla tactics of desperadoes and bandits, they fought desperately to cling to any shred of hope, and their efforts did much to frustrate the Union's attempt to bring the war to a final conclusion.

One of the most bold guerillas was John Mosby. The audacious Mosby defied the stereotypes about outlaws. He read Shakespeare and Plutarch, and, having been kicked out of the University of Virginia for shooting another student, he then studied law.[8]

His experiences in Jeb Stuart's cavalry as a scout and courier inspired him to raise his own company of mounted guerillas in Virginia, where his exploits became legendary. His horsemen haunted the landscape at night, operating with swift surprise, earning Mosby the nickname of the "Grey Ghost." Mosby and his raiders wrought havoc on the Union lines. From his base of operations in northern Virginia, a sympathetic population served as his spies and his refuge. So effective was Mosby in attacking Union supply lines and outposts that the area from the Blue Ridge to the Bull Run mountains was referred to as "Mosby's confederacy." Considerable federal resources were devoted to Mosby's capture. He was shadowed by sharpshooters, and federal orders dictated that any captured ranger was to be shot on the spot. But Mosby retaliated in kind, hanging any federal soldiers that fell into his hands.[9]

Mosby's reputation for mystery and success drew scores of recruits to his cause, and among the conscripts forming Mosby's network appeared a young volunteer whose fate would intersect with Fanny Seward's. His name was Lewis Thornton Powell.

According to his biographer, Betty Ownsbey, Lewis Powell was tall and muscular, and Mosby, who carefully chose his marauders, would have been impressed with this powerful young man and battlefield veteran. A committed Confederate, the seventeen-year-old Powell had joined Company I of the Second Florida Infantry as early as 1861, giving his age as nineteen. He had fought with courage in major campaigns that included Yorktown, Seven Pines, Second Manassas, Antietam, Chancellorsville, and Fredericksburg. Having been wounded and captured in the Battle of Gettysburg on July 2, 1863, Powell was recuperating from his injuries and serving as an army nurse throughout the summer until he escaped on September 7, 1863 and fled south. It was perhaps inevitable that Powell would seek refuge among Mosby's marauders. With the Confederate cause flagging, Powell's fierce loyalty to the South would have made him a natural volunteer with the Grey Ghost, for Powell was described by U.S. Army Hospital steward Samuel S. Bond as "one of the most unyielding of all the rebels."[10]

This unyielding young rebel, whose fate would be entangled with the Seward family, was the polar opposite of Fanny Seward. Powell grew up in a hardscrabble Southern family with few privileges; Fanny grew up in a privileged Northern family with every advantage. Powell's parents, the modest Patience and George, differed from

12. The strapping Lewis Powell, who assumed several aliases, would attempt to assassinate Fanny's father. Library of Congress.

Fanny's parents, the well-connected William and Frances. Powell's parents struggled to provide for their ten children, whereas Fanny's parents bestowed innumerable blessings on their four offspring. As she matured, Fanny's life became one of shy contemplation; Powell's became one of vigorous action.

Still, the similarities between the two young people were also striking. Lewis Powell and Fanny Seward were the very same age, having both been born in 1844. Despite their economic differences, both Lewis and Fanny had grown up among loving families, and Powell's father, a Baptist minister, served, like Fanny's father, as an appropriate role model. Like Fanny's brother Fred, Powell appeared destined to follow in his father's footsteps, taking up religion in the same way that the Seward boy took up law and politics. As children, Lewis and Fanny could have been kindred spirits. Like Fanny Seward, Lewis Powell as a boy was described by his biographer as "sensitive, intense . . . very much an introvert." Like Fanny, he loved animals, earning the nickname of "Doc" from siblings who watched him care for strays and wounded animals. Lewis raised a pet mule that his mother insisted on selling after the animal kicked the boy, breaking his left jaw and causing the loss of a molar. Knowing how attached his son was to this mule, the Reverend Powell interceded, allowing young Lewis to keep this pet. [11] Lewis Powell's loving childhood, like Fanny Seward's, showed no signs of the tragedy that was to come.

As the war interrupted their growing-up years, both Lewis and Fanny became fierce partisans, one for the South, the other for the North. Similarly, both were changed by the war. Fanny's natural sensitivity deepened and her anxieties multiplied, especially about the well-being of her family members, but Fanny never lost a family member to the war. Lewis's losses, however, were devastating. His brother Oliver died in battle, and his oldest brother George lost a limb at Petersburg and was permanently disabled.[12] It is more than likely that the war changed the arc of Powell's life, turning a once-gentle boy into a battle-hardened partisan.

The major difference between these two young people, however, was the difference in their constitutions. Fanny Seward's frail health was legendary; in contrast, every account of Lewis Powell mentioned his brimming good health and imposing physical strength. At seventeen, the youth was already six-feet-one with broad shoulders and a muscular physique, marking him as strong and robust.[13] Even so, there was one more quality besides brute strength that brought Lewis Powell into the midst of John Wilkes Booth's conspiracy. According to Captain Christian Rath, whose prison duties led him into contact with Powell and who eventually became Powell's executioner, the young rebel was also "brave as a lion."[14]

As Northern victories squeezed the Southern cause like a vise, plots and conspiracies sprang up alongside the last-ditch efforts of guerillas and marauders. It is not known when, exactly, Powell became ensnared in the underground activities of John Wilkes Booth, but this much is clear: in November of 1864 he was still serving with John Mosby; by January, 1865, he had left the military, swearing an oath of allegiance to the United States, pretending to be a reformed Confederate soldier, and taking on the false name of Lewis Paine[15]; by March, 1865, Powell had become an official member of Booth's band of conspirators, someone who was seen in Booth's company at Washington bars and restaurants and who showed up at the boarding house of Mary Surratt, where details of the conspiracy plans were being hatched[16]; by April 14, 1865, he had become a central figure in Booth's plan for the night of horrors.

Because his fame as an actor was his best disguise, Booth was able to pursue his clandestine activities with freedom,[17] and after Lincoln's reelection in 1864, when the Southern cause was deteriorating, Booth's passion was inflamed. Not only did Booth break with his brother Edwin, but he intensified his activities on behalf of his beloved South.

One of his schemes, cooked up in late 1864, had at its heart the release of over two hundred thousand Confederate prisoners being held in the North. Their release would mean that thousands of soldiers could replenish the diminishing ranks of the Confederate army. After the fall of Atlanta in September and the reelection of Lincoln in November, however, Booth's plan became more urgent. His idea was to kidnap President Lincoln as he traveled from Washington to his

Soldiers' Home retreat on the outskirts of the city. Booth and his band of conspirators would then hurry the carriage into southern Maryland, ford the Potomac, and spirit the president to Richmond. There they would hold the president for ransom until all the Confederate prisoners had been released. That this was a foolish scheme didn't prevent Booth from pursuing it. In fact, by late October 1864, Booth had bought items like rifles, revolvers, cartridges, daggers, and handcuffs from a New York arms dealer and had enlisted boyhood friends like Sam Arnold and Michael O'Laughlen to help.[18]

It is still unclear, however, when Booth's thoughts turned from kidnapping to murder.[19] What is clear is that Booth, his passions aroused as he watched the Confederacy collapse, felt an increasing urgency to act; after all, the kind of flamboyant acting upon a grand stage that drew the attention of thousands was John Wilkes Booth's métier.

One opportunity presented itself at Lincoln's second inauguration on March 4, 1865. Among the spectators photographed beneath the podium on that blustery day were four men, looking curiously like Booth's conspirators. Another figure, just below the speaking stand, seemed to look like Lewis Powell. Although doubt has been cast on the identities of these men, less doubt surrounded the presence of one man, a handsome man in a top hat, a man standing on a balcony and peering down at the president. That man, in attendance courtesy of Senator Hale's beautiful daughter Lucy, was John Wilkes Booth. On March 4, Lincoln's sentiments about "malice toward none" fell on the deaf ears of his future assassin. Only a month later, after the April 3 fall of Richmond, Booth lamented the lost opportunity of that day: "What an excellent chance I had . . . ," he told a fellow actor, " . . . to kill the president on inauguration day."[20]

Eleven days later, on March 15, Ford's Theatre began to figure into Booth's plans. He reserved the presidential boxes so his conspirators could observe the layout of the theater as they watched an evening performance there. Afterward, Booth feted Powell, Samuel Arnold, and Michael O'Laughlen, as well as John Surratt, David Herold, and George Atzerodt, to a private supper during which they discussed the actor's plan.[21] His ludicrous scheme revolved around Lincoln's next attendance at the theater. O'Laughlen and Herold were to douse the gaslights; Powell and Booth were to restrain the president; Arnold was to help Powell and Booth lower the president onto the stage and into a waiting carriage at the backstage alley; Surratt and Atzerodt were to ferry Lincoln across the Potomac in a boat purchased by Booth. When the conspirators pointed out the impossibility of this scheme and left the restaurant, Booth was dejected and angry.[22]

Even so, two days later, the kidnapping scheme that Booth had been hatching for many months found a way to catch fire. In the morning of March 17, 1865, Booth heard that Lincoln planned to be present that afternoon at an entertainment for wounded soldiers at Campbell Military Hospital. Now, Booth decided, was the time to pursue his former kidnapping plot. Booth determined to waylay Lincoln's carriage as it headed back to Washington, restraining the president and diverting the carriage into southern Maryland. Boyhood friends Arnold and O'Laughlen would help; so would Davey Herold and John Surratt and George Atzerodt. Herold knew the back roads of southern Maryland; Surratt was an experienced Confederate courier; Atzerodt was a boatman who could ferry the president across the Potomac. However, Lewis Powell's use to this conspiracy was critical. A man of his brute size and strength would be needed to overpower the president; after all, Abraham Lincoln, at six feet and four inches tall, still harbored the strength of a former railsplitter. Although by three p.m. the mounted conspirators were heading out to Campbell Hospital in pursuit of their plot, the president, at the last minute, cancelled his hospital visit. Another Booth plan had fizzled.[23]

Now the pace of the Confederacy's final days began to quicken, and so did Booth's sense of urgency. In late March, General Grant and President Lincoln conferred at City Point, Grant's headquarters, about the military and political end game. As March turned to April, Seward's presence was requested there, too, and Fanny accompanied her father on a trip which offered a chilling premonition. From the deck of their party's revenue cutter, Fanny glimpsed the monitor *Montauk*,[24] the ship where, only a few weeks later, the shroud-wrapped body of John Wilkes Booth would be brought and where other members of the conspiracy would be held in custody, wearing the infamous "Lilley irons," handcuffs fashioned from a solid bar that kept the prisoners from putting their hands together.[25]

Meanwhile, General Lee was abandoning Petersburg and heading south to join General Joseph Johnston in North Carolina in hopes of saving his army. As Lee's troops departed and the month of April began, federal forces now occupied the former Confederate positions at Petersburg. Finally, the event so long anticipated by the North and so long dreaded by the South occurred: on April 3, Richmond, the capital of the Confederacy, fell. A jubilant Secretary of War Edwin Stanton sent a welcome order to his wife Ellen: "Petersburg is evacuated and probably Richmond. Put out your flags." Similarly, a joyful Fanny Seward, returning to her diary after an absence of a year and a half, recorded the universal sentiment: "All hearts are rejoicing in the capture of Richmond."[26]

Now, however, the rejoicing that filled the hearts of Northerners fueled the despair of their Southern counterparts. As Northern troops raised their flags over Richmond and federal officers hustled Confederate soldiers into Richmond's notorious Libby Prison, Booth's hope of freeing Southern soldiers to swell the ranks of the Confederate forces was completely dashed. Mired in despair, fierce partisans like Booth could not hear the generous terms of surrender. To them, it seemed not to matter that the Confederate soldiers could peacefully return to their homes, officers keeping their weapons and property, cavalrymen keeping their horses. To them, it seemed irrelevant that Grant furnished Lee's starving army with twenty-five thousand rations of food.[27] All such radical partisans could hear was defeat, underscored by the jubilant celebrations that broke out all over the North, particularly in Washington, DC. Journalist Noah Brooks reported on the jammed saloons and the popping champagne corks on April 3 in a city where "everybody who had a piece of bunting spread it to the breeze."[28]

Although Fanny's father had told a friend in the summer of 1862 that assassination was not an American custom,[29] he could not have forecast the abject despair of the Confederacy at the end of the war. Unfortunately for the South, that despair was underlined by the candles flickering in windows, the flags hanging from public buildings, the newspapers fluttering in fists, and the bands trumpeting patriotic euphoria throughout the North. All too soon, John Wilkes Booth would come to see himself as the hero who would seek retribution for his despairing South.

Now Booth began to imagine himself not as a petty spy and agent for the South but as the embodiment of its salvation, a mythic character to strut the stage not from the proscenium of a fledgling local theater production but from the immortal pages of history. Drinking heavily, consuming as much as a quart of brandy in less than a few hours, Booth seemed to be suffering inner torments. After the fall of Richmond, he railed about mounting a horse and waving a Confederate flag as he tore through the streets of Washington.[30]

On the rainy evening of April 11, two days after Lee's surrender at Appomattox, Booth experienced an epiphany of rage that would ultimately culminate in murder. John Wilkes Booth and his fellow conspirator Lewis Powell stood among the thousands filling the avenue below the White House window, waiting for Lincoln to step onto the balcony to speak to the ecstatic crowds below. From inside the Executive Mansion, journalist Brooks was an eyewitness to the tender scene, recording the events surrounding the final speech President Lincoln would ever make. Holding a candle up to Lincoln's manuscript, which was concealed behind the window drapes, Brooks watched as Lincoln's youngest boy Tad scrambled around his father's feet picking up the pages his father dropped to the floor.[31]

In his speech, Lincoln articulated his reconstruction policy, a policy according generous terms to the ruined South. However, when he mentioned the possibility of awarding the vote to educated blacks or to blacks who had served in the military, Booth became enraged, urging Powell to shoot Lincoln on the spot. Powell refused. In response, Booth muttered that Lincoln had just made the last speech of his life and snarled a vow: "By God," the actor swore, "I'll put him through."[32] It was a vow John Wilkes Booth intended to keep.

# 17

# Prelude to the Night of Horrors

No one was happier that the war was over than Fanny Seward. She had worried about her father and brother Fred working tirelessly through military and political victories and reverses. She had prayed that her brother Will would survive the dangers of the battlefield. She had witnessed the suffering of young soldiers in hospitals and military camps. From the lips of the powerful, she had heard countless tales of valor and defeat that comprised the four-year narrative of civil war.

Given her retiring nature, however, Fanny's was a quiet and reflective joy. Not for her were the shouting and the drum-beating. Instead, Fanny's response was one of reverential reflection. The fall of Richmond on April 3 sent her back to memories of the week before, on March 29, 1865, when she had been aboard the revenue cutter *Northerner* on her visit to City Point with her father as he discussed the final details of the war with Grant. As the waves slapped and danced beneath her boat and the twilight deepened, Fanny reflected on the soldiers who had sailed this same waterway on their way to unknown dangers, penning in her diary her own tribute to the fallen:

> I thought how many vessels they had borne along, what hearts had felt the throb of the waves, what ears had listened to their invitation. What bands of brave, heroic souls had floated down the river to the bay, . . . strong in courage & hope & daring.— . . . but their hearts gave no answering thrill to the throb of the waves, their calm, closed eyes beheld no shores wrapt in the dreamy twilight haze, their ears were deaf to the sweet wave's call—as to the sobs at home. Many of our best and noblest have gone this road, our terrible need has brought us many heroes.[1]

Clearly, this sensitive young woman, like so many of her generation, was grateful for the end of this mighty scourge of war. But Fanny, who had spent the war years so close to those who would determine its success or failure, was especially entitled to a respite. Despite her many privileges, her young life had not been easy, for death or the threat of it had hovered over most of her formative years. Her birth had coincided with the death of her father's beloved mother, and her sex had surely reminded her parents of the loss of their only other baby daughter. She had grown up under the legacy of a strict and forbidding elder in her Grandfather Miller. She had come of age at a time when wrenching national crises were brewing, when fugitive slaves could be rounded up like animals, when blood was being spilled in Kansas, when John Brown was sent to hang. She had watched young Auburn men go off to war and come home in bandages or coffins. She had spent anxious hours worrying about the action on battlefields on which her brother Will risked his life. She had watched her father endure withering criticism and the betrayal of colleagues. She had witnessed this terrible war, in which her family members played leading roles, from both far away in Auburn and up close in Washington. If anyone was entitled to relief from the mighty scourge of war, it was Fanny Seward.

But such relief was not to be, for on the very day after she composed her pensive reverie to the thousands of fallen soldiers whose sacrifices had deeply affected her, a tragedy befell her family which was followed by a series of events from which Fanny Seward would never recover.

It began with an ordinary carriage ride, the kind of excursion that allowed Fanny's father to revive himself in the now-spring air. There were five in the carriage that afternoon: Secretary Seward, Fanny's brother Fred, coachman Henry Key, Fanny's friend Mary Titus, and Fanny herself. The Seward carriage would become the vehicle for an accident that would set in motion a tragic parade of events. Fanny herself, badly shaken by the incident, described what happened as the carriage drove out Vermont Avenue:

> The carriage door . . . kept flying open. The coachman was told to dismount & shut it. While he was doing so the horses started . . . Fred immediately jumped out, thinking to head the horses. Although they were not going very fast he was thrown to the ground. The horses . . . went on increasing their speed. Father had some idea of being able to stop them, & sprang from the carriage in spite of my entreaties. . . . I was on the back seat & could not see whether he reached the ground safely or not. . . . The horses tore along. I had a momentary thought of catching the reins, but they were swinging widely in the air far beyond my reach. . . . I saw the houses & the sidewalk lit with the peaceful sunshine while we seemed to be whirling on to certain destruction. At the alley . . . the horses turned. We brushed against a tree. The brick corner of the house was in front—I was sure we were to be dashed against it and crushed to death. But just there the off horse fell, all crowded in between his mate and the carriage. Before we had time to get out of the carriage, the horse was up again, & we were dashing down the alley, when a soldier headed & stopped the horses, & saved us from being dragged into the stable. As soon as we could get out I hastened back to look for Father, I met a crowd of men carrying him, & I thought he was dead. . . . [2]

When it was over, after the limp body of Fanny's father had been carried into the house, after the doctors had been called and shaken their heads over the battered body of one of the Union's most ardent patriots, after Fanny herself had stepped to the bedroom door to witness her father's bruises and the dear face that was gushing blood, one thing was clear: although the battlefield tragedies of the last four years were now behind her, another tragedy, launched at her own doorstep, was just beginning. Following the fall of Richmond, Lincoln's energies would be devoted to binding up the nation's wounds; now Fanny's energies would be devoted to binding up her father's.

At first, Secretary Seward seemed "insensible." He did not recognize his family members. Then, when he began to slip in and out of consciousness, he seemed "bewildered." Fanny noted that he was "so disfigured by bruises, his face so swolen [sic], that his eyes were closed by immense swellings." Fanny, horrified, could see that he had "scarcely a trace of resemblance to himself."[3]

His anxious family and others hovered and helped. Anna gave Fanny directions for applying a face wash every fifteen minutes. Gus wiped away the blood from his father's nose "that was almost suffocating him." An intimate presence by the bed was Secretary of War Edwin Stanton, who wiped the lips of Fanny's father and "spoke gently to him," behaving "like a woman in the sickroom."[4] That night, Fanny sat by her father's bedside until the early hours of the morning, holding his hand, a gesture that marked their special bond of affection over the years. Fanny's father tossed restlessly, "talking constantly in his sleep."[5]

While Fanny kept vigil over her father, holding his hand in shock and disbelief, the irony of the situation cannot have been lost on her. After all, on April 4, the evening before the carriage accident, the entire city, in celebration of the fall of Richmond, had been illuminated under the order of her father. Surely Fanny's memories of the flags waving, the fireworks exploding, and the bands playing must have mocked her, for the father who helped make possible the surging torrent of celebration, lying in a crumpled heap before her, could not join in the festivities. Even the warm spring air may have underscored the despair of the young woman shut up in the suffocating air of the sickroom. While the rest of the city indulged in euphoric celebration, Fanny Seward sat quietly in an upstairs bedroom, experiencing an anxiety that even four anxious years had not prepared her for: the loss of her beloved father. When, she must have wondered, would this cruel war be over?

On April 7, Fanny's mother and brother Will arrived, having rushed from Auburn at the news. To her sister Lazette, Frances wrote of her shock at seeing her injured husband: "His face is so marred and swollen and discolored that one can hardly persuade themselves of his identity; his voice so changed; utterance almost entirely prevented by the broken jaw and the swollen tongue. It makes my heart ache to look at him." Fanny agreed. "I never saw such agony," she wrote, "it was terrible to witness."[6]

But Fanny's father was attended by the city's most competent doctors, who had been quickly summoned soon after the accident. Dr. Basil Norris, the Army medical director, had first diagnosed a badly dislocated right shoulder and, later, a jaw broken on both sides. Other doctors who rushed to the house and held worried consultations were Dr. Tullio S. Verdi, the Seward's family doctor who had long treated the family, and Dr. Joseph K. Barnes, the Surgeon General who would soon preside over the autopsies of both Abraham Lincoln and John Wilkes Booth.[7]

Dr. Verdi, the thirty-six-year-old Italian-born physician, who practiced homeopathic medicine in Washington, DC, was intimately familiar with the Seward family. He had treated Fred's broken arm only the previous November. He had treated William's dysentery and typhoid fever, contracted while in command at Fort Foote. He had treated Fanny over the years for the multiple fevers, sore throats, and bouts of tonsillitis she suffered, prescribing exercise to bolster her frail constitution and a poultice to soothe her raw throat.[8]

When Dr. Verdi arrived on the scene after the carriage accident, he assessed Seward's condition, describing it as "perilous in the extreme." The face of Fanny's father was alarmingly bruised, swelling closed his right eye, and the right side of his face had turned blue. Seward's lower jaw, fractured bilaterally, hung down so that he was unable to lift it to chew. So swollen and inflamed had the jaw become that Seward could not endure the slightest bandage. In addition, his right arm was fractured near the shoulder. His misery became intense, and a high fever rose, heightening the danger.[9]

While the doctors offered medical support, Seward's friends and colleagues offered emotional support. Fanny's diary captured the sympathetic attentions of her father's powerful political friends. Among these was President Lincoln himself. On April 9, having heard of the accident of his secretary of state, the president cut short his visit at City Point to hurry to Washington. When he arrived, Lincoln must have winced at the sight of his secretary of state lying on the edge of his bed, helpless and swathed in bandages, keeping his sensitive wounded arm free from the intolerable touch of the very bedclothes.[10]

In her diary, Fanny described Lincoln's early evening visit with her father:

> When I went into the room [President Lincoln] was lying on the foot of Father's bed, talking with him. I said good evening & was passing around to my seat on the other side, when I saw a long arm extended back around the foot of the bed, to shake hands in his cordial way. He stayed some time—told us Mr. Stanton had told him he gave father up at first. He told us much about his visit to Richmond, & that one of his last [?] acts was going through a hospital of seven thousand men, & shaking hands with each one.[11]

On that same day, the secretary of war had visited three times. Edwin Stanton, characterized as "old bulldog," had earned this sobriquet for his unrelenting and unapologetic prosecution of the war as well as his unrelenting and unapologetic manner in doing so. Subordinates tiptoed in his presence, aware of the unrestrained wrath that would be unleashed should they prove incompetent or dishonest.[12]

Although Stanton's dogged efforts in pursuit of a Northern victory as secretary of war cannot be overestimated, during times of tragedy Stanton characteristically showed another face. After all, he himself was no stranger to heartache. He had suffered the death of his beloved first wife and the death of his young son during the war; he was himself a severe asthmatic who nonetheless drove himself relentlessly despite his condition. His loyal attention to Seward and his family after the carriage accident and later on gave the lie to his reputation as merely a merciless bureaucrat. In fact, Fanny was moved to record a tender bedroom conversation between Lincoln's secretary of war and her father:

> I shall never forget the scene this morning when Mr. Stanton approached the bed, & father took his hand and in a strong voice cried, 'God bless you Stanton—I can never tell you half ——' 'Don't try to speak,' said Mr. Stanton, whose face I could not see, but from his voice I judged him much affected—'You have made me cry for the first time in my life I believe,' said Father.[13]

Later that same day Mr. Stanton brought around some fruit sent by his wife, and later in the evening the secretary of war made a special trip to the Seward house to give Fanny's father news that she described as "unspeakbly [sic] thrilling & momentous.": *"at 4 o'c today Gen Lee surrendered himself and his army to General Grant.*"[14]

Lee's surrender at Appomattox launched a series of celebrations as yet unprecedented in American history. "The streets were in jubilee," crowed Fanny to her diary the next day, and from the upstairs windows of her father's room, she and her mother watched the "happy people, marching about with flags and bands of music" and heard the "salutes fired by order of Mr. Stanton" and the firing of howitzers by people from the Navy Yard.[15] From the window of her father's sickroom, Fanny could enjoy the illuminations of the public buildings, particularly the words her father had prepared for display on the State Department back in 1861. In his agonies, the secretary himself could not now read its words, but faithful Fanny recorded them in her diary: "The Union saved by fidelity to the Constitution, Faith in the People, & Trust in God."[16]

Seward's recovery, like the war itself, was marked by progress and reverses. On Sunday, the day of Lee's surrender, four days after the carriage accident, the swelling in his face had subsided and he looked more like himself. On Monday, he was able to sit up twice. The following day, he did not seem as strong, and Tuesday's weakness led to a restless night.[17]

Seward's jaw was particularly troublesome not only for him but for his doctors. The surgeons had difficulty keeping it immobile so that the broken ends might knit together. He had to be fed through a tube, a slow, difficult, and painful process. With a painful jaw and a right arm immobilized by splints, Fanny's father "lay helpless on a bed in agony."[18] A raised backrest made it easier for him to move his injured shoulder and arm, providing some relief.[19]

Aware that the bandages swathing his face were uncomfortable and that they were failing to immobilize the jaw, Fanny recorded that

Dr. Norris on Wednesday "secured the fractured jaw by a wire from one tooth to the other." To help him sleep, the doctor prescribed "Valerian & something else," but relief did not come. That night, Fanny noted that he was "delerious [sic]" and "still confused" by morning. But Fanny's father, despite his suffering, proved a cooperative and uncomplaining patient. One of his doctors attested to his astonishingly "stout heart."[20]

Throughout Seward's ordeal, his family rallied around him. They set up a system for caring for him around the clock, for the doctors had determined that his restlessness required a "constant watch." Augustus, Fanny, Fred, and Anna took shifts at the bedside. The family often read to him, Fred and Anna reading him the newspapers and Fanny reading from "Enoch Arden," Tennyson's popular narrative poem about a shipwrecked sailor. A male nurse, thirty-year-old Sergeant George Robinson, convalescing from his own war wounds, was brought in to care for the secretary through the night. Frances also helped, but her weakened physical condition was increasingly challenged by her husband's ordeal. However, Frances declared she had never seen "a family of children more devoted to the care of a parent."[21]

Seward's doctors were equally devoted. Fanny recorded the doctor visits for Thursday, April 13: Dr. Barnes came twice; Dr. Norris during the morning, afternoon, and evening; and Dr. Verdi "3 or 4 times."[22] On Good Friday, April 14, Fanny's father was taking solid food for the first time, breakfasting after a night of restful sleep on "soft egg, milk-toast, shad and coffee." Best of all, Seward's returning strength coincided with an event marking the nation's return to a period of peace. On April 14, an emotional ceremony was taking place in South Carolina, "the ceremony of raising the flag on Fort Sumter, taken from us 4 years ago."[23]

On that day, Fanny had made pencil notations in her pocket diary, wondering absently if she would have anything out of the ordinary to record for the date of April 14.[24] Unsuspecting, Fanny could not have known that she would soon be writing the most gripping diary entry of her life.

The omens were everywhere.

Just that morning, Fred had taken his father's place at a White House cabinet meeting. There he heard President Lincoln recount his strange dream of the night before in which he was "floating" toward an "unknown shore." Lincoln was susceptible to such gloomy premonitions. Once, after another such "ugly dream," Lincoln telegraphed Mary to put son Tad's pistol away. On Election Day of 1860, his bedroom mirror in Springfield caught two images of his face, "one more separate and pale than the other." At the end of March, 1865, Lincoln had dreamed of the White House on fire, and, in another chilling omen, he had been reading *Macbeth*, Shakespeare's bloody tale of political assassination, on his return from City Point to visit Seward in Washington.[25]

Furthermore, there had been unsettling forebodings surrounding the Seward family. In 1864 Seward had been threatened with assassination in an anonymous letter. If poison failed, the letter implied, six men would fire at once, "from a concealed window" using "telescopic rifles." On April thirteenth, a man fitting the description of Lewis Powell was allegedly seen near the family's Lafayette Square home. Private George Robinson, the soldier who was acting as Seward's night nurse, recalled a stranger who came to the dining room window of the Seward house on both April thirteenth and fourteenth. The stranger, who asked about the health of Secretary Seward, matched the description of Lewis Powell. Even John Wilkes Booth, according to fellow conspirator George Atzerodt, had reportedly visited the Seward home prior to April fourteenth and had been seen chatting with a "pretty chambermaid."[26]

Chillingly, one of the letters of condolence sent to Seward was from Martin Ryerson, a friend, businessman, and philanthropist. On April 13 Ryerson wrote of his uncanny apprehension that during this period of approaching peace both Seward and Lincoln "might both be taken from us."[27]

# 18

# Nothing Good about Good Friday

Perhaps the assassination of Abraham Lincoln would never have occurred had it not been for a comment overheard by John Wilkes Booth around noon on April 14. Dropping by Ford's Theatre to pick up his mail, Booth found himself privy to a history-making scrap of news: President Lincoln would be attending Ford's Theatre that evening.[1]

Booth, seeing an opportunity, seized it. He would have the day to plot and plan. He would alert his conspirators about their new assignments. He would rig the theatre's presidential box to allow his entry and exit. He would visit Mary Surratt's boarding house to finalize the details of his escape. He would arrange for a waiting horse at the back alley door of the theatre. He would call a meeting for eight p.m. at the Herndon House, a hotel close to Ford's Theatre and Surratt's boarding house, where the conspirators would coordinate their final plans. Finally, Booth must have crowed, he would have the opportunity to bring down the hated head of the Northern government. Ironically, that unexpected piece of information had provided John Wilkes Booth with a stroke of good luck. As James Swanson, a scholar of the Booth conspiracy, has pointed out, "He would not have to hunt Lincoln. The president was coming to him."[2]

At eight p.m., in a corner of the bar of the Herndon House, where Booth had arranged for Lewis Powell to stay, Booth assigned his cast their roles. George Atzerodt was to kill Vice President Andrew Johnson; Powell was to murder Secretary of State Seward; Booth assigned himself the starring role: he would assassinate Lincoln.[3] Ten o'clock was the appointed hour when Atzerodt would strike Johnson at his hotel, Powell would strike Seward at his home, and Booth would strike Lincoln at Ford's Theatre. That afternoon, leaving his hotel, Booth had bragged to the clerk that "There is going to be some splendid acting tonight."[4]

Soon the curtain would be raised on that performance.

As was her habit, on April 14, 1865, Fanny Seward jotted notes in her pocket diary, notes that, as usual, she intended to expand on at a later time. Fanny considered her pocket notebook to be an invaluable "assistance to memory." "Hurrying" through her life as she did, Fanny was often sorry not to have written down all about the dinner parties and other events immediately after they had taken place. Thanks to her "little notebook," she could capture these details before they had escaped her mind.[5] "[A] tiny three inch piece of paper with a couple of notes" in her pocket diary could result in expansion into "10 pages in her big diary"[6] later on.

Ironically, on the fourteenth of April Fanny recalled wondering absently whether she "should have anything unsual [sic] to enter there later in the day." She could not have known that, three weeks later, she would be expanding on those notes in an attempt to unburden her memory of the most painful experience of her life. During the morning and afternoon of April 14, however, Fanny Seward could not have known how heavy that "weight of recollection" would soon become.[7]

To begin with, Fanny noted in her pocket diary that her father had seemed better that day. During the quiet afternoon, Fanny had sat alone reading to him. Later she had spent some time talking with her resting mother. During that conversation, Fanny confessed to her mother "how any recital of suffering affected & haunted me." Frances admitted that she shared those same feelings.[8] This eerie admission proved an omen of things to come, for this sensitivity to suffering, tested across four years of civil war, would be tested again in the lives of both mother and daughter in the days and weeks ahead.

In the evening the family heard the Navy Yard employees winding their way to the White House in a torchlight parade, and Anna and

Fanny watched from the window as they sang "Rally Round the Flag." After that, Fanny shared a book of soldiers' songs with her sister-in-law, and then the family made "quiet arrangements for the night." Augustus would sleep until eleven o'clock and then sit up during the night with his father. Fanny, along with the nurse George Robinson, would watch over her father while Gus slept.[9]

Fanny, with Sergeant Robinson nearby, had been reading to her father from *Legends of Charlemagne.* Nine days after his accident, the secretary of state was still unable to talk. When Fanny saw that her father was drifting off, she "turned down the gas, laid my book on a stand at the foot of the bed, & took a seat on the other side" of his bed. At about ten o'clock, Dr. Norris made his final visit of the day with his patient, and, leaving the house, "left us all quiet."[10]

While Fanny Seward was settling her father for the night, two men were lurking in the park across the street.

One was the strapping Lewis Powell, the hardened Confederate veteran with the "athletic" and "gladiatorial" physique,[11] the man who kept the skull of a Union soldier as a souvenir, the man who never wounded but "either killed or missed."[12]

The other was twenty-two-year-old David Herold, with a physique as short and slender as Powell's was tall and powerful. Unlike Powell, Herold, who lived with his mother near the Navy Yard, was familiar with the streets of Washington; he would serve as guide through the city streets as he and Powell pursued their mission.[13] Because he also knew the back roads of Maryland like a veteran scout, Herold had earlier been chosen to help with Booth's former kidnapping plot; given his intimate knowledge of the landscape, Herold would have the skill to lead Lincoln's kidnapping party through the Southern countryside. That plan having fizzled, Herold now understood that on the night of April 14 it would be his job to help Powell escape once Seward's foul murder had been committed.[14]

As Powell and Herold paced in the park across from 17 Madison Place, the official address of the Seward house on the east side of

Lafayette Square, they had plenty of time to examine the outside of Fanny's Washington home. The red brick townhouse, only six blocks from Ford's Theatre, was surrounded by so many trees that its occupants could not easily see into the park[15]; thus, the house and grounds provided, ironically, a perfect cover for would-be assassins.

The murderous work of April 14, however, would be accomplished by Lewis Powell, Booth's most valuable recruit and a man fiercely loyal to "Captain Booth." Powell was remembered as having left the meeting at the Herndon House with a "wild look" in his eyes, but the man with the wild look was also well dressed for murder. His clean white overcoat served two purposes: it gave him a presentable appearance, and it concealed the weapons with which Powell was heavily armed. One of those weapons was a heavy 1858 Whitney navy revolver, a gun made popular during the war. The other was a large silver-mounted Bowie knife, made in England for the Confederacy and in common use by blockade runners. It bore the inscription "Real Life Defender" and an alligator motif that harkened back to Powell's first enlistment in a Florida regiment.[16]

The razor-sharp blade of Powell's knife recalled an earlier fear of Fanny Seward. In March of 1863, the North was awash in despair. Several attempts to capture Vicksburg had failed, protests against the Emancipation Proclamation were growing, vocal factions were advocating for peace at any price, and Congress had ordered a draft. During this period, which a Wisconsin officer likened to "the Valley Forge of the war," Fanny's father had badly cut his hand while shaving. Distressing rumors of this accident spread far and wide, and many of the powerful either visited or wrote to express their concern. The hand, bandaged with care by Dr. Verdi, healed steadily, but in this bleak period of the war, Fanny lamented that "Father's hand, upon which so much depended, should be disabled even for a time."[17]

Now, on the night of April 14, a determined young stranger paced in the park across the street from Fanny's bedridden father, concealing a knife with a double-edged point and a ten-inch blade,[18] a weapon more deadly than a razor blade, a weapon intended to permanently disable William Seward's steadfast hands.

Conspirator Lewis Powell had a more challenging assignment than either George Atzerodt or John Wilkes Booth. After all, Atzerodt had merely to slay his victim, Vice President Andrew Johnson, in his apartment at the Kirkwood House, and Booth had merely to slaughter his seated victim, the president of the United States, in the balcony of a theatre which Booth knew well.

In only one respect was William Seward an easy target for Lewis Powell: recovering from his carriage accident, Seward would be bedridden and helpless. In every other respect, Powell's assignment was riddled with unknowns. After all, Powell had to gain entrance to the house without raising suspicion. If he managed to get inside, he then had to locate his victim inside the sprawling mansion, a three-story residence with which he was unfamiliar. Throughout the operation, he had to avoid sounds that would alert the neighbors or the other members of the household. Finally, Powell could not be sure how many family members, government messengers, servants, or nurses would be on the premises, people who could defend the family or run for help.

Powell's mission was undoubtedly made easier by a clever ruse. Herold, whose occupation was as a pharmacist's assistant, was familiar with the butcher paper packages tied with string in which medicines were routinely delivered. Powell, the pair decided, would pose as a messenger from Seward's doctor; his hands would hold a counterfeit package of medicine to be delivered to the secretary of state under doctor's orders.[19]

Ten o'clock approached. Lurking in the darkness, Powell and Herold saw the lights go down in the third-floor bedroom. Only a half-hour earlier, Dr. Verdi had left the house, and now the conspirators watched Dr. Norris depart. As Powell strode across the street to the front door of the Seward mansion, his life was assuming a new trajectory, catapulting him from a childhood as the son of a Baptist minister to an adulthood amidst a group of conspirators determined to avenge the honor of a defeated South. In the wake of his actions, the trajectory of the Sewards' family life would also change.

At the doorstep of the Seward mansion, Powell, his fingers ringing the bell at the same instant that shots were ringing out across town at Ford's Theatre, knew that it was time. Assassination night was about to begin.

The doorbell was answered by William Bell, a nineteen-year-old African American house servant whose official duty was waiter. Unlike most of the servants who worked for the Sewards, Bell had been working for the family for only nine months. The broad-shouldered stranger at the door was dressed in heavy boots, a light overcoat, black pants, and a brown hat. Bell took in the man's coarse black hair and his very red face. He noticed, too, that although the man held a package of medicine in his left hand, he kept his right hand inside his coat pocket. After the stranger stepped inside, Bell closed the door behind him.[20]

Still, nothing seemed suspicious about the stranger, even after he explained that his packet of medicine was from Dr. Verdi and that the doctor had ordered the stranger to give instructions for taking it to Secretary Seward personally.[21] There seemed little to suspect about this request; after all, the stranger even pronounced the doctor's Italian name correctly.[22]

Bell replied that it was against his orders to let anyone up to see Seward but explained that if Powell would give him the directions, he would see that Seward took the medicine properly.[23] It was then that Bell's suspicions were raised, for the stranger kept repeating his request, insisting on going up, and lingering in the hall even as Bell's refusal grew increasingly firm.[24] Finally the stranger left the hall and made for the steps. Watching Powell mount the stairs and hearing his heavy boots thudding on the stairsteps, Bell climbed ahead of him, asking the stranger not to tread so heavily.

It was then that Frederick Seward, Fanny's brother, came out of his room on the third floor and faced the stranger on the steps. When Powell insisted on seeing the secretary, Frederick told him that his father was asleep but that he could be trusted to give his father the medicine. Powell then changed tactics, asking Fred if his father were really asleep. Now, by accident, Frederick gave Powell an important clue. He went to the front bedroom, to "the last door on the left."[25] Opening the door of his father's room to see if he was still sleeping, Fred inadvertently identified the room of Powell's victim.[26]

Fanny, keeping vigil beside her father's bed with Sergeant Robinson, saw her brother open the door and glance at the bed to check on their father. After Fred closed the door, Fanny's father opened his eyes, giving "a little smile of recognition as he saw me at the foot of the bed."

> I do not remember hearing voices outside, but something led me to think that Fred was there with someone else. It occurred to me that he might have some important reason for wishing to see Father awake. Perhaps the president was there, or had sent over. I did not stop to see if father wakened thoroughly, but hastened to the door, opened it a very little, and found Fred standing close by it, facing me. On his right hand, also close by the door, stood a very tall young man, in a light hat & long overcoat. I said 'Fred, Father is awake now.' Something in Fred's manner led me at once to think that he did not wish me to say so, and that I had better not have opened the door. This confused me, & looking around I was glad to see Father going to sleep again. Holding the door as I did, I know the man could not see my father at all, nor could Fred, I think. I do not remember what Fred said to me. The man seemed impatient, & addressing me in a tone that struck me at once as much more harsh & full of determination than such a simple question justified, asked 'Is the Secretary asleep.' I paused to look at my father, & [sic] replied 'Almost.' Then Fred drew the door shut very quickly. I sat down again. I had no means of telling the errand of the man.[27]

Sitting down by the bed and taking up her vigil again, Fanny could not have known that she and her brother had now confirmed for Powell that his helpless victim lay behind that door, guarded only by a delicate young woman.

Outside his father's door, Fred, still resisting Powell's pleas, now grew stern. Impatiently he insisted that "I am the proprietor here, and his son," remembered Bell. "If you cannot leave your message with me, you cannot leave it at all." Then, reluctantly, Powell turned and started back down the steps, Bell scampering a few steps ahead of him.[28]

But the Powell now descending the steps knew something he had not known when he ascended them: the location of his victim. Pretending to leave while Fred returned to his own room, Powell suddenly reversed course, remounting the steps and leaping to Fred's side. Powell, drawing his revolver from his coat, now aimed it at Frederick's head, muttering an oath and squeezing the trigger. "I remember," recalled Fred, "noticing the shape of the pistol, which was that of a Navy revolver. The next instant I heard a click of the lock."[29]

Fortunately for Frederick Seward, Powell's pistol had not fired, sparing Fanny's brother the explosion of a .36-caliber bullet into his brain, an explosion that would have killed him on the spot.[30]

The brutish Confederate who owned a Union skull was now forced to turn his impotent pistol into a weapon of blunt force. Powell now rained savage blows on Frederick's head with the muzzle of the gun, blows so severe that they broke the ramrod.[31]

William Bell, the servant, had watched in horror as Powell bludgeoned Frederick with blows from his revolver. Quickly the family servant ran back down the stairs. Rushing out the front door and heading to army headquarters for help, Bell screamed "Murder!" out into the street.[32]

From inside her father's bedroom, Fanny described what she now heard:

> Very soon I heard the sound of blows—it seemed to me as many as half a dozen—sharp and heavy, with lighter one's [sic] between. There had been an interval of quiet. I did not fully connect this with the person I had seen. I thought they were chasing a rat in the hall, remembering such a chase once. But when the blows continued, I could not tell what it meant, & said to Robinson, who was sitting at the head of the bed, on the side nearest the door, 'What can be the matter? Do go and see.' Then I was afraid something was wrong, and, being impatient to find out, started, myself.[33]

Fanny and Robinson reached the door at the same moment. Suddenly two men, side by side, burst through the door. Instantly Fanny recognized her brother Fred. "The side of his face was covered with blood, the rest very pale, his eyes full of intense expression." Fanny's bloodied brother Fred was unable to speak, having bravely grappled with the assassin in the hallway past his sister's bedroom, past his own bedroom, and into the door of his father's bedroom. "Scarlet ribbons of blood disfiguring his face," Fanny's brother had clung to Powell "with the persistency of a bulldog."[34]

Horrified, Fanny now knew that words were not necessary, for on her speechless brother's "right hand was the assassin."[35]

Powell, with Fred gravely injured, was now free to slaughter his intended victim. However, the Confederate veteran had not counted on coming face to face with George Robinson, a Union veteran, at the door to the bedroom. Quickly realizing that he faced a more difficult obstacle than a fragile young woman, Powell, undeterred, slashed at the sergeant's forehead with his knife, knocking him off balance. With Robinson out of the way, a path to Seward's bed had been cleared.[36]

Fanny could not recall how the stranger's "face looked," but she was sure of two things: "his arms were both stretched out," and he was "rushing toward the bed." Terrified, Fanny saw that the stranger had a pistol in the left hand and a knife in the right. He was lunging straight for her father.[37]

"I ran beside him to the bed," recalled Fanny, "imploring him to stop." Racing Powell to her father's bedside, attempting to throw herself between her father and the assassin, begging him to stop, Fanny shrieked "Don't kill him." Roused by the word "kill," Fanny's father was startled awake. First seeing his daughter's face and then struggling to learn to whom she was speaking, Seward then "raised himself up & had one glimpse of the assassin's face bending over" him.[38]

Now Powell's strong hands pinned the feeble Seward's chest to the bed, but in the dim light of the darkened room the downward stabs and thrusts of the blade missed their target, seeking flesh but often slashing blindly at sheets and blankets and mattress. Finally the double-edged point of Powell's knife found its mark, slicing great gashes into Seward's neck and cheek. Powell then flailed his victim "with all the energy that he had." The vicious blows, made by a blade that felt cold to its victim, unleashed torrents of bloody rain.[39]

Fanny, now in shock, watched in horror by the foot of the bed. Powell's murderous rampage was directed at the person she loved most in the world, the father whom she had scampered after as a little girl, the father who blessed her as a daughter who was "all that a loving father could ask."[40] She remembered thinking, "This must be a fearful dream!" She remembered seeing Fred and Robinson and the assassin "struggling beside the bed." In a kind of out-of-body experience, she absently scanned "all the familiar objects in the room, the bureau, the little stand, the book I had been reading . . . Then I knew it was not a dream." The young woman who could not bear to scald turtles for soup and considered fishing even for amusement "wicked" remembered "pacing the room back & forth from end to end—screaming."[41]

Meanwhile, against the backdrop of Fanny's screams, Robinson regained his footing. The nurse hurled himself onto Powell, grasping him from behind in a vise-like bear hug, struggling to haul Powell off the helpless secretary. Fanny, using the sharp thrusts of her voice's blade as her only weapon at hand, continued to pierce the darkened room with her screams. As the assassin then turned on Robinson, stabbing the nurse in the shoulder as the two men grappled with each other, Powell struck the sergeant under the ear with the butt of his revolver and prepared to ram the knife into the nurse's belly.[42]

Suddenly Fanny's brother Augustus, awakened by the shrill shrieks of his sister, burst into the room. Because of the faint light in the room, Augustus could barely make out the forms of two men, "one trying to hold the other," at the foot of his father's bed. Grabbing onto Powell from behind, Augustus shoved him to the door, and as Augustus and Robinson struggled with Powell, the assassin managed to knife Fanny's brother's head and hand.[43]

While Powell was fighting with both men, Gus heard Powell muttering intensely, "I'm mad, I'm mad!"[44] As Powell was forced into the brighter light of the hallway, Augustus finally had a clear view of the assassin's face. Landing a final blow on Robinson and wrenching free of

Augustus, Powell rushed "headlong down the stairs." On the way down, Powell encountered Emerick Hansell, a messenger from the State Department. Now in the hallway, Fanny vaguely recalled seeing Powell stab at the messenger,[45] wounding him in the back with the point of his knife that sliced through the ribs and barely missed his lungs.

As Powell fled the house, Gus raced to his room, scrambled for his pistol, and dashed to the front door, "intending to shoot the person if he attempted to return."[46] Only after Powell had ridden off on his horse did Gus realize the shocking purpose of Powell's visit: " . . . the man was an assassin who had entered the house for the purpose of murdering my father."[47]

So much had happened so quickly. Fanny shuddered to recall that "all that had taken place" had flashed by "in an instant."[48]

Even so, there was much more to come.

Running from the hall back into the bedroom, Fanny scanned the empty bed and cried out, "Where's father?" At the side of the bed, Fanny found "what I thought was a pile of bed clothes" and then realized that the crumpled heap was her father. Seward had likely rolled off the bed and onto the floor either from the force of the original blows or after Robinson had pulled Powell off his chest. A servant recalled that Fanny screamed, "Oh my God! Father's dead."[49]

Fanny said that her father looked "so gastly [sic] that I was sure he was dead, he was white & very thin [?] with the blood that had drained from the gashes about his face & throat." Indeed, "wrapped in bloody sheets like some latter-day Julius Caesar," Seward did, in fact, look dead. One of his doctors described him as little more than "an exsanguinated corpse." As Fanny attempted to respond to her father, her "feet slipped in a great pool of blood."[50]

Meanwhile, Sergeant Robinson swiftly turned his attention to Fanny's father. Despite his injuries, Fanny recalled, he rushed to the side of the secretary of state. Frantically feeling his wrist, Robinson could not find a pulse. Then, pulling off the secretary's clothes, Robinson felt for Seward's heart, announcing to an anxious Fanny that he heard "his heart still beat." But Fanny's father was bleeding so furiously that Robinson could not tell how seriously he had been wounded. It seemed that the "right cheek was cut clear through so that you could see into his mouth" and the cheek seemed to have "kind of slid down—hung only on the back part."[51]

Standing "faithfully at Father's side," Robinson instructed the stricken Fanny about how to help. He "told me everything—about staunching [sic] the blood with cloths & water," Fanny recalled. Robinson worked from the right side of the bed while Fanny, "kneeling on the bed on the left," across bedsheets slashed and wet with her father's blood, frantically attempted to stanch the blood flow from wounds on the left side of her father's neck. Although her father seemed "almost dead," the stalwart secretary of state was still composed. With great presence of mind, he spoke to Fanny, directing her "to have the doors closed, & send for surgeons, & to ask to have a guard placed around the house."[52]

Now Dr. Verdi arrived. He lived only two blocks away from the Seward mansion, and the waiter William Bell had raced to summon him, shouting, "Oh, come, doctor, Mr. Seward is killed!" The doctor faced five injured men, "all wounded and their wounds bleeding." The men were Secretary Seward, Frederick Seward, Augustus Seward, George Robinson, and Emerick Hansell. With disbelief, Verdi later reflected: "All this the work of one man."[53]

When Dr. Verdi first saw Fanny's father, he was "in his bed, covered with blood, with blood all around him, blood under the bed, and blood on the handles of the doors."[54] His bed was simply "saturated with blood."[55]

As the doctor approached Fanny's father, his feet went "deep in blood." Blood streamed from a gash in Seward's cheek, already painfully swollen from the carriage accident. He had suffered a "frightful wound" about five inches long and two inches deep. The wound had laid the cheek open to flap loosely around the neck.[56] Because he was bleeding so profusely, Verdi feared the jugular vein had been severed.

Determining that this was not so, Dr. Verdi, who knew the family intimately, noticed Fanny and her mother trembling nearby, "almost paralyzed" with fear. He then quickly addressed the "terror" on the faces of all Secretary Seward's family, "evidently expecting that his wounds were mortal." After examining the wounds, Verdi immediately turned to the family and said, "'I congratulate you all that the wounds are not mortal'; upon which Mr. Seward stretched out his hands and received his family."[57]

Having assessed the state of the secretary's injuries, Dr. Verdi then ordered ice applied to Seward's wounds. Fanny, racing down to the butler's pantry for the ice, glimpsed the reporters and servants and neighbors who had begun to gather and were milling around on the landing.[58] In the pandemonium, as Dr. Verdi stood on Seward's right and Fanny again took up her frenzied work on the left, she remembered feverishly "talking & making some exclaimations [sic]" and being cautioned to stay calm by Dr. Verdi, "who was himself greatly excited." Treating the family he knew so well in the aftermath of a bloody rampage, the agitated Dr. Verdi had himself "kept rushing around saying 'Children, children, don't get excited—.'" Sensing the anxiety swirling around him, especially the anxiety of his daughter, Fanny's father extended his hand to her "in a soothing way, as if to bid me be calm, & reassure me."[59] When Fanny's father offered his hand to her, it was another gesture symbolic of the mutual reassurances father and daughter had offered each other across the years. The crisis through which they were now passing, like the crisis of the war itself, had called for the solace of their devotion once again. Crisis had not only inspired their love for each other; it had confirmed it.

The next doctors on the scene were Surgeon General Joseph Barnes and Dr. Basil Norris. As Dr. Norris knelt down to examine the wounds, Fanny heard him mutter something like "[a]ssassination in the vilest form—." Outside her father's door and along the stairway, throngs of people were assembling—"M.C.s, policemen, members of the press—etc." Anna resisted their attempts to enter Fred's room, and Fanny would not allow anyone to enter her father's room. The spectators were "asking us to tell more than we knew ourselves," recalled

Fanny. But Fanny clung to the one fact that meant more to her than any other: "that no artery was severed" and that her father's "wounds were not fatal."[60]

The doctors took charge of their patients, Dr. Norris stitching up "the great gash in father's cheek—" as Fanny painfully listened to her father's moans.[61]

While the doctors attended to her father, Fanny embarked on a frightening survey of the victims in the rest of the house. When Fanny entered Fred's room, she saw her brother "lying bloody & unconcious [sic], on a lounge," realizing that Fred's injuries were "of the most dangerous nature." Fanny's anxious mother confessed to her daughter she was "afraid Fred could not live." Soon the doctors would explain the dangerous nature of Fred's condition. Surgeon General Barnes, who had "attracted a group of brilliant men to the army medical service," would establish that Fred's cranium had been fractured in two places; his original diagnosis noted that Fanny's brother was "bleeding very profusely, exceedingly faint, almost pulseless, and unable to articulate."[62]

When she entered Gus's room, Fanny saw her brother on the bed and learned he had been wounded "five or six times on the forehead and top of the head, and once on the left hand."[63] Gus asked about their father and assured his sister that his own wounds were "not serious." Robinson was now recovering in the room with Gus, dismissing his own wounds as "only flesh wounds," wounds he had ignored as he loyally "insisted on attending to Father."[64]

In Fanny's own bedroom lay messenger Hansell. There the doctors dressed "poor Hansell's back," and Eliza the seamstress attended to this young man who had been stabbed by the fleeing Powell. Also in Fanny's room sat James Donaldson, another messenger for the State Department, who, along with Gus, was planning to share some of the night watch that evening. Donaldson's face was "buried in his hands—" and he was "crying aloud, like a child." The family's mansion, formerly a gathering place for elegant dinners and important guests, had been turned into a noisy trauma center, and Fanny Seward shuddered to observe that "every man I met had blood on his face."[65]

Blood was the ink in which Powell had written his work:

> All the white wood work of the entry was covered with great dashes of blood. . . . It was a terrible sight—there was so much blood everywhere. The drugget on the stairs was sprinkled with it, all the way down to the floor below. On the inner side of the door of Father's room there was, in blood, the distinct impression of a hand, which seemed to have clenched it from without. . . .
>
> . . . . When we found father there was such a pool of blood that our dresses were drabbled in it.[66]

After her father's wounds were dressed, a number of Secretary Seward's colleagues, "distinguished gentlemen" like Secretary of War Edwin Stanton, General Henry Halleck, and Secretary of the Navy Gideon Welles, rushed to his bedside. "As this group stood there Father related in a clear, distinct manner, his recollections of the whole scene—between each and [sic] he drew breath, as one dying might speak, & I feared the effort might cost his remaining strength. . . . It was then that I first heard about the President, one of the gentlemen telling Mother that he was shot."[67]

Sadly, the news about the president was true. Astonishingly, as he was attending to his patients at the Seward mansion, Surgeon General Barnes had been suddenly sent for.[68] That would make two sudden summonses for the good doctor that night. The first, delivered as he was playing whist at the home of his friend Judge David K. Cartter, had been a summons to attend the secretary of state. The second, delivered as he attended the injured at the Seward house, had been a summons to the Petersen House across the street from Ford's Theatre: President Lincoln had been shot.[69] As the Surgeon General left the room, he shook hands with Fanny. Although he assured the young woman that her "Father was safe,"[70] Barnes would soon observe first hand that her father's president and friend, the good Abraham Lincoln, was in grave danger. There would be nothing good to come of this Good Friday.

# 19

# "A Pretty Brave Little Girl Tonight"

Now the "long dark hours" of the night watch began. Taking her seat as at a death vigil, Fanny sat quietly in her father's now silent room. The hushed stillness magnified Fanny's "constant apprehension of some fatal turn" in her father's symptoms.[1] Surely sensitive Fanny could not have failed to interpret every cough, every moan, every movement of the bedclothes as a potential signal of alarm.

She was not aware, however, that a similarly anxious vigil was taking place across town at a humble boardinghouse across from Ford's Theatre. While her father was occasionally given tea, orderlies at Petersen's boarding house were fetching mustard plasters and blankets for the dying president.[2] Through the long night, Fanny undoubtedly whispered endearments, straightened bedclothes, or, as had long been their practice, reached for her father's hand. These were the same sentiments that compelled Lincoln's attending physician, Dr. Charles A. Leale, to reach for the failing president's hand. Both tender gestures had their source in the same sentiment: "to let him . . . know . . . that he was in touch with humanity and had a friend."[3]

The worst thing about the quiet, Fanny admitted, was that it gave her time to think. Her thoughts were "overwhelming" and likely mirrored the anxious reflections of the many doctors and friends who huddled at the dying president's bedside. "The thought that such cruel & inhuman beings, as the man who had attacked my father & brothers, existed" made Fanny shudder. Fanny Seward, herself so devoid of malice that she could not imagine it in others, found it impossible to believe, like Lincoln himself, "that any human being" lived "who would do me any harm." But now both Fanny and her president knew the truth: such evil did exist, and the fact that it abounded in the world, that it had stretched out its hand to squeeze the life out of two unparalleled servants of the nation, made Fanny "wish myself dead, & out of such a world."[4]

Admitting that she was "too shocked to reason," Fanny was nagged through the night by a gnawing fear that "the assassin who had wounded so many might return & finish his attempt." In her fearful state, Fanny "felt suspicious of every unknown face however friendly." In fact, earlier in the night, after Powell had fled, Fanny defied her mother's orders: she went alone to search for other lurking assassins in the attic and on the parlor floor. Despite her fear, Fanny's reasoning had not been flawed. Powell, after all, did have an accomplice in David Herold. Early newspaper reports assumed that all the members of Lincoln's cabinet had been targeted for assassination, and morning rumors swirled that dozens might hang. Even the stout-hearted Edwin Stanton speculated about a far-reaching conspiracy plot, positing that Jefferson Davis, president of the Confederacy, may have masterminded it.[5]

Chillingly, the young woman who admitted that "any recital of suffering affected & haunted me" spent a fearful night reciting scenes that would both affect and haunt her for the rest of her days. While she hovered at her father's bedside or paced the floorboards of his room, her mind retraced the scenes of suffering experienced only a few hours before, recollections that were bathed in blood:

> Blood, blood, my thoughts seemed drenched in it—I seemed to breathe its sickening odor. My dress was stained with it—Mother's was drabbled with it—it was on everything. The bed had been covered with blood—the blankets & sheet chopped with several blows of the knife.[6]

Swathed in the recollection of bloody deeds as horrific as those in the theater tragedies she knew by heart, Fanny was likely haunted by

Shakespearean images of bloody daggers and bloody hands, images that now served as matching symbols of the drama from her own personal version of *Macbeth*. Given her own fascination with the theater, Fanny could not have failed to recognize the dramatic elements leading to the horrific scene she had just witnessed: the trick of a package of medicine, a handsome coat disguising weapons, an assassin shouting "I'm mad." As she retraced the nightmarish scene of that terrible night, over and over she repeated the haunting and familiar line from *Macbeth*, the line she had so often heard spoken on the stage of the theater that she so deeply loved. Throughout the long dark night that loomed like a nightmare, the words "I have supped full on horrors" echoed in her mind like a silent scream.[7]

Inevitably, blessedly, "night wore away," and as "the gray light of morning came," other words of poetry came to Fanny's mind. Over and over fluttered the words from Tennyson's "In Memoriam": "Risest thou then gray dawn again."[8] Against the backdrop of such a bloody night, the appearance of a gentle morning struck Fanny as incongruously surreal: " . . . that light should come, & the sun rise, & the birds sing & the green leaves rustle in the trees, seemed strange in such a world."[9]

In the early morning, Dr. William Notson, an assistant surgeon from the U.S. Medical Corps, substituted for Dr. Norris at Seward's bedside. The doctor showed Fanny a card. It announced the sobering news that "the president was growing worse." Fanny could not have known that soon Surgeon General Barnes, who had provided faithful service at her father's side only a few hours before, would be closing the eyes of Abraham Lincoln and crossing "the pulseless hands . . . across the motionless breast."[10]

That morning a somber but faithful visitor appeared at Seward's bedside. He was Edwin Stanton, the secretary of war. Having just given a herculean effort to concluding a war, he now faced the prospect of burying his beloved president and launching a manhunt for the assassins. Standing at the bedside of a friend and respected cabinet member, staring in disbelief at the bandages covering Seward's slashed and bloodied face, surely even this stoic public servant must have shuddered before all that he had experienced in less than twelve hours. After all, Stanton had visited the Seward household only the evening before, leaving sometime around nine p.m. to attend a serenade scheduled to take place at his own home. Later, getting ready for bed, Stanton heard his wife Ellen screaming downstairs, "Mr. Seward is murdered!" Racing to the Seward mansion and observing the chaos there, Stanton was soon torn away by news of President Lincoln's assassination, and he was forced to fight the crowds swarming around Ford's Theatre to reach the president.[11] When Surgeon General Barnes informed Stanton that Lincoln's wounds were fatal, the reputedly impassive Stanton was reported to have collapsed into a chair and "wept like a child."[12]

Fanny recalled that Stanton announced to her mother that the president had "died at 7," personally delivering the "shocking news" to the Seward family "within two hours." To Fanny's mother, Frances, fell the duty of informing the secretary of state. Quietly, "while Mr. Stanton was there by the bed," Fanny's mother "said very gently to Father—'Henry—the President is gone.'"[13]

Despite his injuries and his inability to talk, Fanny concluded that her father "seemed to know the meaning" of Stanton's news, taking it "calmly." Perhaps Fanny's father was recalling the image of the president who had lounged across the bed on his return from Richmond, that same bed now streaked with blood. Perhaps he was remembering that he had once called Lincoln "the best and wisest man he [had] ever known." From Fanny's account, it seems clear that he understood what journalist Noah Brooks acknowledged: a "great and loving heart was still."[14]

Then, displaying the valiant resilience that so characterized him, Fanny's father reached for the white slate and pencil he had been using to communicate ever since his carriage accident. Fanny watched her father struggling to make himself understood by writing words to Stanton and the family. Alas, Fanny conceded that "owing to his exhausted state, & to his broken arm, it was almost impossible for him to write" anything that "could be read."[15] Miraculously, despite his broken body, the spirit of Fanny's father remained unshattered.

Fanny listened to the conversation between her mother and Edwin Stanton. "Are *you* safe Mr. Stanton," Frances Seward asked, "as if apprehensive of danger to him." "Not any more than anyone else," Mr. Stanton replied. After Stanton indicated that his wife, Ellen, was waiting in the library, Fanny went down to visit, and it was then that Fanny presented the evidence which she had discovered after the assault on her father. While Surgeon General Barnes was in attendance and Dr. Norris was stitching Seward's cheek, Fanny had found some things of importance:

> [B]etween the door & the bed, just in front of the wash-stand, a hat which I supposed to be Payne's*—as it afterwards proved to be—I showed it to Anna, & by her advice put it in the bureau drawer. The washbowl on the stand had the bottom broken out when I first looked at it. Near where I found the hat, the pistol was picked up—I found Robinson looking for the priming on the floor—he said it was missing, and if stepped on might do mischief—he soon found it.[16]
> [**Note: Fanny is using one of Lewis Powell's aliases here.]*

Immediately Stanton "took charge of both" items, recognizing them as important evidence. Fanny also took the opportunity to inform Stanton of her "fear" that there was no guard at the back door. Stanton, remembered Fanny, was "very kind," but he was also characteristically efficient, quickly ordering another guard to the house with "instructions to come to me, & to place the guard where I said."[17]

Another morning visitor was Dorothea Dix, who came over "quite early . . . & saw Mother & Father." Earlier, Dix had sent the family a note, "offering to be of assistance, & to send one or more women nurses." During this visit, Fanny's father was able to make himself understood by writing a message for Miss Dix on his slate. Fanny copied down his words: "Neither the friends nor the enemies of our America have left me anything to complain of. The friends of America ought to have watched Mr. Lincoln better. His life however is the forfeit. The Nation will do him Justice."[18]

On the morning of April 15, however, Justice seemed out of reach. Instead, the "friends of America" experienced a day in which nature, offering a "cheerless cold rain," reflected the emotions of the capital.

Washingtonians, both "horrified and excited," raced through the streets, learning "that Mr. Lincoln had been shot and killed, in the midst of his friends, by the side of his wife, at the acme of the people's joy." The bells began to toll the grim announcement, and the city was plunged into "deep, universal mourning." Where only shortly before, the capital had been glittering with grand illuminations and exploding with fireworks, now "broad folds of funeral drapery"[19] shrouded a mourning city.

Throughout the day, at the house on Lafayette Square, Fanny's father continued to try to communicate on his slate. Faithful Fanny recorded his words, leaving "blanks where the words were illegible." The other sentences he struggled to write included these fragments:

> ——— the blows inflicted before or after the assault on you, Augustus, & Frederick, I was fast asleep and only saw Fanny ——— up, and the assassin. I next ——— ——— and would kill me. Then the blow, dashing blood in floods. . . . I saw all my strength was weakness last night. I thought that if I had still reserved forces I should make them take me safely through in two or three days. I am very moderate. I have drunk tea all day—making no point of it.[20]

Those disjointed fragments were the last words Fanny recorded in her diary about the events of April 14 and 15, 1865. She would not pick up her diary again until June 17, when another family tragedy was fast approaching.

Meanwhile, over the days and weeks to come, both Seward and Frederick were closely attended by physicians and family members. As the nation awaited the burial of its president and the capture of his assassins, William and Frederick Seward struggled to recover from their hideous wounds.

Fanny's father's condition was serious. For days he fluctuated between partial consciousness and stupor. The injuries from his carriage accident had been serious enough, but to them had been added "the frightful wounds inflicted by the assassin's knife." Surgeon General Barnes identified three distinct wounds: a gash in the right cheek that swept to the angle of the jaw, another stab wound on the right side of the neck, and a final stab wound on the left side of the neck. Dr. Verdi concluded that his patient's real danger was from loss of blood, weakening him and making it more difficult for him to recover from the shock.[21]

Treating Seward's wounds presented challenges to the doctors. Because of the prior injury to the jaw from the carriage accident, Seward's new wound added to the inflammation in his already swollen cheek, rendering "the union of the bones more difficult."[22] After several unsuccessful attempts to stabilize his jaw, eventually New York dentist Dr. Thomas Gunning was called in. Gunning fashioned a splint to align the lower jaw; the splint was held in place by a contraption made of rods affixed to a headcap.[23]

In the tumultuous world outside the quiet sickrooms of Fanny's father and brother, historic events were taking place. Vice President Johnson was inaugurated, Lincoln's funeral train was crossing the country, the assassins were arrested, and Jefferson Davis was captured, while Fanny's father was still immobile. Although Seward would later refer to a "vague and dreamy memory of being propped up with pillows, and drawn to the window, to witness the passing funeral pageant of the president" with its "great black catafalque" and "nodding sable plumes," there is no question that he was still "physically too weak to grasp its full significance."[24] While these events were occurring, "Seward had almost no use of his mending right arm. His face was swollen, and a high collar only partially concealed the scars left by Paine's knife. The iron brace that held his broken jaw in place made speech difficult."[25]

Yet the indefatigable secretary of state, aided by Fanny, her father's "almost inseparable companion," ultimately recovered; but he emerged from his ordeal as a permanently disfigured man. Assistant Secretary of War Charles A. Dana described him as "one of the most horrible spectacles that the human eye ever beheld." His face was disfigured by long scars, and the slash to his jaw created a sagging mouth that slid downward on the right side into the chin. Ever after, when being

13. Seward's face was permanently disfigured after the assassination attempt. Collections of the Seward House Museum, Auburn, NY.

photographed, he preferred turning "the scarred half of his face away from the camera."[26]

Still, Seward returned to the world with his equanimity intact. As he gallantly received President Johnson and his cabinet on a visit to his home on May 9, the iron frame stabilizing his jaw made it almost impossible for him to talk. Even so, by June he was returning to work for short periods, his shoulder still crippled and his left arm and hand still weak. He described himself as a "bruised reed and the marvel is that I am not broken in pieces."[27]

However, the most critically injured of those wounded in the Seward household that night was Fanny's brother Frederick. Stanton, telegraphing General Sherman, predicted that Seward might recover but that Frederick was likely to die of the wounds he received from the assassin. When Doctor Verdi first examined Fred after the attack, Fred was conscious but had great difficulty in articulating. Fred, recognizing the doctor, kept placing his finger on the back of his head, mumbling, "It is, it is." After Verdi examined the wound, he turned to Fred and asked, "You want to know whether your skull is broken or not?" Fred replied, "Yes." Verdi replied, nodding "Yes" in response. Not long after, Fred lapsed into a coma, not to awaken for another sixty hours. Dr. Verdi feared Frederick's wounds would be fatal.[28]

Fanny's brother Fred had suffered at least two vicious blows to the head that crushed the left parietal and the left frontal bone. Both wounds exposed the brain. Forever after, Frederick would wear a skullcap to disguise these wounds.[29]

Fortunately, Fred Seward, like his father, would recover. He regained consciousness, and splinters of bone were removed from his brain periodically. In two weeks' time Fred was conscious, and speaking clearly and distinctly. Medically, the greatest concern was from hemorrhages of his wounds.[30] Still, Frederick's overall recovery was slow. He only left the house after two months, and it would be six months before he returned to work at the State Department.[31]

As Fanny's father and brother slowly returned to health, surely the family had time to recount the series of fortunate coincidences that had assured their survival. After all, Powell, in injuring five people in the Seward mansion that night, earned the dubious honor of becoming, like one of Macbeth's assassins, the "best o' the cut-throats."[32] As Seward biographer John M. Taylor has pointed out, Powell had wounded more people in a single assassination attempt than any other such villain in American history.[33]

Undoubtedly, the most fortunate circumstance occurred when Powell's revolver malfunctioned. But other circumstances favored the Sewards' survival and foiled the assassin's plans.[34] Foremost among them was the unexpected presence of Sergeant George Robinson in

William Seward's sickroom. Wounded in Virginia in May of 1864, Robinson, a farmer before he enlisted with the Eighth Maine Volunteer Infantry, was slated to be transferred back to his home state when he was assigned on April 13 to serve as Seward's nurse, the day before the assassination attempt.[35] A braver soldier could not have been found. Despite the brief nature of his service with the family, Robinson, who "had submitted himself repeatedly to the punishment of Powell's knife," clung to the assassin with the ferocity of a soldier on the battlefield. There is no doubt that this courageous sergeant "would not have abandoned his patient until Powell stabbed him to death."[36]

Furthermore, once the assassin had escaped, Robinson had vigorously worked in conjunction with Fanny to sustain his patient's life. For his efforts, he was rewarded with a clerkship, a pension, a farm, a gold medal, and the knife Powell used in his murderous attempt.[37] Moreover, just as the misfiring of Powell's gun saved Frederick Seward's life, there can be no doubt that the presence of Sergeant Robinson in the Seward bedroom that night prevented the death of Fanny's father.

The bravery of each of the Seward children also helped to avert tragedy that night and gave the lie to any assumptions that the Seward siblings might have been merely privileged blue bloods. Frederick was determined to protect his father even in the face of his own serious head wounds, and Augustus, once alarmed, rushed to intercede. But gentle Fanny Seward also exhibited extraordinary courage that terrible night. She raced Powell to her father's bedside, attempting to warn her father and fend off his attacker. She screamed, "Don't kill him," rousing the dozing secretary. She continued to scream, alerting her brother Augustus to the danger and arousing the rest of the household. She did not leave her father's room until the three men wrestled themselves out into the lighted hallway. Although in shock from what she was witnessing, she still had the presence of mind to minister to a father drenched in blood and hemorrhaging from his wounds. She fetched sheets to keep him warm. She fetched shirts to keep him clean.

14. The presence of Sergeant George Robinson in Seward's bedroom helped to save the life of Fanny's father. Collections of the Seward House Museum, Auburn, NY.

She kept curious bystanders out of his room. She more than earned the accolades of the presiding surgeon Dr. Norris, who declared, "You have been a pretty brave little girl tonight."[38]

Above all, it was she who had earlier created the circumstance that, outside of the misfired gun and the bedside presence of a brave soldier, most assuredly guaranteed her father's survival. Settling her father for the night, she had turned down the gas, inadvertently creating a darkened room in which evil might be more easily thwarted. In that darkened room, Powell perhaps mistook Seward's backrest for his body; in that darkened room, Powell slashed wildly at the ghostly outlines of sheets and bedclothes, often missing his target; in that darkened room, Powell found it more difficult to grapple with the apparition-like forms of Robinson and Frederick and Augustus.

Still, in addition to her heroic actions, Fanny's mere presence at her father's side, a presence that had been the habit of her lifetime, may have done more than anything else to preserve her father's life. Without hesitation, this delicate young woman attempted to insert herself between her father and his assassin. Later, Powell is reported to have said that if he could have "made up his mind to strike her [Fanny] out of his way, he could have accomplished his purpose upon the Secretary." As it was, "her face between his weapon and her father disarmed him; he had not the heart to take her life also."[39] Fanny's behavior on that dreadful night of horrors had been "all that a loving father could ask."[40]

## 20

# "This Baptism of Blood"

In the days following the assassination, while the Sewards struggled to recover, Washington churned with competing identities: it was the scene of a crime, the center of a new government, the source of rumor and gossip, the hub of a grieving nation. But the mood overarching these competing forces was one of revenge.[1] And no one would be better equipped to seek revenge on Lincoln's murderers than Secretary of War Edwin Stanton. He would apply the same resolute obsession that led to the North's victory in the war to the capture of Lincoln's assassins.

Although John Wilkes Booth and David Herold had cleverly eluded the authorities, on the night of Monday, April 17, the authorities were handed their first major break: they apprehended Lewis Powell. On that very day a handbill describing him had been issued:

> "Height 6 feet 1 inch, hair black, thick, full and straight; no beard . . . cheeks red on the jaws; . . . 22 or 23 years of age; . . . —large eyes . . . brows not heavy, but dark; . . . complexion healthy; nose straight and well formed; . . . hands soft and small; fingers tapering; shows no signs of hard labor; broad shoulders; taper waist; . . . strong looking man; manner not gentlemanly, but vulgar. . . ."[2]

The vulgar and ungentlemanly assassin had spent an uncomfortable few days since his attack on the Seward family household. Abandoned by his accomplice Herold, over the weekend Powell had wandered in the woods north of Fort Lincoln in his bloodstained clothing, sleeping by night in a cedar tree.[3] By Monday night, however,

Powell, dazed and hungry, decided to seek help at the home of Mary Surratt, the boarding house in which many of the details of the assassination plot had been hatched.[4]

Mounting the steps to 541 H Street, Powell had attempted a rude disguise. He had thrown away his bloody coat and wrapped his head in a torn section of his undershirt. In his hand was a pickaxe acquired from his wanderings around Washington. He could not have known that inside the house were police officers preparing to take Mary Surratt into custody. Once inside, Powell concocted a lie for the authorities, attempting to pass himself off as a day laborer hired to dig a trench for Mrs. Surratt. But Mary Surratt also lied, denying she had ever met the young man before. The truth was that they both knew each other, they both had been involved in the conspiracy plot, and that they both recognized that this association spelled their doom. Trapped in a tangle of mutual lies, journalist George Alfred Townsend wrote that both Powell and Surratt had now "dug a trench deep and broad enough for them to lie in forever." Soon servant William Bell, summoned from the Seward house, identified his employer's attacker. Later, in the wee hours of the morning, Augustus Seward was called on to confirm Bell's identification. By the morning of April 18, Powell was chained aboard an ironclad in the Potomac River.[5] His luck had run out.

But the Seward family's luck was soon to run out, as well. Augustus's wounds proved minor, the elder Seward was healing, and Fred would survive. But the assassin who had injured five people in a single attack would yet cause at least one casualty.

When Frances Seward hurried to Washington after her husband's carriage accident in April of 1865, she had been ill for many years. Her health in the previous year had especially worried Fanny. In a letter to her father on the first of August in 1864, Fanny had described the Auburn homestead as "a hospital." For several days, the South Street clinic included her mother, aunt, and two injured soldiers: her brother Will and his friend MacDougall. Fanny stated that her mother had an "unusually ill turn—caused or prolonged by a cold. Today she has had much pain in the face—but her cough is gone." A couple of weeks later, Fanny was still concerned: her mother had "neuralgia and some fever every day"; the family speculated that her illness was prompted by her "intense anxiety about Will" and the fierce fighting in which he had participated during the summer at Monocacy. Seven days later, Frances continued with "restless nights" and the "almost daily attacks of neuralgia which are reducing her strength very much." Alarmed, Fanny confessed to her father that "I feel very anxious that Mother's health should fall back to what it was years ago. I daresay she has not told you how sick she has been."[6]

Frances was not only sick; she was also worried. Frances, of course, had always been a worrier. When Gus traveled to Key West, Frances worried over his safety, "troubled by every wind that blows," and fretting over "the frequency of shipwrecks at this season of the year."[7] Even from the relative safety of Auburn, Frances worried. When her elderly Aunt Clara died suddenly in the fall of 1862, she was overcome with what Fanny perceptively called "mental emotion," suffering heart palpitations so severe that "she was near falling & about to swoon" as she "followed the coffin into the vault."[8] Understandably, however, the autumn of 1862 had been a particularly emotional time for Frances, for a first grandchild had been born and the baby's father, Frances's beloved son, had marched off to war. The concurrent death of an aged and ever-present aunt likely intensified an already wrenching period in the family.

The war, naturally, increased Frances's tendency to worry, but worry throughout the war she did. She dreamed of her family being blown up in the Capitol.[9] She obsessed about Fred's wounds and her certainty about the outcome: "He will die."[10] Many of her worries were justified. She shared them with women all over the country who worried about their soldier husbands, brothers, fathers, nephews, and sons. Frances's concerns for Will were especially acute, for her impetuous son threw himself into things, and those things now included battlefields. Although her husband and sons Augustus and Fred were serving the war effort away from the fighting, Washington was hardly an oasis of safety, and in 1864, with Jubal Early knocking at its doors, it seemed less safe than ever. Still, Frances's children, understanding the connection between their mother's worries and her health, conspired to keep her worries to a minimum.

However, before the carriage accident in April of 1865, the war was clearly winding down, and now the South Street house had become the source of contention and worry for Frances Seward. For decades, throughout her husband's long absences and her own long illnesses, the house had proved a source of safety and stability for her. Plans to expand on this sanctuary or to change it in any way always met with resistance from Frances. In the summer of 1862, for instance, she rejected plans to add on to the homestead, fearing it would lose its "rural character." She would not allow the sacrifice of "the old cherry tree planted by 'Grandpa' and the home of the robins for nearly 40 years."[11]

Now, in the spring of 1865, more serious plans to build an addition on the house were afoot, proposed again by the very family members who had abandoned it, as Frances thought, for Washington. In fact, so indignant was Frances about these latest changes that she wrote to Fanny, suggesting that her father and brother Fred build a house "somewhere on the Hudson," a house that would be "like that in Washington—where you all seem happy."[12] The implication behind Frances's words was that the family was finding happiness in a place without her.

The truth was that even loyal Fanny had become increasingly "happy" in Washington, settling herself there in October of 1864 and satisfied to remain.[13] One Seward biographer even suggested that Fanny had taken this extended visit to her father's home "over her mother's objections."[14] Perhaps Frances felt the sting of Fanny's choice.

Wrapped in a cloak of resentment and addressing her concerns through the daughter most likely to feel sympathy with or loyalty to her mother's wishes, Frances declared to Fanny that she would simply stay in the Auburn house with her sister Lazette, observing that her children were not likely to find the Auburn homestead as "agreeable . . . as we who have never *lived* elsewhere."[15] The issue of changes to the house revealed Frances's resentment of the attraction of life in

Washington as well as her continued rejection of it. Ironically, Frances was so committed to her quiet life in Auburn that she seemed to be subtly pushing away the family that she loved in order to maintain the South Street house as she wished. In the spring of 1865, there was much tension in the family over this issue.

However, that tension evaporated instantly as Frances received word of her husband's life-threatening carriage accident.

When Frances arrived in Washington, Fanny noted that her mother "had been sick on the way . . . & was in the greatest anxiety about father." Even though Fanny had prepared her mother for her first look at her battered husband, Frances was "still . . . much shocked" by his condition. Characteristically anticipating the worst, Frances "explained" to Fanny the dangers of "congestion & inflammation," dismissing Fanny's perception, reiterated by the doctors, that "there was no danger in his situation." Fanny confessed to her diary that her mother's alarming diagnosis, so contrary to the doctors', "made me feel very badly."[16]

The strain of watching over her husband through long nights of bedside care following his carriage accident took its toll on Fanny's mother.[17] After the assassination attack, however, Frances fell "ill . . . perhaps with palpitation." Confessing to Fanny that she was afraid "Fred could not live," Frances "showed feeling & anxiety that must have been anguish."[18] When she had rushed to Washington to care for her injured husband, Frances Seward was unprepared, physically and mentally, for what she would experience. She was about to enter the period of the most intense "mental emotion" of her life.

Following the attack, Frances, like all of the family members, took their turns at the bedsides of William and Frederick. A doctor remained in the house at all times. But the father healed more quickly than the son, and by May 21, Fanny was reporting that he was able to play a little whist and scan the papers in the parlor.[19] When the Grand Review of the Army took place on May 23, Seward was well enough to sit by the window and look down on the parading troops. General Sherman recalled taking off his hat and waving to Seward at his window. Still bandaged and weak, the secretary of state returned his wave.[20]

But in the tension of opposites that had so characterized the Seward marriage, as Seward's health improved, Frances's declined. To an Auburn friend, Mrs. Seward wrote that she had been "confined to my bed since I commenced this letter. The wearing anxiety I feel about Mr. Seward and Frederick consumes my strength . . . This baptism of blood seems to have obliterated much of my previous existence."[21]

By late May, Mrs. Seward's decline had become alarming, especially to Fanny. Since the assassination attempt, concerns about the health of William and Fred had been intense and unrelenting. To Thurlow Weed, her husband's long-time political ally and friend, Frances confessed that she felt as if she had "two hearts, one throbbing for Henry, and the other for Frederick."[22] That throbbing heart beat against a backdrop of momentous changes: Lincoln's White House funeral on April 19, Booth's dramatic death at Garrett's farm on April 26, the start of the military trial of the conspirators on May 10, the Grand Review disbanding the Union armies on May 23.

Taking up her diary on June 17, after a two-month hiatus since Powell's invasion of her household, Fanny recorded her anxieties about her mother. Now the family was taking turns at the bedside of Fanny's mother just as they had with her father and brother. For months the Seward household had been turned into a hospital with hushed bedside vigils, night shifts, and visiting doctors. Like a nurse observing the condition of her patient, Fanny's diaries now recorded the daily progress of this new failing patient. For example, although her mother claimed to feel better, taking some tea, Fanny observed that she "seemed very feeble." Surgeon General Barnes was heartened when he took her pulse, informing Fanny that her mother "had improved" during the "last 24 hours." That observation did not jibe with Fanny's own. To Fanny, her mother was mostly "weak & languid—sleeping much."[23]

Now Fanny and "dear Will" often huddled together, sharing their mutual worries about their mother. Will seemed "impressed with [the] same fears as mine," wrote Fanny. Brother and sister feared the worst. Despite the doctor's recent encouragement and their father's hopes that Frances was improving, Fanny and Will "could not see improvement—she seemed to us to be wasting away, thinner, weaker every day." She was eating very little, and the doctor "pressed the . . . point of nourishment."[24]

On the night of June seventeenth, Gus sat beside his mother, fanning her for a long while. On a trip downstairs, Fanny saw Edwin Stanton visiting with their father. Stanton exhibited his characteristic kindness to the family, kissing Fanny "very kindly," taking "both my hands in both his, holding them while we all spoke, & pressing them many times, so very, very kindly, as did my heart good—& gave me new strength." She confessed to her father and his friend that she was terribly frightened about her mother.[25]

Still, the doctor's evening report said that Frances was better. This news made a grateful Fanny feel like God was "giving me back my Mother." She vowed: "Oh I will try to be a comfort to her in the days that are to come." Relieved, Fanny thanked God "for his tender mercy . . . in bringing all that I love safely away from their near approach to the unseen hand." This rhapsodic passage represented one of the few times Fanny had confessed to deeply meaningful religious sentiments in her diary, but running through this passage about godly comfort was an undercurrent of fear, the terrifying fear of losing her mother. Fanny confessed, too, about the comfort provided by her diary. For almost the first time, she acknowledged its importance as emotional solace. "Because I have no human friend at hand into whose ear to pour these little thoughts—How I talk to my little diary!"[26]

The following day, a Sunday, was Will's birthday. Fanny had slept on the camp bed while others sat up with her mother, who had an "awful night." The nurses claimed Frances rested well, but Fanny learned that her mother had been troubled by "dreadful dreams." Despite her worries for her mother, Fanny sought out Will, remembering the importance of his birthday. Giving him a "birthday kiss" and asking "if he was too old to wear a rose in his button-hole," loving Fanny pinned him with "the handsomest & most fragrant blush rose I had been able to find." With his side whiskers trimmed and a rose in his button-hole, it must have been a comfort for Fanny to observe "good, & gentle, & strong & considerate & kind" Will looking "so handsome!"[27]

Despite Frances's restless night, however, the surgeon general's breakfast visit pronounced Frances "decidedly better—her pulse better, sounder, fuller, 'more of it.'"[28] Doses of false hope were being dispensed as a kind of medicine.

Three days later, Frances Seward's lifetime of worry was at an end, and Fanny's mother became "the one victim of the assassin who had not been directly touched by his knife."[29] Her son Frederick described June 21, 1865, as "the longest and saddest day of that long sad year."[30] The woman whom her daughter Fanny had called "my affinity" was gone.

While Fanny's mother was clinging to life, the assassination conspiracy trial had been taking place. Lewis Powell, whose actions had so devastated the Seward family, took center stage. After all, Booth was dead, and only the second most murderous of the assassins was alive to receive the wrath of the nation. Called the "mystery man" of the assassination for his assumption of various aliases while he was a conspirator, Powell, also known as "Paine" or "Payne," became at the trial "the observed of all observers." Prior to the trial, Alexander Gardner, the preeminent photographer and a colleague of Mathew Brady, took more pictures of Powell than of all the other conspirators, producing *cartes-de-visite* images for public consumption.[31]

There was every reason for the public to be mesmerized by the assassin with the "gladiatorial frame" and the "brawny, muscular chest." All eyes were on the young, handsome conspirator with the "good face" and the "unusually large and liquid" gray eyes. Powell also added to his allure by sitting immovably in the docket throughout the trial and refusing to show even the slightest flicker of emotion. His unswerving stoicism marked the Seward assassin as "a thoroughbred amongst dray horses."[32]

Facing a public ravenous for details, Powell evoked characterization straight out of Victorian melodrama. He was rumored to be from a family of notorious desperadoes. Observers concluded that "neither intellect nor intelligence" could be discerned in his face. He offered a singular specimen of "the massive robustness of animal manhood in its most stalwart type." A "Christian lady," inspired by the bearing of the stoic prisoner in the courtroom's sweltering heat, passed him a handkerchief and a note indicating that she and others were keeping him in their prayers.[33]

Even prayer was unlikely to help Lewis Powell. Although Powell's lawyer was William E. Doster, a graduate of Yale and Harvard law schools as well as a brigadier general promoted for his service during the war, this skilled advocate assessed his client's chances as "none at all." Aware that the military nature of the trial meant he would have to prove his client's innocence in the face of his presumed guilt, Doster understood the forces arrayed against Powell: the public mood required that "somebody must be hanged for example's sake." The lawyer explained the efficacy of his defense as "firing pistol shots against siege guns."[34]

For two weeks during the trial, Powell was silent, even with his lawyer. "He would sit bolt upright with the back of his head against the wall; his two manacled hands spread out on his knees, staring straight forward at the crowd . . . ," remembered his lawyer. But when William Bell identified Powell as Seward's assailant, Doster detected a "thaw."[35] The testimony of George Robinson also finally moved the immovable Powell. Listening with "rapt attention" as the wounded Robinson gave an "emotionally charged account" of the assassination attempt, Powell, with red face and clenched teeth, watched with more interest than he had yet shown as Robinson handled the knife[36] which Powell had raised against Fanny's father.

During a private interview at Powell's request, Doster was then treated to a "rambling history" of the young Confederate's life story. Surprisingly, Powell asked about the condition of Frederick Seward and confessed to his attorney that "he was sorry he had hurt the young man and owed him an apology."[37]

Desperate for a defense, Doster thought he might try an insanity plea. After all, Powell had shouted "I'm mad" during the Seward attack, and it had been sheer lunacy to attempt such a bold assault with so little advance planning in an unfamiliar house filled with so many people. But Doster's defense witnesses were unhelpful. A Dr. Nichols, who had agreed to testify to his "grave doubts" about Powell's mental stability, was called away at the last minute, and Powell's "well-known constipation," doubtfully presumed as a symptom of insanity, did not fly. Near the end of the trial, Powell's best hope seemed to be the magnanimity of his victim, William Seward. Rumors flew that Seward might ask for the young man's pardon, on the grounds that a victim cannot outlive his attempted murderer. Technically, perhaps, Powell's charge should have only been assault and battery. However, when Frances Seward suddenly died during the course of the trial, any hopes for Powell died with her.[38]

In a little over two weeks after Frances's death, on July 7, 1865, Lewis Powell, along with three other conspirators, was hanged. On the evening of July 6, Powell had personally asked for the counsel of Reverend Dr. Abram Dunn Gillette, expressing remorse for his crimes and accepting the justice of his punishment. In a touching gesture, Dr. Gillette presented Powell with the gift of a straw hat to protect him against the heat as he made his death march to the gallows. When a puff of wind swept off Powell's hat, Gillette returned it to the condemned man. "Thank you, Doctor," said Powell only moments from his own death, "I shall not need it much longer."[39]

# 21

# Not "Over Well"

It was not like Fanny to wait so long to answer a letter. Her cousin Amanda Schooley had written a few weeks after the assassination attempt, and it was January, 1866, before Fanny was finally able to answer.

After all, so much had happened in the tragic year of 1865, Fanny explained. First there had been "all the trial of last April," Fanny's understated description of the assassination attack. Then there had been all the trial of June with her mother's death. Frances's funeral had been held in Auburn, where the town closed down for the services and the streets were clogged with mourners. All eyes were on the sad figure of William Henry Seward, supported by his daughter Fanny on one arm and his wife's sister Lazette on the other. At the cemetery, as the clergyman uttered "dust to dust, ashes to ashes," a little bird twittered a fitting tribute from a tree branch over Frances's grave.[1]

Perhaps the worst trial of all had been the grief and the memories. To her cousin Amanda, Fanny described the process of her mother's passing:

> She suffered much in her illness—but the end was as peaceful as falling asleep. . . . As long as her strength was needed to attend my father & brother, she kept up, though suffering intensely from anxiety—when they became better, her health failed—and she sank very rapidly. She . . . bore her illness with the sweetest patience. The day before she died all pain seemed to leave her—'I am so comfortable!' she said and 'I only want to see you all look happy.' After that she had more to suffer; but at last lay still and beautiful, only breathing more and more lightly till she ceased to breathe at all. It comforts me to think that she can never suffer any more.[2]

Of the trial of her own health, Fanny characteristically said very little. Since her mother's death, Fanny's health had also been failing, and her family had been alarmed. After Frances's Auburn funeral, Aunt Lazette had kept a close eye on Fanny, penning almost daily reports to Fanny's father in Washington. On July 4, Fanny's fever had finally left and she was able to take a drive. But by July 10, Fanny had again spent two days debilitated by a fever that had returned. By the 11th, Aunt Lazette was dosing Fanny's fever with the quinine recommended by Dr. Norris, and Fanny needed Will's help just to climb the stairs. By August 24, Lazette was "quite anxious" about Fanny and was hoping that Fanny could go to Washington to seek the advice of Dr. Norris, who "understands her constitution better than any other of the physicians there." Fanny herself, in writing to her cousin, explained self-effacingly that "my manner has been so broken up, & my health so indifferent that I have not been able to write as much as I should otherwise have done."[3]

Sadly, Fanny's health was more than indifferent. Although her doctors were slow to realize it, she was seriously ill, in the early stages of consumption, a disease that struck fear into the hearts of nineteenth-century Americans. Mid-century, when Fanny Seward was alive, death from consumption, or tuberculosis, reached its height. The image of the disease in the popular imagination was somewhat "spiritual," one in which the pale skin, glittering eyes and sudden flush of low-grade fever of the moribund was seen as something admirable, even noble. Louisa May Alcott's *Little Women* described the face of dying sister Beth, a consumptive, in this way: " . . . there was a strange transparent look about it, as if the mortal was being slowly refined away, and the immortal shining through the frail flesh with an indescribably pathetic beauty." Consumption seemed to claim the literary attention of nineteenth-century writers as well as the lives of some of its most important authors, like Henry David Thoreau.[4]

These images obscured the horrific experience of the disease, as well as the truth that real understanding of this scourge was minimal. Tuberculosis was not thought to be contagious until 1865, and the tubercle bacillus was not isolated until 1882.[5] The sanatorium "cure," which recommended rest in isolated areas like that of Saranac Lake, New York, where the air was pure and the landscape peaceful, came into vogue only during the second half of the century, but real progress in curing the disease began only the 1940s, when streptomycin was discovered.[6]

The symptoms of consumption, which largely affected the lungs, were well known. They included coughing, intermittently at first and then incessantly later on. Blood-flecked sputum was present in the early stages, and then foamy, bright red hemorrhages occurred as the disease progressed. Fever and night sweats dogged patients, as did weight loss, exhaustion, heart palpitations, and chest pain.[7]

These were all symptoms that Fanny Seward experienced as her disease progressed during 1866. She had serious fits of coughing. She had chest pain and headache. She had fevers in the morning and fevers at night that left her exhausted. She had nausea and dizziness when she tried to write. She had pains in her back, side, and chest.[8]

But perhaps neither her family nor her doctors realized how sick she truly was, or perhaps they were afraid to face the truth. At one point, whooping cough was suspected; at another, lobular pneumonia or pleurisy. No one seemed to have mentioned the fatal word "consumption." Whatever the case, there was little anyone could do. Fanny was told to keep water steaming on the stove to moisten the air. She was instructed to keep the furnace heat low to avoid stimulating her cough. Quinine was prescribed for fever. Iron was prescribed for fatigue. Brandy was taken at the first sign of a chill.[9] The remedies seemed inconsequential.

But Fanny herself still exhibited the fortitude that saw her climbing the ramparts at Fort McHenry or sleeping in a tent in General Hooker's camp. When she spent August of 1865 at the shore in Cape Island, New Jersey, Fanny delighted in the people so eager for her father's autographs that "they ask in advance for the envelopes." Despite having experienced an unusually sick spell in January, 1866, Fanny thoroughly enjoyed the dizzying carriage drive through Rock Creek with Mary Grier. Even though the coachman was "not overcareful," Fanny determined to be "very merry." She participated in an excursion to Mount Vernon, even though just walking up the hill forced the twenty-one-year-old Fanny "to rest on the porch with the elder ladies." She was proud of her progress when she felt well enough to wear a dress or shop for button boots and a sailor hat. In the face of often immobilizing discomfort, Fanny Seward modestly explained that she had not been "over well."[10]

Unlike her mother, who was never reluctant to worry her family about her health, Fanny had always shrugged off her ailments with aplomb. She once noted that Doctor Boyce, for instance, was "trying his hand at my incorrigible throat," wondering absently if it might one day "carry me off." She laughed at the "great fuss" she once made over a tooth filling. She referred to her frequent sore throat as "my old enemy." Irrepressible as ever, Fanny tried to ease her family's worries about her. She told her father to think of her not "on the sick but the convalescent list."[11]

Despite her uncomplaining nature, Fanny's symptoms were often incapacitating, and she was often disappointed by their restrictions. When a flag was dedicated in memory of Abraham Lincoln, Fanny was too ill to attend the ceremony, and her family had to leave her behind. She wanted to picnic at the lake with Will and Jenny and their children on the Fourth of July, but she was so tired she had to rest all day. She hoped to attend afternoon church but was "altogether unable." Even though her Aunt Lazette called her "quite a belle with foreign ministers and members of the cabinet," Fanny was no longer attending the dinners and balls of dignitaries, but receiving visits from the powerful at home. On New Year's Day, Fanny received a flower bouquet from the Executive Mansion. Perhaps that gift served to heighten her awareness that President Johnson's reception began at "11 o'c—" and that she sat in the Seward house behind shuttered blinds, too ill to attend.[12]

By 1866, Fanny was only twenty-one years old, and she was not resigned to illness as her mother had been. Sick as she often was, young Fanny Seward wanted to live. To that end, she shared with her father a plan for going to the West, where the air would be better for her lungs.

With Dr. Norris's encouragement, she dreamed of visiting Charlotte Cushman in Rome, delighting in building these "air castles."[13]

As she always had, she applied her flagging energy in the interest of her family. She worried about Fred. Near the Christmas season in 1865, although Fred was at work three hours a day, splinters of bone were still working loose from head wounds that still gaped. By the spring and fall of the next year, Fred's wounds still chafed below the cap he wore to hide them, and his "pulsing brain" was still painfully visible. About her father she was equally worried. She wrote congratulating him on being released from "the bondage of cap & splint" a few weeks after her mother's death. Yet she knew her father, still wrapped in bandages, presented a "maimed, haggard and distorted figure," and had to be carried upstairs to his chair at the State Department. Although by year's end he was working as hard as ever and had regained his ability to speak, his face was still scarred by his injuries, his right arm virtually useless, and his overall strength seriously compromised. Amazingly, Fanny's father remained as cheerful as ever.[14]

Fanny gamely tried to support her father by filling her mother's role as political confidante, requesting to be "instructed in politics." Undoubtedly recognizing that Fanny possessed a literary, not a political, sensibility, her father kindly replied that he wanted to spare her the "anxieties, in a field in which you can do no effectual labor." Fanny ministered to him through a sick spell in March of 1866, even though she was not well herself. As was his nature, Seward recovered quickly, to the delight of a daughter bid goodnight by being taken in his arms and smothered in "a succession of the warmest kisses."[15]

But Fanny clearly grieved the loss of her mother. She tried to preserve her memory by collecting her papers. She shared photographs of Frances with those to whom her mother had been close. She visited her mother's grave in July, heartened that the severe winter had not killed the ivy; she visited again in the fall, even though the damp weather confined her to her carriage. She considered the requests to write her mother's biography, recognizing that "no task could be more delicate" and keeping aspiring biographers at bay.[16]

She read over the tributes that came, tributes that consoled but also served to remind her that she no longer had her mother's "unfailing sympathy & pure guidance." She felt complimented when Mary Grier shared that Fanny opened a door using the same "mannerisms" as her mother. Frequently she felt her "dear Mother's presence," and was cheered by remembering that her mother had promised "to go with me everywhere." In February of 1866 on a visit to Philadelphia, she wrote a poem in her mother's memory. "Come Near" referenced Fanny's own weary longing for her mother's loving presence, offering a tribute to the "mother dearest" who offered "courage, comfort, strength and cheer." Still, on the anniversary of her mother's death on June 21, 1866, she confessed to her diary that she would not attempt "to write of the thoughts it brings."[17]

The thoughts Fanny did write about during this final period of her life centered on religion. Fanny was jotting down excerpts from Bible passages, especially those which lifted her spirits. "Thou shalt not be afraid for the terror by night," she wrote, "nor for the arrow that flieth by day." Copying down Biblical passages allowed her to remind herself that "this God is our God for ever and ever: he will be our guide even unto death."[18]

Except for Fanny's mother Frances, however, the Sewards had not been fervently religious. They were not the every-Sunday churchgoers who attended services faithfully. Fanny enjoyed the morning prayer service when she was in Washington, but since it came at breakfast time, she chose sharing the hour with her father instead.[19] Although family members attended as often as they could, sometimes the press of events or the disruption of illness kept the Sewards away from Sunday services.

Fanny characteristically appreciated the church atmosphere of music and flowers; however, she often had reservations about the substance of religion itself. In this she was like her father, who preferred religious tolerance to religious doctrine. To Fanny, true religion emphasized "the love of man towards God," recognizing that "real love" was more important than "religious forms."[20]

Civil War Americans made up a religious nation that believed God "actively intervened" in everyday life: God caused the corn to wither, the foals to thrive, and the larder to be full or empty. Still, in the 1860s and 1870s, Americans were attending church less frequently than those of earlier generations, and only about half the nation attended church regularly. Some regarded attendance as a duty; others, a bore. In that spirit, Fanny reported on Mr. Platt's sermon over Christmas in 1860 as "shorter & better than usual." Often women "dragged along" whichever family members they could. Such was the case with William Seward. He had been accused of lacking religion, and one of his biographers suggested that he "allowed himself" to be baptized in the Episcopal Church, as if the decision had not been his own.[21]

Fanny, whose mother had worked hard to influence her on religious matters, sighed in a letter to her father about the gift of a church history from a Mrs. Rudd, who, Fanny feared, intended to "give me a good many talkings about church matters." Fanny had also confessed to her dislike of the bishop's "prosy sermons." Although several passages in her diary attest to Fanny's enjoyment of church services, perhaps this young woman felt like Emily Dickinson, who disliked notions of "Paradise—Because it's Sunday—all the time."[22]

Interestingly, Fanny's diaries reveal some strikingly independent thinking on the topic of religion. In a book about the afterlife, which she had picked up as a young teen, the author had described Heaven as much like earth, "where the people eat, drink, and sleep—attend Oratorios—and . . . study the fine arts." Although Fanny claimed the ideas were "strange," she decided the proposal was "an improvement on the old idea of Heaven—." She was skeptical of a sermon on infant baptism, confused about how "such vows could be truly performed." Of a sermon on "eternal punishment," she wrote curtly: "Did not like it."[23]

Fanny's Christianity was realistic. Its purpose was to improve behavior and inspire good works. Its emphasis was therefore on this world, not the next. More than once she pronounced her satisfaction with a sermon because it was "practical." Many clergy of Fanny's day shared this emphasis on practical Christianity, seeking to shape the character of their congregants in daily life, not threaten them with images of the flames of hell in the afterworld. Fanny found that the rewards of religion could be practical, too. When she was sad, she cheered herself by reading Isaiah. She recommended "humbling oneself before God" as an antidote to melancholy.[24]

But melancholy was one thing, failing health another. On some level, Fanny Seward must have sensed that she was dying. In fact, she had written a poem on that subject on January 3, 1866, when she was especially sick.[25] Perhaps that is why, in the spring of 1866, Fanny entertained the invitation to be confirmed from the Reverend John Vaughen Lewis, pastor of St. John's Episcopal Church.[26]

Anna, her sister Molly, and Fanny attended Mr. Lewis's church service, the first of the confirmation season, and Fanny met privately with the reverend, explaining her dilemma: she had a desire to be confirmed, but she also had many reasons why she "ought not to." The minister, perhaps sensing the fragile state of her health, explained to her that she needed "to put on that armor for the battle which I will have to fight through life."[27] Attending a church service soon after, Fanny confessed to having been "refreshed and helped." Taking the step toward confirmation had helped her feel less "groping alone in the darkness."[28]

The Fanny Seward who was confirmed on Sunday, March 25, 1866, had needed the consolation of religion. She had been groping alone in the darkness for a long time. She had faced an assassin that threatened her father and two of her brothers. She had lost her mother in the aftermath. She was losing control of her own health to periods of fever, coughing, and chills. Now the "sense of help"[29] she so desperately needed was perhaps on the way.

Without question, religion proved a comfort to Fanny Seward in the spring of 1866. So was a visit from Ellen Perry, nicely timed to support Fanny during Passion Week and her first communion experience. But where Fanny's newfound faith promised spiritual fidelity, Fanny was soon forsaken by the material reality of her weakening body. She had shortness of breath, and the "old pains" in her back and chest returned. After she became "slightly delirious thro' [sic] the night," she was confined to bed for two weeks. Her energy was flagging. She wanted to go to church, but she could not sit up for long.[30] As spring moved into summer and she returned to Auburn, Fanny's health declined even further. The strongest evidence of her decline was that she abandoned her diary for the month of April, and the entries in May through July grew shorter and shorter.

By August, the family was seriously alarmed. Aunt Lazette was recommending the remedy of a "saffron bag" filled with frankincense to place on the chest and ward off chills. But Will and Jenny suspected Fanny's situation required more serious interventions. Will, writing to both his father and Dr. Norris, was "almost sure that her difficulty was more than ordinary fever." To Dr. Norris, Will provided a complete explanation of her symptoms, requesting his advice. Fanny herself had been frustrated that she had required "so much waiting upon." She had been able only to "lie down, or drive out propped by a pillow." As a result, Fanny's father made immediate arrangements to send Dr. Norris to Auburn.[31]

Engaging Dr. Norris was a wise decision. In his company Fanny felt the "soothing power" she needed. She was comfortable with the doctor, who had praised her on assassination night as "a pretty brave little girl." After the assassination attempt, she had developed a relationship with the doctor in which she could confess her worries, particularly when her mother was dying. Although Dr. Norris warned Fanny that she needed to guard her health, he was relatively optimistic in his diagnosis, finding only a "prolonged [or protracted] respiration" at the top of each lung. Dr. Norris suspected some "sub-acute inflammation" but declared "no occasion for immediate alarm." Still, good Dr. Norris's advice sounded merely palliative. He suggested that Fanny stay in her room until the afternoon, breakfast before she tried to get up, and sit down when she got tired.[32]

Throughout the ups and downs of her illness, Fanny was cheered by the attentions of family and friends. During the challenging spring in Washington, she reported on the devotion of her sister-in-law Anna and her friend Ellen Perry. Fred read to her. Her brother Gus gathered wild flowers for her and sat with her every evening. She noted the visits of "Dear Father," who sometimes visited several times a day. As spring moved into summer and Fanny returned to Auburn, Fanny's father was writing her as frequently as ever from Washington, sometimes even daily. Those letters often reprised their mutual love for nature, as the secretary described the "music" of the "mosquito concert" or provided instructions for making the parrots talk: "put the cage into the breakfast-room, and let them hear the clatter of knives, forks, and children's tongues, which makes the music of the feast." As ever, father and daughter delighted in each other.[33]

At the end of August, however, the Seward family was plunged into political campaigning again. President Andrew Johnson was making a campaign tour to stump for moderate Republican candidates in the upcoming election cycle, and Fanny's father had organized this tour for him.[34] This "Swing Around the Circle" tour made a stop in Auburn on August 31, 1866.

The presidential campaign party was entertained at the Seward home, assembling in the parlor prior to the official reception. Fanny was bothered by the damp, so she sat beside the hall door to the library for a while and then moved into the upper front room to hear President Johnson make his address on the front steps. Catching glimpses of General Custer, Admiral Farragut, and General Grant, it had almost seemed like a campaign reception from the old days.[35]

But the presidential visit took its toll on the fragile Fanny. At midnight, Johnson was addressing "a delegation—20 car loads—just come from Syracuse." By the time everyone left, the table was being set for breakfast. After breakfast, the crowd departed for the depot, and "in a few moments . . . the carriages rolled away to the early western train." During the festivities, Fanny had seemed stronger than she had in a while, although her limitations prevented her from standing. After the event was over and while the household attempted to return to normal, Fanny collapsed with high fever and a cold.[36]

However, during the final part of the campaign trip, tragedy struck. Fanny's father fell ill with what appeared to be cholera. A telegram from Gus from Latrobe, Pennsylvania, announced that her father was "dangerously ill." The family rushed to his side in separate trains; Fanny was accompanied by a doctor as a special protection for her own fragile health.[37] The family met up with the Secretary in Harrisburg, Pennsylvania, where they hoped to journey to Washington together—if the secretary survived.[38]

When they entered the car carrying Fanny's father, Fanny was shocked. "He was so emaciated," she wrote, "that he looked as on the night of the assassination." He could no longer speak, and "his skin had the coldness of death—he was in the collapse state of the cholera." The doctors offered no hope. Fanny sat across the aisle from his makeshift bed, where her father lay across the seats; later a couch was prepared for Fanny directly across from her father to keep her from being fatigued. In that position, with her head across from his, she could watch his face and "from time to time catch a glance of recognition & affection from him."[39]

Even now, gravely ill as he was, Seward's instinct was to protect his daughter as he always had. After all, he had risked his own life during a horrific carriage accident, "hoping to . . . arrest the horses before Fanny and Mary Titus were dashed to pieces." On assassination night, he had confessed that he knew Powell "was seeking his life," but he "feared most for Fanny, and with a great effort rose up in his bed to interpose his shattered frame as a protection." Now, so ill that he was not expected to live, he was comforted by the intimate presence of the daughter who had meant life itself. In his desperate distress, Fanny's father now extended his hand to her, and she caressed it with tender affection.[40] As they had during times of crisis and times of calm across the years, they continued to reach out for each other.

Then, as he had so many times before, Seward rallied. He took broth, and Fanny reported that although "he looked like a dying man" still, his face became "*less* deathlike." Gradually he began to talk, to put on his glasses, to observe the passing scene, even to ask for the newspapers. When they reached Washington, Secretary Stanton met the car personally, having arranged for an ambulance and stretcher and having alerted the servants in Lafayette Square to prepare for his coming.[41] Soon the crisis of health for Fanny's father had passed. As irrepressible as ever, he returned to work with his formidable vigor.

But Fanny Seward had never shared her father's vigor. All too soon she would leave her love of literature, her pleasures in Washington, her family, and especially her beloved father behind. She would spend the final weeks of her life in the house on Lafayette Square. Her last diary entry was written in Washington on Sunday, October 7, 1866. "This is the first time since the 1st of July," she wrote, "that I have been well enough to attend church on Communion Sunday."[42] She would write her last letter on October 11, 1866, a letter to her dear brother Will.

By October 29, 1866, the daughter who had been all that a loving father could ask was dead.

Emily Howland had shared Christmas dinner with the Sewards, visited with the family on several occasions, and been supported by the family in her efforts to promote equality for African Americans, but she had been unaware that Fanny had been ailing. Howland was the young woman who hailed from Cayuga County near Auburn in upstate New York, and who undertook groundbreaking work both by teaching at the school for free black girls and by working at the contraband camp established in Washington. In a letter to her mother, Howland explained the details of Fanny's death as well as anyone could have. She did not mention consumption, only "an attack of fever . . . from which she had no strength to rally. It seems it came on six weeks ago when her Father was ill with Cholera."[43]

Miss Howland paid her respects at the Seward home, where she looked at "the fair young face in the coffin covered with white flowers." Fanny's father looked "pale and feeble and old." Aunt Lazette had reported that the secretary "could not believe that death was near until very shortly before the last. Then for a short time self-control gave way and natural grief burst forth. This trial came closer to his heart than any other could."[44] At the service, held at 3:30 on October 31, the church was filled with generals, ambassadors, cabinet members, and even President Andrew Johnson, dignitaries who had "gathered about the remains of one of the most innocent and pure of human beings."[45]

Fanny's "poor stricken father" was "trembling" as he "tottered up the aisle scarcely able to walk."[46] Perhaps he was remembering that letter he had written to Fanny upon her thirteenth birthday, the letter that expressed his fondest hope that he would live to "protect and advise" her and that she would live to support his "tottering steps" as he aged. Tragically, his foreboding that he might not live to protect her and that she might not be spared to support him came to pass.[47] Although Fanny's death had not come on a battlefield, surely her wartime experiences had exacerbated an always frail constitution, and her loss mirrored the suffering in thousands of homes of Civil War Americans.

Snuffed out like brief candles, the promising lives of scores of the nation's youth, like Fanny Seward, had not lived to support the steps of their bereft and aging parents. Not long after her funeral, in a letter to his son Will, Seward described Fanny's death as "the grief that can find no consolation."[48]

Before Fanny died, a famous painter had been hired by Seward to paint her portrait. His name was Emanuel Leutze, an artist renowned for his heraldic painting of *Washington Crossing the Delaware*.[49] In addition, while work on the Capitol dome was evolving, Leutze was composing a six hundred square foot historical panorama for the building. *Westward the Course of Empire Takes its Way* extolled the virtues of American expansion.[50]

Patrons enabled the talented young German immigrant to study in Europe at the Dusseldorf Academy, where he developed his interest in historical painting,[51] a style that combined the imagination and allegory of romanticism with the drama and patriotism of nationalism.[52]

Leutze was a man after William Seward's own heart. Energetic, enthusiastic, and restless, Leutze could balance a cigar and a palette before a canvas, then take a break by romping wildly with his big barking dog. Not surprisingly, the red-bearded artist and the beak-nosed politician became friends.[53]

Both Fanny and the artist fell ill before the painting was completed, so Leutze had to finish the composition after Fanny died. The soft, romantic brush strokes he used echoed the tenderness that was Fanny's character, yet the lavender shades of Fanny's gown projected a subdued, mournful spirit of loss. The fall leaves to the right of Fanny's figure hinted at the October autumn of Fanny's death, and the morning glory vines to the left hinted at nature's seasonal resurrections. The symbolism of Fanny's approaching death was suggested in the sky darkening above her head, and the soft parting in the clouds implied that, after death, Fanny had been taken to a better place.[54]

The presence of Leutze in Seward's life after the tragic deaths of both his wife and daughter must have been a comfort to him. Furthermore, the respect Seward held for his artist-friend was reflected by the fact that Fanny's father requested Leutze to design the headstones for the graves of Fanny and her mother. Frances's design was "a white marble tomb, surmounted by a cross in bas-relief." Fanny's was similar, differing only in the use of a vine twining the cross instead of the draped tear-vase of her mother's design.[55]

Like a portent straight from *Macbeth*, Harriet Tubman was said to have experienced a supernatural premonition about Fanny Seward's death. Tubman had had such visions before. Prior to the start of the Civil War, a prominent black abolitionist lamented to Tubman that neither of them would see emancipation before they died. Clinging to the images in a dream of only the night before, Tubman shared her vision of a coming war that would free the slaves. Tubman assured her friend, "You'll see it, and you'll see it soon."[56]

According to Sarah Bradford's biography, at the time of Fanny's death Tubman had reportedly seen "a chariot in the air, going south, and empty, but soon it returned, and lying in it, cold and stiff, was the body of a young lady of whom Harriet was very fond, whose home was in Auburn, but who had gone to Washington with her father." Terrified, Tubman "ran to the house of her minister, crying out: 'Oh,

15. This painting, finished after her death, memorializes the brief candle that was Fanny Seward's all-too-short life. Collections of the Seward House Museum, Auburn, NY.

Miss Fanny is dead!'" Chillingly, word of Fanny's death had just been received.[57]

The drama of Tubman's alleged foreboding was in keeping with the drama of the life of Fanny Seward and the period in which she lived. No dramatist could have imagined the reality that was the life of Fanny Seward or the details that would make the aftermath of its performance so memorable.

Seven years after Fanny's death, Edwin Booth finally opened the trunk that his brother John had left behind. Inside were costumes and wigs and swords. One by one, Edwin Booth tossed the items into the fire: the Roman toga worn to play Julius Caesar, the black robe worn by Shylock, the belted sword worn in the role of Iago. Edwin Booth, who had once dined with the targets of his brother's fiendish plot, was left like his brother's victims to be haunted for the rest of his days by the most ignoble role his brother John ever played.[58] In another dramatic irony, after Edwin died in 1893, all three floors of Ford's Theatre collapsed as his train was steaming north to his burial place. More than twenty people died.[59]

Another grisly finale to Fanny's life concerned the would-be assassin Lewis Powell. His corpse had once been thought lost, but in 1993 his head turned up in the anthropology collection of the Smithsonian Institution, its identity subsequently confirmed by the FBI. The identification had been aided by the loss of a molar on the left jaw, caused by an errant kick from a pet mule. Powell's head was taken to Florida, placed in a tiny coffin, and buried on Veterans' Day in 1994. Author James Swanson mordantly quipped that Powell was now resting "if not in peace, then in pieces."[60]

During the drama of the Civil War, William Seward had been a protagonist, Fanny Seward a bit player. Still, the bit player nurtured no dreams of playing Lady Macbeth; she was content in her minor role. Fittingly, she had played that role well. As Edwin Booth had observed, she was not one of those actors whose best talents were scorned by their hunger to play Hamlet.[61]

She had been born the privileged daughter in a progressive political family that felt called to serve, whose service did not isolate them from but exposed them to tragedy. She had been the quiet and retiring girl who had listened intently and observed keenly at the dinners and balls of the powerful. She had not auditioned for the part of frail young adult, yet she did not let her ill health keep her away from camps and soldiers, from receptions and open houses, from the theater and the portrait gallery. She had undertaken the role of devoted companion to a mother whose death had left her bereft and alone. She had provided solace to a father whom she adored and who, before her eyes, had been savagely attacked. She had been a tenderhearted girl who had developed reserves of toughness that allowed her to minister to her father's gaping wounds, her womanly skirts soaked with blood. She had shied away from the role of radical feminist, yet in a radical act of her own, she had been as irrepressible in her own way as her father had been in his: she had dared to nourish dreams of becoming a writer, and she had dared to keep a diary.

Fanny Seward's life, like those of thousands of her contemporaries, had been a brief candle that had sputtered out too soon. She would not live to witness future events either small or large. She would never know whether niece Nelly's white cat learned not to sleep in the coal bin. She would not be able to wear the crape bonnet "of the newest fashion" that Jenny was having made for her. She would not witness the arrival of the set of De Quincey's works at the library in Auburn. She would miss seeing her father presented with the tribute of a cane, a gift carved from the handrail of the stairway leading to his office and representing the touch of presidents, diplomats, cabinet officers, and congressional representatives across the decades. She would not thrill to discover how much her growing niece would sound like her Aunt Fanny. "Mama bought me a beautiful canary bird," Nelly reported in a letter to her grandfather. "He sings very sweetly . . . I send you a great many kisses and love." She signed it "Your little Nelly" in a voice that sounded all too familiar.[62]

Fanny would not live to witness her father's final political triumph in the purchase of Alaska, nor would she ever gaze on *Negotiations for the Purchase of Alaska*, Emanuel Leutze's dramatic historical portrait of that event. She would miss the satisfaction of knowing that her brother Fred would survive to live a long and useful life. She would not experience the increasing freedoms for women that blossomed after the war, particularly the opportunities for them to write and publish.

Thankfully, however, Fanny would be spared the urgent telegram sent in October of 1872 from Will in Auburn to Fred in Washington: "I consider father's condition quite alarming, a fever has set in which cannot be controlled. You had better come at once." She would also miss the second telegram with its even graver news: "Father died at three o'clock." Fanny would not be present to hear her dear, dear father's final words: "Love One Another."[63] But perhaps that didn't matter; after all, the daughter who had been all that a loving father could ask had already heeded that higher law.

*Acknowledgments*

*Notes*

*Bibliography*

*Index*

# Acknowledgments

My father, whose passion was the Civil War, prepared me for Fanny Seward. When I was a child, my family and I made numerous roadside stops at Civil War battlefields, and my mother kept a special pair of shoes in the car for slogging across them, accessories she called her "battlefield shoes." A budding writer even as a child, I was most attracted to the stories my father told about the Civil War. Through him, I learned that men's sideburns, in a kind of historical word swap, were named for General Ambrose Burnside, and that "hookers," those ladies of the evening found in every historical period, had something to do with the dashing General Joseph Hooker. My father's favorite story was about Confederate General John B. Gordon, wounded five times in the battle of Antietam, the final wound a direct blow to his face; in my young mind there was no more vivid image than that of brave General Gordon holding his cap to his head and watching it fill up with his own blood.

As I grew into a writer, penning award-winning novels for young adults, history was always part of the story: the civil rights movement, the McCarthy era, the growth of suburbia in the 1950s. When I researched a novel called *Uncommon Faith*, centered around the Underground Railroad and Northern women's abolition efforts, I learned much about the antebellum era, and that soil was preparing me for the seeds of Fanny Seward.

Like most Americans, I had never heard of Fanny Seward. I vaguely associated the name "Seward" with her father and the 1867 purchase of Alaska, known as "Seward's Folly." Again, like most Americans, I was well aware of Booth's murder of President Lincoln in Ford's Theatre on April 14, 1865, but I was completely unaware that there were other assassinations planned for that very evening for other members of Lincoln's cabinet, including William Henry Seward, Fanny's father and Lincoln's secretary of state.

Still, until I read Doris Kearns Goodwin's *Team of Rivals*, I knew little about Seward and nothing about his daughter. That book and another historical marvel, James Swanson's *Manhunt: The 12-Day Chase for Lincoln's Killer*, whetted my appetite for learning more about Fanny, whose young face and piquant comments kept peeking out between the lines of both works. After all, I had been a writer of historical fiction for young adults, and this young adult had experienced life in the front row of the theatre of the Civil War. Even better, I learned that Fanny had kept a diary, one of those primary source documents beloved by historians, that recorded her eyewitness accounts of events of the Civil War, including the assassination attempt on her father. Most exciting of all was that there had been no book yet published about this privileged young woman; I saw that there was much new historical ground to break.

The first serious step on my journey began when I read Patricia Carley Johnson's 1964 dissertation, "Sensitivity and Civil War: The Selected Diaries and Papers, 1858–1866, of Frances Adeline (Fanny) Seward." Johnson provided a remarkable overview of Fanny's life as the youngest daughter in a progressive political family during a momentous time in history. Best of all, Johnson had provided information about contemporaries of Fanny whose identity would be difficult to locate without her painstaking work. She is owed a debt of gratitude by all researchers, including myself, who have come after her.

Captivated, I began to read in earnest, at first general interest books on the period, then primary source materials. Most helpful were the volumes left behind by William Seward's son Frederick and the impressive biography of his father by Glyndon Van Deusen. I devoured the microfilmed version of Fanny's dairies from the William Henry Seward Rare Books Special Collections & Preservation Department at the University of Rochester (New York) until my eyes grew blurry. My travels to Rochester, where the Seward papers are housed, introduced me to Fanny's poetry and prose, but a visit to the family home of the Sewards in Auburn, New York, introduced me to my best research source, Jennifer Haines, then-Director of Education for Seward House. She helped me explore the rich resources of the Seward mansion, introducing me to facts both well-known and obscure, and patiently responded to my many e-mails and queries over a period of many years. We soon began to refer to each other as FOFs, Friends of Fanny. It is to this enthusiastic young historian that I have dedicated this book.

As the work progressed, there were many setbacks along the way. The first was of my own creation. The final manuscript was nearly six hundred pages, and no publisher would be willing to take on such a hefty volume without major excisions. Consequently, I was forced to carve much out of my final manuscript: Fanny and her mother Frances's adoring friendship with Senator Charles Sumner; Fanny's intense but short-lived friendship with Sue Ward; and Fanny's many descriptions of parties, dresses, and manners of Washington society during the Civil War. However, this reality taught me that history's mountain is incredibly steep, and that I could be satisfied with establishing a foothold.

Historians of the future will not want for material to explore about the Seward family. For instance, William Seward's letters have never been published, and I found his microfilmed handwriting almost impossible to read, so I had to rely on his son Fred's version of his letters, often undated and surely carefully excised. This difficulty pointed the way to a new and important area of research: the publication of the letters of William Henry Seward. In addition, Fanny's diaries and letters had never been published in their entirety, so I was left to piece information together under many constraints; future historians would find a worthy object of research in preparing these documents for publication. I am hopeful that one day a diligent researcher will write a dissertation on Fanny's intriguing unpublished writings; space allowed for only cursory analyses here. Equally fitting as a subject for future historians is Fanny's mother, Frances Seward. Every bit as complex and fascinating as her famous husband, Frances left a rich legacy of letters awaiting researchers of the future. In short, there are still other worlds of Seward history to explore.

I am grateful to the many people who helped me shape this book. I am indebted to Karen Bove, who patiently shared her knowledge of the Perry family, whose daughter Ellen was Fanny Seward's best friend. I benefited from the scholarship of Pat Pfleiger, PhD, West Chester University of Pennsylvania; she is an expert on nineteenth century periodicals for children, and clarified much about Fanny's early writings in *Merry's Museum.* Deirdre C. Stam's research on Fanny's reading habits was invaluable, and Scott William Anderson's dissertation corrected my original vision of Auburn as a sleepy little town.

Kate Clifford Larson's scholarship on Harriet Tubman, particularly her relationship to the Seward family, is exceptional, and thanks also go to Beth Crawford of Crawford & Stearns Architects and Preservation Planners for sharing part of the research and documentation work for the Harriet

Tubman home. Betty Ownsbey's work on Lewis Powell was also critical to the telling of Fanny's story, as was the generosity of Laurie Verge and Joan Chaconas and Marjorie Patten of the Surratt House Museum in Clinton, Maryland; they provided important historical details about Lewis Powell as well as information about the George Atzerodt confession.

Andrew Roblee, Facilities Manager at Seward House, and Lori Birrell, Manuscript Librarian at the University of Rochester, were vital sources of photographic and citation advice. I am indebted to everyone at Syracuse University Press, especially the diligent Deanna McCay, for their attention to detail and their adherence to the highest standards of scholarship. I am grateful to Jeffrey Heard and Sonya Kirkwood and Winnie Tseng of Sinclair Community College for the time they spent obtaining obscure material in support of my research. I am also indebted to the reference librarians at the Dayton and Montgomery County Public Library and Wright Memorial Public Library. I thank Sheila Filler for always acting interested in the project, and Mary Connolly, who stitched up a Civil War quilt based on period fabrics to help me keep going.

I wish to thank the extraordinary historians and writers who have either encouraged my work or volunteered to serve as peer reviewers for early drafts of the manuscript. Primary among them is Walter Stahr, the author of the masterful biography *Seward: Lincoln's Indispensable Man*. He provided generous line-by-line comments on the manuscript, and his incisive remarks have made this a better book. He is that rare individual that, thankfully, the world still produces: a gentleman and a scholar. Naturally, any mistakes that remain in the book are entirely my own.

Above all, I am indebted to the irrepressible Jennifer Haines, fellow Friend of Fanny (FOF) and devotee of history's higher laws.

# Notes

### Abbreviations

Seward family members are referenced in the following way:

| | |
|---|---|
| Augustus | Augustus Henry Seward |
| Fanny | Frances A. "Fanny" Seward |
| Frances | Frances A. (Miller) Seward |
| Fred | Frederick William Seward |
| Lazette | Lazette M. (Miller) Worden |
| WHS | William Henry Seward |
| Will | William Henry Seward Jr. |

Frequently used papers and published resources are abbreviated as follows:

| | |
|---|---|
| DFS | Diaries of Fanny Seward. William Henry Seward Papers. Rare Books, Special Collections, and Preservation Department, University of Rochester. Microfilm Reel 198. Boxes 134–135, Section IV F. |
| PCJ I | Patricia Carley Johnson, "Sensitivity and Civil War: The Selected Diaries and Papers, 1858–1866, of Frances Adeline (Fanny) Seward." PhD diss., University of Rochester, 1964. |
| PCJ II | Johnson, Patricia Carley. "'I Could Not be Well or Happy at Home . . . When Called to the Councils of My Country': Politics and the Seward Family." *University of Rochester Library Bulletin* 31, no. 1 (Autumn 1978). |
| SP | William Henry Seward Papers. Rare Books, Special Collections, and Preservation Department, University of Rochester. The Seward family correspondence can be found on Microfilm Reels 112–124. Fanny Seward's letters to her family are contained on Reel 116. |

Seward I — Seward, Frederick W. *William H. Seward: An Autobiography from 1801 to 1834 with a Memoir of his Life, and Selections from his Letters, 1831–1846.* New York: Derby and Miller, 1891.

Seward II — Seward, Frederick W. *Seward at Washington, as Senator and Secretary of State: A Memoir of his Life, with Selections from his Letters, 1846–1861.* New York: Derby and Miller, 1891.

Seward III — Seward, Frederick W. *Seward at Washington, as Senator and Secretary of State: A Memoir of his Life, with Selections from his Letters, 1861–1872.* New York: Derby and Miller, 1891.

SR — Seward, Frederick W. *Reminiscences of a War-Time Statesman and Diplomat, 1830–1915.* New York: G. P. Putnam's Sons, 1916.

VD — Van Deusen, Glyndon. *William Henry Seward.* New York: Oxford University Press, 1967.

*Note: Quotations from Fanny Seward's writings preserve her original grammar, spelling, and punctuation; only the occasional change has been made in the interest of clarity.

### 1. In the Shadow of Death

1. Taylor, *William Henry Seward*, 38. This was Cornelia Seward, 1835–1836.
2. Seward II, 46.
3. SP, WHS to Frances, August 4, 1850.
4. Seward II, 182.
5. SP, WHS to Fanny, December 10, 1857.
6. Thomas and Hyman, *Stanton: The Life*, 352.
7. Winik, *April, 1865*, 203.
8. DFS, April 13, 1865.
9. Carpenter, *Six Months*, 293.
10. DFS, April 5, 1865. Note: There are varying accounts of the accident; Fanny's account has been preferred here.
11. Taylor, *William Henry Seward*, 240.
12. DFS, April 5, 1865.
13. Taylor, *William Henry Seward*, Preface, ix–x.
14. Olive Risley Seward, *W. H. Seward's Travels Around the World*, 778.
15. DFS, April 12, 1865.
16. DFS, April 14, 1865.
17. Winik, *April, 1865*, 118.
18. DFS, April 9, 1865.
19. Brooks, *Washington, D.C., in Lincoln's Time*, 195.

20. Ibid., 213.

21. Swanson, *Manhunt*, 1.

22. Ostendorf, *Lincoln's Photographs*, 209. The picture referenced is O–109; Ostendorf identifies it as taken by an "unknown cameraman," although it is grouped with other Gardner photos.

23. SR, 255.

24. Brooks, *Washington, D.C., in Lincoln's Time*, 215.

25. DFS, April 14, 1865. The full title of the book is *Legends of Charlemagne or Romance of the Middle Ages* by Thomas Bulfinch. Fanny's copy was published in 1863.

26. Ibid.

27. Note: the last doctor to visit that night was Dr. Basil Norris, an army medical officer. Other doctors had also been attending Secretary Seward while he recovered from his carriage accident. They included Surgeon General Dr. Joseph K. Barnes, who also attended Lincoln at his death bed, and Dr. Tullio S. Verdi, the Sewards' family doctor and a Washington homeopath.

28. Swanson, *Manhunt*, 52.

29. DFS, April 14, 1865.

**2. From Innocence to Experience**

1. An exceptional source for information on Fanny Seward's diaries and the life she lived as the youngest member of the Seward family is the PhD dissertation of Patricia Carley Johnson (Rauch), "Sensitivity and Civil War: The Selected Diaries and Papers, 1858–1866, of Frances Adeline (Fanny) Seward," University of Rochester, 1964.

2. VD, 118.

3. SP, Frances to Lazette, November 29, 1858.

4. DFS, December 25, 1858.

5. DFS, September 1, 1861.

6. Baker, *Works*, vol. 4, 292–93.

7. DFS, August 1, 1859, molasses; DFS, January 10, 1861, dancing; December 28, 1858, manners; April 3, 1859, pets; January 16, 1863, photography.

8. DFS, January 5, 1859.

9. DFS, February 10, 1860.

10. DFS, December 28, 1858, Bell; March 18, 1859, bullfights; December 25, 1858, pistols; March 7, 1860, fish.

11. SP, Frances to Lazette, March 3, 1860.

12. DFS, January 5, 1859, rubbers; April 30, 1859, collar; February 25, 1861, skating.

13. DFS, January 5, 1859.

14. DFS, February 27, 1861.

15. DFS, December 28, 1858.

16. DFS, March 27, 1859, church service; March 3, 1859, rude boy; March 26, 1859, defects.

17. SP, Fanny to Will, May 28, 1857.

18. DFS, January 11, 1860.

19. DFS, January 17, 1863.

20. DFS, February 5, 1863.

21. DFS, March 2, 1859.

22. DFS, January 25, 1862.

23. DFS, March 22, 1862.

24. Stam, "Growing up with Books," 196–97.

25. DFS, February 8, 1863, *Paradise Lost*; April 1, 1860, Longfellow; February 12, 1861, *Vanity Fair*; March 1, 1861, *Marble Faun*; February 22, 1859, *Dombey and Son*; January 24, 1860, *Bleak House*; September 10, 1861, *Great Expectations.*

26. DFS, March 1, 1861.

27. Kasson, *Rudeness and Civility*, 39.

28. Stam, "Growing up with Books," 201, ailing; 202–203, gifts; 193, pages.

29. DFS, December 9, 1860, Will; February 18, 1863, Sue Ward; October 12, 1862, Ellen Perry; February 15, 1861, mother; February 5, 1863, Swayne; December 22, 1862, Lazette.

30. SP, Fanny to Frances, April 20, 1855, bird; DFS, December 31, 1858, end-of-year; DFS, January 4, 1859, scene.

31. SP, Fanny to Frances, April 21, 1855, poem; *Merry's Museum and Parley's Magazine* (New York: S. T. Allen & Co.), December 1856, 175. Fanny's story was called "Our Watchie: A True Story," and she submitted it under the pen name of "Pansy"; SP, Frederick to Frances, December 16, 1856, pride; DFS, February 1, 1861, little face; DFS, February 18, 1861, extracts.

32. SP, Fanny to WHS, July 1856, no day given.

### 3. Being a Seward

1. The birth and death dates for Fanny's most significant family members are William Henry Seward (father) 1801–1872; Frances Adeline Miller Seward (mother) 1805–1865; Augustus Henry Seward (brother) 1826–1876; Frederick William Seward (brother) 1830–1915; William Henry Seward Jr. (brother) 1839–1920; Elijah Miller (grandfather) 1772–1851; Clarinda Miller (great aunt) 1793–1862; Lazette Maria Miller Worden (aunt) 1800–1875.

2. DFS, December 25, 1858.

3. DFS, December, 1859, no day given.

4. DFS, April 15, 1860.

5. DFS, December 31, 1858.

6. DFS, February 16, 1864.

7. DFS, January 19, 1859.

8. VD, 258.

9. DFS, December 28, 1861.

10. SP, Fanny to Charlotte Cushman, July 12, 1866, younger; Seward II, 203, remarks; SP, Fanny to WHS, August 1, 1864, solace.

11. Jennifer Haines, Former Director of Education at Seward House, e-mail correspondence to the author, November 30 and December 5, 2006.

12. DFS, December 26, 1858, piano; March 3, 1860, McLeod; April 26, 1859, grace; March 19, 1859, cake.

13. SP, Frances to WHS, June 20, 1856.

14. SP, Lazette to Fanny, January 23, year uncertain, likely 1857 or 1858. Note: Rover's very tiny letter and envelope are still preserved in their original at Seward House.

15. SP, Fanny to Will, June 10, 1857.

16. VD, 258; 269.

17. VD, 261.

18. Seward II, 183.

19. DFS, March 9, 1860, Adams; January 11, 1860, dislike; February 9, 1859, announcement; January 26, 1859, livery.

20. DFS, Christmas, 1858, Barrett; PCJ I, 220, n. 109, Freeman; DFS, January 16, 1859, Bogart.

21. Leech, *Reveille in Washington*, 66.

22. DFS, February 22, 1860.

23. PCJ II, 2.

24. SP, Frances to Lazette, June 11, 1847.

25. PCJ II, 5.

26. SP, WHS to Frances, December 31, 1860.

27. DFS, October 14, 1863.

28. SP, Frances to Lazette, November 7, 1848.

29. VD, 92.

30. VD, 264.

31. DFS, April 25, 1859, slippers; April 29, 1858, cheese; April 28, 1859, friend; April 30, 1859, bonnet; December 1859, no day, closet; May 9, 1859, hoopla.

32. Seward I, 62.

33. PCJ II, 1–2.

34. PCJ II, 10.

35. PCJ II, 9–10.

36. PCJ II, 10–11.
37. SP, Fanny to Frances, April 26, 1855.
38. VD, 405.
39. VD, 403.
40. DFS, December 30, 1858.
41. VD, 407.
42. Seward III, 494.
43. DFS, December 28, 1858.
44. SP, Frances to Augustus, January 6, 1854.
45. SP, Frances to Fred, February 27, 1865.
46. SP, Fanny to WHS, December 1853, no day given.
47. SP, Fanny to Frances, May 13, 1855.

### 4. "My Affinity"

1. Anderson, "Entrepreneurs and Place"; Hall, *History of Auburn*. Anderson's dissertation registers the vitality of Auburn as an early model of entrepreneurial capitalism; Hall's history chronicles Auburn's significant people, events, and institutions.

2. DFS, January 19, 1861.

3. VD, 92.

4. DFS, February 15, 1861, read; SP, Fanny to WHS, May 15, 1864, strolled; SP, Fanny to WHS, June 29, 1862, and SP, Fanny to Frances, May 1, 1854, weddings, anniversaries, babies; SP, Fanny to WHS, May 15, 1864, Ladies' Aid; SP, Fanny to WHS, July 20, 1861, sewing, tea, visited.

5. DFS, December 25, 1858, dearest; DFS, January 16, 1859, considerate; SP, Fanny to Frances, October 1853, no day given, kiss; SP, Fanny to Frances, February 11, 1864, affinity.

6. SP, Frances to WHS, June 5, 1863.

7. SP, Frances to WHS, March 17, 1849.

8. DFS, March 14, 1862.

9. DFS, March 10, 1863, diphtheria; February 20, 1859, always looking; February 21, 1859, cold; December 28, 1860, sleigh ride; December 22, 1862, face.

10. DFS, December 25, 1860.

11. Conrad, *The Governor and his Lady*, 53.

12. DFS, May 9, 1863, Indian meal; July 12, 1866, brandy; Jan 8, 1866, gin and water; January 7, 1866, raw cotton.

13. VD, 30–31, gynecological, reading; Taylor, *William Henry Seward*, 102, pavement; VD, 267, gaslights, piano; SP, Frances to Lazette, March 17, 1859, insensitivity; Taylor, *William Henry Seward*, 37, tumor; VD, 266, deranged.

14. Fisher, *House of Wits*, 238.

15. Lutz, *Emma Willard*, 76.

16. Stam, "Growing up with Books," 198.

17. Ibid., 193.

18. DFS, January 5, 1859, geography; DFS, January 26, 1860, music; SP, Fanny to WHS, May 25, 1862, lilies and roses; DFS, January 2, 1859, "aufully"; DFS, December 1859, no day, "delecatly"; DFS January 19, 1860, "parler"; DFS, January 24, 1860, "quaters."

19. DFS, June 1, 1859.

20. DFS, March 23, 1860.

21. DFS, April 28, 1862, singing; DFS, March 3, 1860, painting; DFS, March 11, 1859, music; DFS, January 16, 1861, afternoon; SP, Fanny to WHS, January 17, 1862, letters; DFS, January 25, 1862, native speaker.

22. DFS, January 4, 1859.

23. SP, Elizabeth Parsons to Frances, November 3, 1849, girl; SP, Frances to WHS, May 23, 1853, John; SP, Frances to WHS, July 23, 1852, funeral; DFS, December 25, 1858, pudding.

24. Baker, *Works*, vol. 1, 51–93.

25. SP, Fanny to Frances, April 12, 1853, sketch; SP, Fanny to WHS, December 1853, no day given, puzzle; "Understanding" (Seward House), display.

26. DFS, December 26, 1858.

27. DFS, February 20, 1859.

28. DFS, April 30, 1862.

29. Clinton, *Harriet Tubman*, 36.

30. Ibid., 37.

31. Ibid., 116.

32. SP, WHS to Frances, November 18, 1855. Note: On the old kitchen and woodshed as stops on the Underground Railroad, see Lewis, "Underground Railroad"; and Seward II, 258.

33. Seward II, 257.

34. WHS to Frances, November 18, 1855.

35. Larson, *Bound for the Promised Land*, 40–41.

36. Drew, *A North-Side View of Slavery*, 30.

37. Larson, *Bound for the Promised Land*, xvii.

38. Garrison Family Papers, Martha Coffin Wright to Ellen Wright Garrison, December 30, 1860.

39. Larson, *Bound for the Promised Land*, 155.

40. Ibid., 163. Note: For details about the property through the years see Crawford, Harriet Tubman Home Chronology.

41. Larson, *Bound for the Promised Land*, 163, brother Will. Cf. Crawford, 2, citing Rebecca Green, "History of Harriet Tubman and Her Brick House," Cornell

University, Ithaca, New York, 1998, unpublished research; Larson, *Bound for the Promised Land*, 166–167, charm and humor; ibid., 184, not to have pressed.

42. Larson, *Bound for the Promised Land*, 164–65.

43. Ibid., 203–212.

44. Larson, *Bound for the Promised Land*, 196–202, subject of debate; Martha Coffin Wright to Francis Wright, May 28, 1862, Garrison Family Papers, Fanny's aunt; Larson, *Bound for the Promised Land*, 197, Seward house to live.

45. DFS, March 4, 1859, dollar; April 4, 1860, friend; February 12, 1860, muff; March 28, 1862, read.

46. SP, WHS to Frances, January 18, 1861.

## 5. Almost "President" Seward

1. DFS, November 1859, no day given.
2. Kauffman, *American Brutus*, 104.
3. DFS, November 1859, no day given.
4. DFS, January 9, 1861.
5. Baker, *Works*, vol. 4, 292–93.
6. Stanton, *Random Recollections*, 215.
7. DFS, May 16, 1860.
8. Andrews, "How We Got Lincoln," 1.
9. DFS, May 17, 1860.
10. DFS, May 18, 1860.
11. Stanton, *Random Recollections*, 216.
12. Stahr, *Lincoln's Indispensable Man*, 186–87.
13. Seward II, 130.
14. Andrews, "How We Got Lincoln," 1.
15. Taylor, *William Henry Seward*, 7–10.
16. DFS, May 18, 1860.
17. DFS, May 19, 1860.
18. Seward II, 452.
19. Ibid.
20. VD, 229.
21. VD, 268.
22. Fanny's diaries mention the Wide-Awakes daily from September 3–8, 1860.
23. Nicolay and Hay, *Abraham Lincoln: A History*, 268.
24. DFS, September 8, 1860, carriage ride; September 14, 1860, steamer; September 9, 10, prima donna; September 5, 1860, Lansing; September 30, 1860, St. Louis.
25. Goodwin, *Team of Rivals*, 262.

26. SR, 140–42.

27. SP, WHS to Frances, January 23, 1861, civil war; Stahr, *Lincoln's Indispensable Man*, 3, all sections; DFS, December 31, 1860, above the union [sic].

28. Villard, *A Journalist's Story*, 52–53, roped; Nelson and Sheriff, *A People at War*, 51, actress; Seward II, 502, reveille.

29. Arnold, "The Baltimore Plot," 123–28.

30. Nelson and Sheriff, *A People at War*, 51.

31. Seward II, 550.

32. Stahr, *Lincoln's Indispensable Man*, 240–41, 246–47.

33. DFS, March 4, 1861.

34. DFS, March 5, 1861.

35. DFS, March 11, 1861.

36. DFS, May 19, 1861.

37. Massey, *Bonnet Brigades*, 32, aid societies; SP, Fanny to WHS, September 10, 1862, lint; SP, Fanny to WHS, October 1, 1862, barrel.

38. Massey, *Bonnet Brigades*, 31.

39. SP, Fanny to Lazette, December 8, 1861.

40. SP, Fanny to WHS, November 9, 1862, dressing gowns; Fanny to Lazette, March 14, 1863, contrabands; Fanny to WHS, May 15, 1864, shirts; Fanny to WHS, October 4, 1864, Titus.

41. Nelson and Sheriff, *A People at War*, 234, sewing societies; Strouse, *Alice James*, 133, Colonel; Myerson and Shealy, *The Journals of Louisa May Alcott*, 105, those who can.

42. DFS, May 19, 1861.

43. Ibid.

44. Ibid.

**6. Washington Prepares for War**

1. DFS, September 1, 1861.

2. Ibid.

3. Ibid.

4. Seward II, 553.

5. DFS, May 19, 1861.

6. Burlingame, *Abraham Lincoln: the Observations*, 51.

7. Wert, *The Sword . . . Potomac*, 12–13, action; Burlingame, *Abraham Lincoln: the Observations*, 75, powder; Denney, *The Civil War Years*, 58–60, wine.

8. Denney, *The Civil War Years*, 60.

9. Nicolay and Hay, *Abraham Lincoln: A History*, 92.

10. Seward II, 599.

11. DFS, September 1, 1861.

12. Ibid.

13. From James M. Nihiser to his Wife, July 24, 1861. Quoted in Wert, *The Sword . . . Potomac*, 22.

14. Henry, "Eyewitness to the Civil War."

15. DFS, February 9, 1863.

16. SP, WHS to Fanny, December 10, 1857.

17. Lockwood and Lockwood, *The Siege of Washington*, 34.

18. VD, 269.

19. DFS, September 1, 1861.

20. Ibid.

21. Epstein, *Lincoln and Whitman*, 9.

22. Goodwin, *Team of Rivals*, 13.

23. Taylor, *William Henry Seward*, 2.

24. Goodwin, *Team of Rivals*, 6.

25. Ostendorf, *Lincoln's Photographs*, 210.

26. DFS, September 1, 1861.

27. DFS, September 2, 1861, passport; September 8, 1861, Bull Run; September 4, 1861, Columbiads.

28. DFS, September 8, 1861.

29. DFS, September 3, 1861.

30. From the *Wisconsin Daily Patriot* (June 27, 1862), quoted in Gaff and Gaff, "The Dread Reality of War," 67, jack mules; DFS, September 6, 1861, horses; DFS, September 2, 1861, regiment.

31. Goodwin, *Team of Rivals*, 388.

32. Ibid., 430.

33. VD, 255, eyes; Taylor, *William Henry Seward*, 2, bird; VD, 255, parrot.

34. From John H. Burrill to his parents, July 5, 1861, quoted in Davis, *Lincoln's Men*, 47, fence; From Samuel Alexander to Agnes Alexander, November 25, 1861, quoted in Davis, *Lincoln's Men*, 58, Pritty; Burr, *Russell H. Conwell*, 130, feathers; Hendrick, *Lincoln's War Cabinet*, 15, pantaloons.

35. Taylor, *William Henry Seward*, 189–90.

36. Ibid., 186–87.

37. DFS, September 9, 1861.

38. Keckley, *Behind the Scenes*, 58, thread; Taylor, *William Henry Seward*, 187, appointment; Goodwin, *Team of Rivals*, 387, overshadow; Ibid., 315, hotel; VD, 337, resented the help.

39. VD, 282–83, place; Goodwin, *Team of Rivals*, 385, couple only; Taylor, *William Henry Seward*, 188, spending habits; Hendrick, *Lincoln's War Cabinet*, 187, forbade her coachman.

40. From Mary Todd Lincoln. Quoted in Turner and Turner, *Mary Todd Lincoln*, 370.

41. Badeau, *Grant in Peace*, 358–59.

42. VD, 340.

43. DFS, September 9, 1861.

44. Lockwood and Lockwood, *The Siege of Washington*, 226.

**7. 1862: The Dismal Year**

1. VD, 92, California; Roe, *The Ninth New York Heavy Artillery*, 436, student; SP, Frances to Lazette, December 29, 1849, languages; VD, 144, horses.

2. DFS, March 12, 1861, and September 4, 1862, fire alarm; May 1, 1862, depot; October 12, 1862, interests.

3. DFS, September 12, 1862.

4. Seward III, 100.

5. DFS, September 22, 1862.

6. DFS, March 30, 1862.

7. DFS, May 25, 1862.

8. DFS, September 21, 1862.

9. McPherson, *Battle Cry of Freedom*, 326.

10. PCJ I, 532, n. 298, coast; Seward III, 73, plates; DFS, April 9, 1862, campaign.

11. DFS, September 21, 1862.

12. DFS, September 22, 1862.

13. DFS, August 29, 1862, sick; DFS, August 30, 1862, Owasco; Brooks, *Washington, D.C., in Lincoln's Time*, 16, boots; DFS, September 1, 1862, Second Bull Run.

14. SP, WHS to Fanny, August 2, 1862.

15. Seward II, 497.

16. SP, WHS to Fanny, December 29, 1860.

17. Seward II, 635.

18. Ibid., 575.

19. SP, Fanny to WHS, January 20, 1861, little girl; Fanny to WHS, January 8, 1861, chattering; Fanny to WHS, April 7, 1861, geese; Fanny to WHS, April 28, 1861, flags.

20. Hamilton, "A Call to My Country-Women", 347.

**8. Two Emancipations**

1. DFS, December 22, 1862.

2. DFS, May 3, 1862, blues; May 11, 1862, insufficient; May 16, 1862, more peaceful.

3. DFS, January 1, 1863.
4. DFS, March 8, 1858.
5. DFS, January 1, 1863.
6. Ibid.
7. Ibid.
8. Staudenraus, *Mr.Lincoln's Washington*, p. 253.
9. DFS, September 22, 1862.
10. SP, Frances to Lazette, December 29, 1849.
11. DFS, January 27, 1859.
12. DFS, January 28, 1859.
13. Baker, *Mary Todd Lincoln*, 197, withdrawn; DFS, March 2, 1860, in her room; DFS, January 29, 1859 and DFS, March 16, 1859, socialize.
14. SP, Frances to Lazette, January 1, 1859.
15. SP, Frances to Lazette, December 29, 1849.
16. DFS, January 1, 1861.
17. Seward III, 151.
18. Nicolay and Hay, *Abraham Lincoln: A History*, 164.
19. Seward III, 214.
20. Seward III, 117.
21. SR, 227.
22. Nicolay and Hay, *Abraham Lincoln: A History*, 164.
23. Seward III, 151.
24. DFS, January 1, 1863.
25. From James Abraham to Mary Abraham, March 5, 1863, Abraham Papers, Civil War Times Illustrated (*CWTI*), U.S. Army Heritage and Education Center (USAMHI). Quoted in Davis, *Lincoln's Men*, 105.
26. Goodwin, *Team of Rivals*, 549.
27. Breault, *The World of Emily Howland*, 49.
28. DFS, January 4, 1863.
29. Breault, *The World of Emily Howland*, 52.
30. DFS, March 10, 1863.
31. DFS, January 1, 1863.

### 9. Turning Points

1. Goodwin, *Team of Rivals*, 598, Friday nights; DFS, January 14, 1863, one o'clock; DFS, February 4, 1863, working ones.
2. DFS, January 1, 1862, fat; ibid., rest; January 12, 1863, deaf; January 20, 1863, hummingbird.
3. DFS, January 14, 1863.

4. VD, 269.
5. DFS, February 16, 1864.
6. DFS, February 16, 1863.
7. DFS, February 13, 1863.
8. DFS, January 15, 1863.
9. Nicolay and Hay, *Abraham Lincoln: A History*, vii.
10. Nicolay and Hay, *Abraham Lincoln: A History*, vii, Presidency; Burlingame, *Abraham Lincoln: the Observations*, 35, ante-room; Nicolay, *Lincoln's Secretary*, 88, impassable.
11. DFS, September 1, 1861.
12. DFS, September 9, 1861 at the White House.
13. DFS, January 1, 1863.
14. DFS, January 9, 1863.
15. VD, 407, interested; Nicolay, *Lincoln's Secretary*, 114–15, emaciation; Epstein, *Lincoln and Whitman*, 149, goatee; Nicolay, *Lincoln's Secretary*, 85, quoting; DFS, January 1, 1862, cousin.
16. DFS, January 15, 1863.
17. DFS, January 16, 1863.
18. DFS, January 15, 1863.
19. DFS, January 16, 1863.
20. DFS, January 19, 1863.
21. DFS, February 2, 1863.
22. DFS, May 2, 1863.
23. DFS, April 26, 1863.
24. DFS, April 26, 1863.
25. DFS, December 28, 1861.
26. Seward III, 161, ministers; DFS, April 26, 1863, *Carrie Martin;* SR, 229, ferry; DFS, April 26, 1863, ladies; Seward III, 161, clothing.
27. DFS, April 26, 1863.
28. Wert, *The Sword . . . Potomac*, 229.
29. DFS, April 27, 1863, handsomer; Brooks, *Washington, D.C., in Lincoln's Time*, 56, cheery; DFS, April 27, 1863, bed-room.
30. DFS, April 26, 1863.
31. DFS, April 27, 1863.
32. SR, 232.
33. DFS, April 27, 1863.
34. Ibid.
35. Ibid.
36. DFS, May 1, 1863.
37. Ibid.

38. McPherson, *Battle Cry of Freedom*, 638.

39. Williams, *Lincoln and His Generals*, 232.

40. DFS, May 6, 1863.

41. Wert, *The Sword . . . Potomac*, 237.

42. Ibid., 252.

43. Brooks, *Washington, D.C., in Lincoln's Time*, 57.

44. From Henry Van Aernum—My dearest Lis, July 15, 1863, Van Aernum Papers, USAMHI. Quoted in Wert, *The Sword . . . Potomac*, 308.

45. DFS, June 15, 1863.

46. Agassiz, *With Grant and Meade*, 73.

47. DFS, June 29, 1863.

48. DFS, June 15, 1863, used to be; July 4, 1863, ever knew; ibid., brighten.

49. DFS, July 7, 1863.

50. SP, Box 132, Janet Watson Seward, 16.

51. Nelson and Sheriff, *A People at War*, 187. OK.

52. Marten, *Civil War America*, 147.

53. Ibid., 149–151.

54. Seward III, 175–176.

55. SP, Frances to WHS, July 18, 1863.

56. SP, Frances to WHS, June 28, 1863.

57. SP, Frances to WHS, July 12, 1863, negroes; Frances to WHS, July 18, 1863, threats; Fanny to WHS, July 26, 1863, Auburn.

58. SP, Frances to Fred, July 23, 1863, loved; Frances to WHS, July 18, 1863, assist them; Fanny to WHS, July 26, 1863, protection.

59. SP, Frances to Fred, July 23, 1863.

60. SP, Frances to WHS, July 24, 1863

61. SP, Fanny to WHS, July 26, 1863.

62. PCJ I, 105, n. 22.

63. SP, Fanny to Lazette, February 1, 1863.

64. SP, Fanny to WHS, June 19, 1864.

65. SP, Fanny to WHS, 1864, no day or month given.

66. DFS, July 11, 1863.

67. Boyden, *Echoes from Hospital and White House*, 143–44.

68. Ownsbey, *Alias "Paine"*, 15.

**10. Loss and Consolation**

1. DFS, April 14, 1865, haunted; December 28, 1861, letters; January 25, 1863, stalwart; September 1, 1862, precious.

2. Volo and Volo, *Daily Life in Civil War America*, 99.

3. Drew Gilpin Faust, *This Republic of Suffering*, xi.

4. Werner, *Reluctant Witnesses*, 8–9, underage; 12, too long; 8, dogs; 2, boy soldiers.

5. Werner, *Reluctant Witnesses*, 94, sewer; ibid., 79, city; from the diary of Lida Lord, "Diary of a woman during the siege of Vicksburg," quoted in Werner, *Reluctant Witnesses*, 80, eggs.

6. Werner, *Reluctant Witnesses*, 51, coffee; ibid., 52, turnip tops; ibid., 89, soup; Abraham Lincoln to Fanny McCullough, December 23, 1862, in Basler, *Collected Works*, 17, expect it.

7. Marten, *The Children's Civil War*, 7–9.

8. DFS, December 30, 1858.

9. From Private George Alphonso Gibbs, Eighteenth Mississippi Infantry Regiment, quoted in Werner, *Reluctant Witnesses*, 1.

10. PCJ I, 221, n. 114, Cemetery; n. 113, friends; n. 112, merchant.

11. DFS, August 31, 1860, election; SP, Fanny to WHS, August 30, 1863, wonders; DFS, August 1, 1859, candy; DFS, April 22, 1859, plates; DFS, March 27, 1866, photographs.

12. DFS, December 1859, no day given, safe; March 12, 1863, grieving; June 6, 1863, Baptist Church; March 29, 1866, communion; June 17, 1865, talk.

13. Werner, *Reluctant Witnesses*, 155, Dickens; Diary entry of Emma LeConte, quoted in Werner, *Reluctant Witnesses*, 155, sadness all around; DFS, May 11, 1862, beset her.

14. Fite, *Social and Industrial Conditions*, 256, n. 4.

15. DFS, February 18, 1863, *Miserables*; SP, Fanny to WHS, January 20, 1861, history; DFS, October 12, 1862, inspired.

16. Leech, *Reveille in Washington*, 66–67.

17. Winthrop, *Life in the Open Air*, 221, love-taps; 255, ventilation; 263, Uncle Sam.

18. Leech, *Reveille in Washington*, 86.

19. Nelson and Sheriff, *A People at War*, 234, gallery; Sutherland, *Expansion of Everyday Life*, 14, tunes; Kasson, *Rudeness and Civility*, 217, curiosities; Epstein, *Lincoln and Whitman*, 96, reception.

20. DFS, February 13, 1863.

21. Nicolay, *Lincoln's Secretary*, 167.

22. Panzer, *Mathew Brady and the Image of History*, 4.

23. DFS, March 15, 1860; DFS, December 30, 1861; DFS, April 5, 1862.

24. Panzer, *Mathew Brady and the Image of History*, 21.

25. Ibid., 1.

26. DFS, January 15, 1859.

27. DFS, March 24, 1859, *School for Scandal;* January 13, 1862, *Othello;* March 20, 1863, *Macbeth;* March 21, 1863, *Richard III.*

28. DFS, January 27, 1860.

29. DFS, January 13, 1862.

30. DFS, February 24, 1859, Murdoch; PCJ I, 292, n. 114, Davenport; DFS, April 6, 1860, Mary Stuart; PCJ I, 784, n. 362, Wallack.

31. Bode, *American Popular Culture*, 13, American theater; From William Forrest, mentioned in Bode, *American Popular Culture*, 18, King Lear; Bode, *American Popular Culture*, 16, out of favor.

32. Ruggles, *Prince of Players*, 118–119.

33. Clinton, *Mrs. Lincoln: A Life*, 198.

34. Colfax, *Life and Principles of . . . Lincoln*, 12.

35. Goodwin, *Team of Rivals*, 612.

36. Culley, *Diary Literature*, vii, 8th Child; McCarthy, "A Pocketful of Days," 288, baby Willie; ibid., bath.

37. DFS, September 12, 1862.

38. DFS, September 11, 1862.

39. Seward III, 184.

40. DFS, December 24, 1861.

41. Culley, *Diary Literature*, 3–4.

42. Cashin, *The War Was You and Me*, 239.

43. DFS, December 9, 1862.

44. DFS, April 4, 1862.

45. DFS, January 23, 1866.

46. SP, Fanny to WHS, September 27, 1864.

47. Taylor, *William Henry Seward*, 19.

**11. "The Work I Cannot Choose But Take"**

1. DFS, March 1, 1861.

2. DFS, May 8, 1862.

3. SP, "Laura," Box 133.

4. Jennifer Haines, e-mail correspondence to author, November 10, 2009.

5. DFS, April 30, 1863, dancing room; SP, Fanny to WHS, November 17, 1861, trees; DFS, September 15, 1860, curtains.

6. DFS, January 29, 1863.

7. Ibid.

8. DFS, January 1, 1859.

9. DFS, September 4, 1861.

10. DFS, January 31, 1863.

11. DFS, February 16, 1860, curled up; September 10, 1861, half shut; December 27, 1861, grey.

12. DFS, April 27, 1863.

13. DFS, April 29, 1863.

14. DFS, September 20, 1862.

15. DFS, September 22, 1862.

16. Drew Gilpin Faust, *This Republic of Suffering*, 25.

17. DFS, September 22, 1862.

18. Ibid.

19. Drew Gilpin Faust, *This Republic of Suffering*, 29.

20. DFS, September 22, 1862.

21. SP, Fanny to Lazette, August 19, 1857.

22. Frank, 210.

23. Clinton, *Mrs. Lincoln*, 198, Swisshelm; Marbut, *News from the Capital*, 95, Washington correspondent; Clinton, *Mrs. Lincoln*, 181, Redden; Marbut, *News from the Capital*, 250, man's name; ibid., National Press Club.

24. DFS, April 5, 1862, fire instead; January 3, 1863, finery; May 25, 1862, limbs.

25. SP, Box 135.

26. Ibid.

27. Ibid.

28. Ibid.

29. SP, Box 133.

30. SP, WHS to Fanny, November 18, 1865, good beyond; DFS, February 25, 1861, all the rest; From Nathaniel Hawthorne to his publisher William D. Ticknor, quoted in Ticknor, *Hawthorne and His Publisher*, 141, worth reading.

31. Pattee, *The Feminine Fifties*, 51.

32. Ibid., 52–53.

33. Ibid., 66.

34. George Stade, "Men, Boys and Wimps," the *New York Times Book Review*, August 12, 1984, 22, quoted in Shapiro, *Unlikely Heroines*, 2.

35. Pattee, *The Feminine Fifties*, 56, best seller; From Nathaniel Hawthorne to his publisher William D. Ticknor, quoted in Ticknor, *Hawthorne and His Publisher*, 141, scribbling women; Pattee, *The Feminine Fifties*, 57–58, wipe a tear; letter From Artemus Ward, quoted in Pattee, *The Feminine Fifties*, 307, weeps.

36. Shapiro, *Unlikely Heroines*, 134.

37. SP, Box 133.

38. Jennifer Haines, e-mail correspondence to author, November 5, 2009.

39. SP, Fanny to Frances, February 11, 1864.

## 12. The Marriage Option

1. Donald, "*We are Lincoln Men*", 103–04.

2. DFS, January 22, 1863.

3. Ibid.

4. Ibid.

5. DFS, January 15, 1863.

6. DFS, February 12, 1859.

7. DFS, April 9, 1862.

8. DFS, January 24, 1863, Parker; January 29, 1863, McClellan; January 17, 1863, Montgomery.

9. DFS, January 29, 1863.

10. Ibid.

11. DFS, April 24, 1863.

12. PCJ, 754, n. 223.

13. DFS, April 24, 1863.

14. Ibid.

15. DFS, April 27, 1863.

16. Ibid.

17. Wert, *The Sword . . . Potomac*, 6, Green Mountain Boys; Sutherland, *Expansion of Everyday Life*, 5, leggings; McPherson, *Battle Cry of Freedom*, 323, circus; Volo and Volo, *Daily Life in Civil War America*, 139, Northern soldier.

18. DFS, April 24, 1863, all he can; From the diary of Theodore F. Upson, July 6, 1882, quoted in Winther, *With Sherman to the Sea*, 19, better enlist; DFS, March 29, 1863, best part.

19. Sutherland, *Expansion of Everyday Life*, 3, petticoats; DFS, April 24, 1863, shame; DFS, January 14, 1863, shirking.

20. Volo and Volo, *Daily Life in Civil War America*, 102.

21. Stoddard, *Inside the White House*, 224–226.

22. SP, Fanny to WHS, November 9, 1862.

23. Brooks, *Washington, D.C., in Lincoln's Time*,4.

24. Epstein, *Lincoln and Whitman*, 123.

25. Ibid., 128–29.

26. DFS, November 28, 1862.

27. SP, Fanny to WHS, August 1, 1864.

28. SP, Fanny to WHS, August 16, 1864.

29. SP, Fanny to WHS, October 4, 1864.

30. PCJ I, Appendix B, 1047–51.

31. Ibid.

32. SP, Box 133.

33. DFS, January 14, 1863.

34. Perrine, "The Dashing Kate Chase," 11.

35. DFS, May 7, 1862.

### 13. The Sewards on Women

1. DFS, January 22, 1863.
2. Ibid.
3. Welter, "The Cult of True Womanhood," 167.
4. Strouse, *Alice James*, 43.
5. DFS, January 22, 1863.
6. Nye, *Society and Culture in America*, 50.
7. Welter, "The Cult of True Womanhood," 158.
8. Tyler, *Freedom's Ferment*, 432.
9. Bode, *American Popular Culture*, xiv.
10. Woodward, *Mary Chesnut's Civil War*, 168.
11. Moffat and Painter, *Revelations: Diaries of Women*, 271.
12. DFS, January 15, 1861.
13. DFS, December 17, 1861.
14. McPherson, *Battle Cry of Freedom*, 480.
15. Leepson, *Desperate Engagement*, 146.
16. Sutherland, *Expansion of Everyday Life*, 91.
17. Elizabeth Cady Stanton, *Eighty Years and More*, 194.
18. Ibid., 196.
19. Jennifer Haines, e-mail correspondence to author, October 21, 2008.
20. DFS, January 12, 1863.
21. DFS, April 29, 1862, useful, unmarried; SP, Frances to WHS, September 30, 1848, self-reliant; SP, Excerpt from Frances's Scrapbook, containing clippings on women's rights topics, bonnets, and cloaks; Garrison Family Papers, Martha Coffin Wright to Lucretia Mott, September 8, 1855, not to be married.
22. DFS, April 29, 1862.
23. SP, Fanny to Frances, February 11, 1864.
24. DFS, April 29, 1862.
25. James, *Notable American Women*, 486–87.
26. Nelson and Sheriff, *A People at War*, 122, over 50; Leepson, *Desperate Engagement*, 145–146, facilities; Seward III, 192–93, blood like water; Nelson and Sheriff, *A People at War*, 116, flow.
27. McPherson, *Battle Cry of Freedom*, 478, rolling bandages; Nelson and Sheriff, *A People at War*, 116, morals; Davis, *Lincoln's Men*, 122, compassion.
28. DFS, March 30, 1862.
29. Denney, *The Civil War Years*, 145.
30. DFS, March 27, 1862.
31. McPherson, *Battle Cry of Freedom*, 477.

32. McPherson, *Battle Cry of Freedom*, 486–487, injuries or disease; ibid., 487, pneumonia; Sutherland, *Expansion of Everyday Life*, 20, get over it.

33. Leech, *Reveille in Washington*, 210–11.

34. Goodwin, *Team of Rivals*, 611.

35. Dudden, *Women in the American Theatre*, 77, adulation; ibid., 85, limelight; Clinton, *Mrs. Lincoln*, 206, Commission.

36. DFS, October 9, 1863.

37. Nicolay, *Lincoln's Secretary*, 81.

38. DFS, October 9, 1863.

39. Ibid.

40. From the *New York Times*, 19 Feb. 1876, 7, quoted in Leach, *Bright Particular Star*, 44, pantheress; DFS, October 17, 1863, strength; Dudden, *Women in the American Theatre*, 91–92, indignation.

41. Dudden, *Women in the American Theatre*, 89.

42. DFS, October 9, 1863, headstrong; October 18, 1863, wink; October 19, 1863, poetry.

43. DFS, October 12, 1863, possess; October 13, 1863, diffidence; October 12, 1863, tenderness.

44. Dudden, *Women in the American Theatre*, 98, Stebbins; Fisher, *House of Wits*, 491, Hosmer; ibid., 302, undrape models in.

45. Dudden, *Women in the American Theatre*, 97, perversion; Reynolds, *Waking Giant: America*, 208, homosexual; Dudden, *Women in the American Theatre*, 98, discreet.

46. Dudden, *Women in the American Theatre*, 82–83, actors; ibid., 100, manipulative; ibid., 83, especially its women; ibid., 84–85, America; ibid., 100, greatness.

### 14. Connections to Catastrophe

1. DFS, October 10, 1863.

2. John T. Ford, cited in Leech, *Reveille in Washington*, 277.

3. DFS, October 10, 1863.

4. Ibid.

5. Ibid.

6. Swanson, *Manhunt*, 12.

7. DFS, October 10, 1863.

8. Titone, *My Thoughts Be Bloody*, 305.

9. DFS, February 10, 1860, Lucy Hale; PCJ I, 279 n. 54 romantically linked; DFS, April 6, 1862, destiny.

10. DFS, March 11, 1864.

11. Titone, *My Thoughts Be Bloody*, 59, caul; Giblin, *Good Brother, Bad Brother*, 13, poetry; Titone, *My Thoughts Be Bloody*, 83, babysitter.

12. Giblin, *Good Brother, Bad Brother*, 20–21.

13. Wilmeth and Bigsby, *The Cambridge History*, 368.

14. Giblin, *Good Brother, Bad Brother*, 44.

15. Ibid., 73.

16. Giblin, *Good Brother, Bad Brother*, 9, free blacks; Titone, *My Thoughts Be Bloody*, 211–12, John Brown; Giblin, *Good Brother, Bad Brother*, 63, banished; Clarke, in Alford, *John Wilkes Booth . . . Memoir*, 82, South.

17. Titone, *My Thoughts Be Bloody*, 336–37.

18. Giblin, *Good Brother, Bad Brother*, 101.

19. Titone, *My Thoughts Be Bloody*, 282–83.

20. DFS, March 11, 1864.

21. Ibid.

22. Ibid.

23. Ibid.

24. Interview with Sir Charles Wyndham, quoted in Wilson, *John Wilkes Booth*, 15.

### 15. When This Cruel War Is Over

1. Winik, *April, 1865*, 179.

2. Trudeau, *Bloody Raids South*, 341.

3. SP, Fanny to WHS, May 15, 1864.

4. Wert, *The Sword . . . Potomac*, 333.

5. SP, Fanny to WHS, June 1, 1864.

6. SP, Box 132, Janet Watson Seward, 26.

7. Ibid.

8. Ibid., 27.

9. SP, Fanny to WHS, June 19, 1864.

10. SP, WHS to Fanny, November 30, 1862, attached to him.

11. SP, Box 132, Janet Watson Seward, 14.

12. Taylor, *William Henry Seward*, 233, VI Corps; Sutherland, *Expansion of Everyday Life*, 21, show of battle; Werner, *Reluctant Witnesses*, 17, skeleton's toes.

13. Leepson, *Desperate Engagement*, 3.

14. Ibid., 26–28.

15. Thomas and Hyman, *Stanton: The Life*, 319.

16. Leepson, *Desperate Engagement*, 85.

17. Ibid., 109.

18. Taylor, *William Henry Seward*, 233.

19. Leepson, *Desperate Engagement*, 119.

20. Seward II, 233.

21. Ibid.
22. SP, Box 132, Janet Watson Seward, 28.
23. Ibid., 29.
24. Ibid.
25. Ibid., 30.
26. Thomas and Hyman, *Stanton: The Life*, 319.

**16. A Conspiracy Evolves**

1. Goodwin, *Team of Rivals*, 654.
2. Seward III, 242–44.
3. Channing, *Confederate Ordeal*, frontispiece.
4. Ibid., 160.
5. DFS, January 22, 1863, hardships; Werner, *Reluctant Witnesses*, 52, raspberry leaves; DFS, January 22, 1863, a pair.
6. Channing, *Confederate Ordeal*, 149.
7. From Mary Chesnut, Journal entry for March 5, 1865, quoted in Woodward, *Mary Chesnut's Civil War*, 744.
8. Winik, *April, 1865*, 155.
9. Ibid., 156–57.
10. Ownsbey, *Alias "Paine"*, 11, nineteen; 13–14, Fredericksburg; 18, fled south; 18–19, rebels.
11. Ownsbey, *Alias "Paine"*, 3–4, role model; 9, taking up religion; 7, introvert; 7, keep this pet.
12. Ibid., 148.
13. Ibid., 11.
14. From Captain Christian Rath to John A. Gray, quoted in Gray, "Fate of the Lincoln Conspirators," 634.
15. Ownsbey, *Alias "Paine"*, 33.
16. Steers, *Blood on the Moon*, 83.
17. Ibid., 58.
18. Giblin, *Good Brother, Bad Brother*, 93–94, Confederate army; Kauffman, *American Brutus*, 134, released; Swanson, *Manhunt*, 23, foolish scheme; Kauffman, *American Brutus*, 160–61, O'Laughlen to help.
19. Ownsbey, *Alias "Paine"*, 67.
20. Ownsbey, *Alias "Paine"*, 45, like Lewis Powell; Swanson, *Manhunt*, 2, peering down; Winik, *April, 1865*, 345, Lucy; John Wilkes Booth, quoted in Laughlin, *Death of Lincoln*, 60, kill the president.
21. Steers, *Blood on the Moon*, 84.
22. Giblin, *Good Brother, Bad Brother*, 110–111.

23. Steers, *Blood on the Moon*, 85, Campbell Military Hospital; Giblin, *Good Brother, Bad Brother*, 102, railsplitter; ibid., 111, fizzled.

24. DFS, April 4, 1865.

25. Swanson, *Manhunt*, 353.

26. Goodwin, *Team of Rivals* 709, saving his army; Wert, *The Sword . . . Potomac*, 403, Petersburg; Thomas and Hyman, *Stanton: The Life*, 351, flags; DFS, April 4, 1865, Richmond.

27. Wert, *The Sword . . . Potomac*, 409.

28. Brooks, *Washington, D.C., in Lincoln's Time*, 244.

29. VD, 412.

30. Giblin, *Good Brother, Bad Brother*, 113.

31. Brooks, *Washington, D.C., in Lincoln's Time*, 254–55.

32. From John Wilkes Booth to Lewis Powell as reported by Powell to Thomas T. Eckert. See "Impeachment of the President," House Report 7, 40 Cong., 1 Sess. (1867), 674. Quoted in Hanchett, *The Lincoln Murder Conspiracies*, 37.

### 17. Prelude to the Night of Horrors

1. DFS, April 4, 1865.

2. DFS, April 5, 1865.

3. Ibid.

4. Ibid.

5. DFS, April 6, 1865.

6. Seward III, 270, news; ibid., 271, heart ache; DFS, April 8, 1865, witness.

7. Seward, III, 270, both sides; Verdi, "The Assassination," 47, the family; Hatch, "Lincoln's Doctors," 46, Booth. Note: Barnes would also attend President Garfield after his assassination in 1881.

8. Verdi, "The Assassination," 47, broken arm; ibid., 46, Fort Foote; DFS, April 10, 1863, throat.

9. Verdi, "The Assassination," 47.

10. Seward III, 271.

11. DFS, April 9, 1865.

12. Thomas and Hyman, *Stanton: The Life*, 377–78.

13. DFS, April 9, 1865.

14. Ibid.

15. DFS, April 10, 1865.

16. DFS, April 11, 1865.

17. DFS, April 9, 1865, like himself; April 10, 1865, twice; April 12, 1865, night.

18. Verdi, "The Assassination," 47.

19. Taylor, *William Henry Seward*, 243.

20. Lattimer, "The Stabbing," 110, immobilize; DFS, April 12, 1865, one tooth to another. Note: Fanny never mentions a protective brace or collar supporting her father's jaw, often cited as offering protection from Powell's later knife wounds; ibid., relief did not come; DFS, April 13, 1865, still confused; Verdi, "The Assassination," 48, stout heart.

21. Verdi, "The Assassination," 47, constant watch; DFS, April 13, 1865, newspapers; DFS, April 14, 1865, sailor; DFS, April 13, 1865, male nurse; DFS, April 9, 1865, ordeal; Seward III, 271, care of a parent.

22. DFS, April 13, 1865.

23. DFS, April 14, 1865.

24. Ibid.

25. SR, 255, unknown shore; Jean H. Baker, *Mary Todd Lincoln*, 237, Tad's pistol, two images; Randall, *Mary Lincoln: Biography of a Marriage*, 374, on fire; Goodwin, *Team of Rivals*, 723, *Macbeth*.

26. VD, 413, rifles; Ownsbey, *Alias "Paine"*, 71, stranger. Note: this report is questionable, as Powell, in one account, claimed to have first learned the details of the assassination plot on the evening of April 14; Chaconas, "Unpublished Atzerodt," 20–21.

27. SP, Ryerson to Fred, April 13, 1865.

### 18. Nothing Good about Good Friday

1. Swanson, *Manhunt*, 10–12.

2. Ibid., 13.

3. Giblin, *Good Brother, Bad Brother*, 117.

4. Kauffman, *American Brutus*, 223.

5. DFS, January 14, 1863.

6. Jennifer Haines, e-mail correspondence to the author, February 24, 2007.

7. DFS, April 14, 1865.

8. Ibid.

9. Ibid.

10. DFS, April 14, 1865, *Charlemagne*; SR, 258, unable to talk; DFS, April 14, 1865, all quiet.

11. Poore, *The Conspiracy Trial*, 1:12.

12. Maxwell, "The Bizarre Case of Lewis Paine," 226.

13. Swanson, *Manhunt*, 29.

14. Ibid., 25.

15. Ownsbey, *Alias "Paine"*, 76, Madison Place; Kauffman, *American Brutus*, 22, Ford's Theatre; VD, 269, into the park.

16. Taylor, *William Henry Seward*, 242, Captain Booth; Swanson, *Manhunt*, 29, wild look; Lattimer, *Kennedy and Lincoln . . . Assassinations*, 101–105, regiment.

17. Letter from a Wisconsin officer, Major Rufus R. Dawes, Sixth Wisconsin Infantry, December 25, 1862, recipient not known, quoted in McPherson, *Battle Cry of Freedom*, 590, Valley Forge; SP, Fanny to Lazette, March 14, 1863, healed steadily; DFS, March 13, 1863, even for a time.

18. Brooks, *Washington, D.C., in Lincoln's Time*, 269.

19. Pitman, *Assassination of President Lincoln*, 96, assistant; Swanson, *Manhunt*, 52, delivered; Doster, *Lincoln and Episodes*, 269, doctor.

20. Poore, *The Conspiracy Trial*, 1:474–77.

21. Ibid., 1:472.

22. Swanson, *Manhunt*, 53.

23. Poore, *The Conspiracy Trial*, 1:472.

24. Pitman, *Assassination of President Lincoln*, 161. Note: Bell would not have been aware of Powell's earlier violence toward a Negro servant, striking her and threatening to kill her after she had balked at a request to clean up his room; Powell's own signed statement said, "I whipped a colored woman . . . because she insulted me." Cf. Prior, "Lewis Payne, Pawn," 9.

25. Taylor, *William Henry Seward*, 243.

26. Lattimer, "The Stabbing," 107.

27. DFS, April 14, 1865.

28. Poore, *The Conspiracy Trial*, 1:472–73.

29. *Record of Trial of John H. Surratt*, vol. 1, 251.

30. Swanson, *Manhunt*, 57.

31. Lattimer, "The Stabbing," 110.

32. Poore, *The Conspiracy Trial*, 1:473.

33. DFS, April 14, 1865.

34. DFS, April 14, 1865, intense expression; Lattimer, "The Stabbing," 108, father's bedroom; Ownsbey, *Alias "Paine"*, 79, bulldog.

35. DFS, April 14, 1865.

36. Poore, *The Conspiracy Trial*, 1:480.

37. DFS, April 14, 1865.

38. Ibid.

39. Poore, *The Conspiracy Trial*, 2:3, cheek; *Record of Trial of John H. Surratt*, vol. 1, 265, energy that he had; VD, 414, rain.

40. SP, WHS to Fanny, December 10, 1857.

41. DFS, April 14, 1865.

42. *Record of Trial of John H. Surratt*, vol. 1, 262–63.

43. Poore, *The Conspiracy Trial*, 2:6.

44. Pitman, *Assassination of President Lincoln*, 156.

45. DFS, April 14, 1865.

46. Poore, *The Conspiracy Trial*, 2:6.

47. Ibid., 7.

48. DFS, April 14, 1865.

49. DFS, April 14, 1865, blows; Lattimer, "The Stabbing," 109, chest; DFS, April 14, 1865, dead.

50. DFS, April 14, 1865, throat; Taylor, *William Henry Seward*, 245, Caesar; Verdi, "The Assassination," 49, corpse; DFS, April 14, 1865, blood.

51. *Record of Trial of John H. Surratt*, vol. 1, 264, heart; DFS, April 14, 1865, beat; *Record of Trial of John H. Surratt*, vol. 1, 265, part.

52. DFS, April 14, 1865.

53. Verdi, "The Assassination," 48, killed; Pitman, *Assassination of President Lincoln*, 157, bleeding; Verdi, "The Assassination," 50, one man.

54. Pitman, *Assassination of President Lincoln*, 157.

55. Niven, 493.

56. Verdi, "The Assassination," 49.

57. Pitman, *Assassination of President Lincoln*, 157.

58. Hatch, "I'm Mad! I'm Mad!", 36.

59. DFS, April 14, 1865.

60. Ibid.

61. Ibid.

62. DFS, April 14, 1865, could not live; Warner, *Generals in Blue*, 21, medical service; Pitman, *Assassination of President Lincoln*, 157, articulate.

63. Poore, *The Conspiracy Trial*, 2:6.

64. DFS, April 14, 1865.

65. Ibid.

66. Ibid.

67. Ibid.

68. Ibid.

69. Hatch, "Lincoln's Doctors," 43.

70. DFS, April 14, 1865.

### 19. "A Pretty Brave Little Girl Tonight"

1. DFS, April 14, 1865.

2. Swanson, *Manhunt*, 110.

3. Leale, "Lincoln's Last Hours," 12.

4. DFS, April 14, 1865, existed; Donald, *Lincoln*, 577, any harm; DFS, April 14, 1865, such a world.

5. DFS, April 14, 1865, parlor floor; Swanson, *Manhunt*, 142, hang; Leonard, *Lincoln's Avengers*, 11, masterminded it.

6. DFS, April 14, 1865. Note: a swatch of the bloody sheet is on display at Seward House.

7. Ibid. Note: The line is from *Macbeth*, Act V, Scene V. The line is more accurately "I have supped full *with* horrors."

8. Ibid. Note: Tennyson's actual words are "Risest thou thus, dim dawn, again."

9. Ibid.

10. PCJ I, 928, n. 147, Medical Corps; DFS, April 14, 1865, growing worse; Warner, *Generals in Blue*, 21, closing the eyes; *While Lincoln Lay Dying*, 6, motionless breast.

11. Thomas and Hyman, *Stanton: The Life*, 396–97.

12. Turner, *Beware the People Weeping*, 63.

13. DFS, April 14, 1865.

14. DFS, April 14, 1865, calmly; Nevins and Thomas, *The Diary of George Templeton Strong*, vol. 3, 292, ever known; Brooks, *Washington, D.C., in Lincoln's Time*, 260, still.

15. DFS, April 14, 1865.

16. Ibid.

17. Ibid.

18. Ibid.

19. Leonard, *Lincoln's Avengers*, 10, cold rain; Verdi, "The Assassination," 50, people's joy; Brooks, *Washington, D.C., in Lincoln's Time*, 260, funeral drapery.

20. DFS, April 14, 1865.

21. Seward III, 278, knife; Pitman, *Assassination of President Lincoln*, 307, neck; ibid., 158, shock.

22. Pitman, *Assassination of President Lincoln*, 158.

23. Lattimer, *Kennedy and Lincoln . . . Assassinations*, 106.

24. Seward III, 278.

25. Taylor, *William Henry Seward*, 250.

26. Verdi, "The Assassination," 46, companion; Lloyd Lewis, *Sherman: Fighting Prophet*, 575, spectacles; Swanson, *Manhunt*, 377, camera.

27. Taylor, *William Henry Seward*, 246, short periods; Conrad, 398, weak; From WHS to James Watson Webb, August 9, 1865, private collection, quoted in Taylor, *William Henry Seward*, 250, broken in pieces.

28. SR, 260, assassin; Pitman, *Assassination of President Lincoln*, 157, sixty hours; Verdi, "The Assassination," 49, fatal.

29. Lattimer, "The Stabbing," 108.

30. Seward III, 280.

31. Lattimer, "The Stabbing," 108.

32. *Macbeth*, Act III, Scene IV.

33. Taylor, *William Henry Seward*, 245.

34. Note: One area of controversy involves the theory that Seward was protected by a metal brace or cervical collar that deflected the assassin's knife (Kauffman, *American Brutus*, 26; Francis Wilson, *John Wilkes Booth*, 122). The most thorough discussion of the issue concluded that such a device was not worn by the Secretary (Lattimer, "The Stabbing," 112). Taylor dismisses the cervical collar idea (Taylor, *William Henry Seward*, 245). Most importantly, other eyewitnesses to the event do not mention a collar, and Fanny, who kept careful notes of her father's condition and progress, never mentions any kind of protective cervical device. Frederick, however, testified that his father was "half raised by one of those frame works which are made for the accommodation of the sick" (*Record of the Trial of John Surratt*, vol. 1, 250). Ownsbey suggested that this device, made of metal, might have deflected Powell's blade (Ownsbey, *Alias "Paine"*, 216, n. 12).

35. Cooney, "Seward's Savior," 93.

36. Swanson, *Manhunt*, 372.

37. Turner, *Beware the People Weeping*, 195–96.

38. DFS, April 14, 1865.

39. *Baltimore Sun*, "Death of Miss Seward," obituary, October 31, 1866.

40. SP, WHS to Fanny, December 10, 1857.

**20. "This Baptism of Blood"**

1. Means, *The Avenger Takes His Place*, 106–7.

2. Ownsbey, *Alias "Paine"*, 90.

3. Doster, *Lincoln and Episodes*, 269.

4. Ownsbey, *Alias "Paine"*, 88.

5. Ownsbey, *Alias "Paine"*, 88–93, met the young man before; Townsend, *The Life, Crime, and Capture*, 46, forever; Ownsbey, *Alias "Paine"*, 100–101, Potomac River.

6. SP, Fanny to WHS, August 1, 1864, cough is gone; Fanny to WHS, August 16, 1864, anxiety about Will; Fanny to WHS, August 25, 1864, sick she has been.

7. SP, Frances to Augustus, January 6, 1855.

8. DFS, September 7, 1862.

9. VD, 407.

10. SP, Frances to Lazette, June 2, 1865.

11. SP, Frances to Fred, July 29, 1862.

12. SP, Frances to Fanny, March 1865—no day given.

13. VD, 410.

14. Taylor, *William Henry Seward*, 239.

15. SP, Frances to Fanny, March 1865—no day given.

16. DFS, April 7, 1865.
17. DFS, April 9, 1865.
18. DFS, April 14, 1865.
19. Seward III, 281.
20. Ibid., 282.
21. Ibid., 280.
22. Ibid., 286.
23. DFS, June 17, 1865.
24. DFS, June 18, 1865.
25. DFS, June 17, 1865.
26. Ibid.
27. DFS, June 18, 1865.
28. Ibid.
29. Conrad, 398.
30. Seward III, 285.
31. Ownsbey, *Alias "Paine"*, 1–2, Paine or Payne; Poore, *The Conspiracy Trial*, 1:12–13, observers; Swanson, *Manhunt* and Weinberg, conspirators, 15; Swanson, *Manhunt*, 353, consumption.
32. Poore, *The Conspiracy Trial*, 1:12–13, gladiatorial; Brooks, *Washington, D.C., in Lincoln's Time*, 269, chest; Ibid., gray eyes; Ownsbey, *Alias "Paine"*, 122, horses.
33. Ownsbey, *Alias "Paine"*, 2, melodrama; Poore, *The Conspiracy Trial*, 1:12–13, desperadoes; ibid., intelligence; ibid., stalwart type; Ownsbey, *Alias "Paine"*, 132, prayers.
34. Steers, *Blood on the Moon*, 219, during the war; Doster, *Lincoln and Episodes*, 257, none at all; ibid., 259, example's sake; ibid., 263, siege guns.
35. Doster, *Lincoln and Episodes*, 265.
36. Ownsbey, *Alias "Paine"*, 124.
37. Doster, *Lincoln and Episodes*, 265.
38. Ibid., 267, did not fly; ibid., 270, battery; ibid., 269, died with her.
39. Ownsbey, *Alias "Paine"*, 138–39, punishment; ibid., 143, gallows; ibid., 144, longer.

**21. Not "Over Well"**

1. SP, Fanny to Amanda Schooley, January 26, 1866, last April; Seward III, 285, on the other; ibid., 286, grave.
2. SP, Fanny to Amanda Schooley, January 26, 1866.
3. SP, Lazette to WHS, July 4, 1865, take a drive; Lazette to WHS, July 10, 1865, returned; Fanny to WHS, July 11, 1865, quinine; Fanny to WHS, July 11, 1865, stairs; Lazette to WHS, August 24, 1865, physicians there; Fanny to Amanda Schooley, January 26, 1866, have done.

4. Caldwell, *The Last Crusade*, 9, height; from Louisa May Alcott, *Little Women*, Chapter 36, 395, beauty; Caldwell, *The Last Crusade*, 18–20, Thoreau.

5. Caldwell, *The Last Crusade*, 11.

6. Ibid., 12–13.

7. Ibid., 8.

8. DFS, January 1–4, 1866, coughing; January 6, 1866, headache; January 20 and 21, 1866, exhausted; January 23, 1866, to write; February 1 and April 30, 1866, chest.

9. DFS, January 1, 1866, whooping cough; April 30, 1866, pleurisy; January 10, 1866, moisten the air; January 22, 1866, furnace; June 2, 1866, quinine; January 27, 1866, iron; July 12, 1866, brandy.

10. SP, Fanny to WHS, August 29, 1865, envelopes; DFS, January 23, 1866, merry; DFS, May 25, 1866, elder ladies; DFS, April 30, 1866, dress; DFS, May 22, 1866, sailor hat; DFS, January 17, 1866, over well.

11. DFS, May 6, 1862, carry me off; DFS, March 31, 1859, tooth filling; SP, Fanny to WHS, November 9, 1862, enemy; SP, Fanny to WHS, November 24, 1865, convalescent list.

12. DFS, March 13, 1866, behind; DFS, July 4, 1866, all day; DFS, May 13, 1866, unable; SP, Lazette to Janet Seward, January 19, 1866, cabinet; DFS, January 1, 1866, attend.

13. DFS, January 3, 1866.

14. SP, Fanny to Will, December 14, 1865, gaped; DFS, May 11, 1866, chafed; DFS, September 13, 1866, painfully visible; SP, Fanny to WHS, July 11, 1865, splint; Seward III, 284, distorted figure; ibid., 327, as ever.

15. SP, WHS to Fanny, July 25, 1866, politics; SP, WHS to Fanny, July 18, 1866, labor; DFS, March 9, 1866, kisses.

16. SP, WHS to Fanny, November 25, 1865, papers; DFS, January 4, 1866, close; DFS, July 10, 1866, ivy; DFS, September 12, 1866, carriage; SP, Fanny to WHS, August 29, 1865, at bay.

17. SP, Fanny to WHS, August 11, 1865, guidance; DFS, January 22, 1866, mannerisms; DFS, January 12, 1866, everywhere; SP, Box 135, cheer; DFS, June 21, 1866, brings.

18. DFS, January 28, 1866.

19. DFS, March 1, 1866.

20. DFS, December 26, 1860, flowers; Taylor, *William Henry Seward*, 13–14, doctrine; DFS, May 25, 1862, forms.

21. Sutherland, *Expansion of Everyday Life*, 79, intervened; ibid., 79, full or empty; ibid., 80, regularly; DFS, Christmas 1860, than usual; Sutherland, *Expansion of Everyday Life*, 83, dragged along; Taylor, *William Henry Seward*, 38, his own.

22. SP, Fanny to WHS, October 12, 1862, church matters; SP, Fanny to WHS, November 17, 1862, sermons; Emily Dickinson, "I never felt at Home—Below," #413 in Johnson, *The Complete Poems of Emily Dickinson*, 321–22.

23. DFS, January 3, 1859, Heaven; DFS, April 27, 1862, performed; DFS, January 8, 1860, like it.

24. DFS, February 24, 1861, practical; Sutherland, *Expansion of Everyday Life*, 82, afterworld; DFS, May 11, 1862, melancholy.

25. DFS, January 3, 1866. Note: Fanny mentions "Dying" in this diary entry but does not explore its contents.

26. PCJ I, 1006, n. 64.

27. DFS, March 20, 1866.

28. DFS, March 22, 1866.

29. DFS, March 23, 1866.

30. DFS, March 29, 1866, experience; April 30, 1866, old pains; May 1, 1866, two weeks; May 13, 1866, for long.

31. SP, Fanny to WHS, August 4, 1866, chills; SP, Will to WHS, August 6, 1866, advice; SP, Fanny to WHS, August 7, 1866, pillow; DFS, August 11, 1866, Dr. Norris to Auburn.

32. DFS, June 17, 1865, power; DFS, April 14, 1865, girl; DFS, June 17, 1865, dying; DFS, August 14, 1866, health; DFS, alarm; SP, Fanny to WHS, August 19, 1866, tired.

33. DFS, May 2, 1866, a day; SP, WHS to Fanny, July 16, 1866, concert; SP, WHS to Fanny, July 15, 1866, feast.

34. Stahr, *Lincoln's Indispensable Man*, 471.

35. DFS, August 31, 1866.

36. DFS, September 1, 1866, train; August 31, 1866, standing; September 1, 1866, cold.

37. DFS, September 14, 1866.

38. DFS, September 15, 1866.

39. DFS, September 15, 1866.

40. Seward III, 279, to pieces; *New York Times*, "The Attempt to Assassinate Seward," protection; DFS, September 15, 1866, affection.

41. DFS, September 15, 1866.

42. DFS, October 7, 1866.

43. Breault, *The World of Emily Howland*, 11, Cayuga County; ibid., 6, girls; ibid, 52, Washington; Emily Howland Papers, #2681, Emily Howland to Hannah Howland, October 31, 1866, Cholera. Note: The coroner recorded the cause of Fanny's death as "bilious remittent fever." The *New York Tribune* reported that it was typhoid. The underlying cause, however, was tuberculosis (VD, 416–17).

44. Emily Howland Papers, #2681, Emily Howland to Hannah Howland, October 31, 1866.

45. Ibid.

46. Ibid.

47. SP, WHS to Fanny, December 10, 1857.

48. SP, WHS to Will, November 14, 1866.

49. Bode, *American Popular Culture*, 63.

50. Ibid., 50.

51. Ibid.

52. Marcoccia, "Emanuel Leutze."

53. Ibid. Note: In 1859 Leutze painted two portraits of Fanny's father. Of the first, Fanny wrote in her diary about her dissatisfaction with Leutze's early rendering because it lacked "father's kind expression, benevolent mouth or mild blue eyes" (DFS, March 28, 1859). The second painting, finished in 1861, was found in the artist's studio after his death.

54. Marcoccia, "Emanuel Leutze."

55. Ibid.

56. Interview of Harriet Tubman by her biographer, Sarah Bradford, quoted in Bradford, *Harriet, the Moses of Her People*, 92–93.

57. Ibid, 143.

58. Giblin, *Good Brother, Bad Brother*, 181–182.

59. Ibid., 221.

60. Kauffman, *American Brutus*, 391, FBI; Ownsbey, *Alias "Paine"*, 7, mule; Swanson, *Manhunt*, 380, pieces.

61. DFS, March 1864—no day given.

62. SP, Lazette to Janet Watson Seward, January 19, 1866, coal bin; SP, Fanny to Janet Watson Seward, September 29, 1866, bonnet; SP, Fanny to Will, October 11, 1866, library; SR, 145, cane; SP, Cornelia "Nelly" Seward to WHS, February 9, 1868, canary.

63. SP, Telegram, Will to Fred, October 10, 1872, at once; SP, Telegram, Will to Fred, October 11, 1872, three o'clock; Seward III, 508, Another.

# Bibliography

Agassiz, George R., ed. *With Grant and Meade from the Wilderness to Appomattox: Letters of Colonel Theodore Lyman*. Lincoln: University of Nebraska Press, 1994.

Alcott, Louisa May. *Little Women*. Boston: Little, Brown, 1926.

Allen, Thomas B. *Harriet Tubman, Secret Agent: How Daring Slaves and Free Blacks Spied for the Union during the Civil War*. Washington, DC: National Geographic Society, 2006.

Anderson, Scott William. "Entrepreneurs and Place in Early America: Auburn, New York, 1783–1880." PhD diss., Syracuse University, 1997.

Andrews, Peter. "How We Got Lincoln." *American Heritage* 3, no. 7 (November, 1988): 1.

Angle, Paul M., ed. *Abraham Lincoln: A History by John G. Nicolay and John Hay*. Chicago: University of Chicago Press, 1966.

Arnold, Isaac Newton. "The Baltimore Plot to Assassinate Abraham Lincoln." *Harper's New Monthly Magazine* 37 (June 1868): 123–28.

Attie, Jeanie. *Patriotic Toil: Northern Women and the American Civil War*. Ithaca, NY: Cornell University Press, 1998.

Badeau, Adam. *Grant in Peace: From Appomattox to Mount McGregor, a Personal Memoir*. Hartford, CT: S.S. Scranton, 1887.

Baker, George E., ed. *The Works of William H. Seward*. Vol. 1. New York: Redfield, 1853.

Baker, George E., ed. *The Works of William H. Seward*. Vol. 4. Boston: Houghton Mifflin, 1884.

Baker, Jean H. *Mary Todd Lincoln: A Biography*. New York: W.W. Norton, 1987.

*Baltimore Sun*. "Death of Miss Seward." Obituary, October 31, 1866.

Bancroft, Frederic. *The Life of William H. Seward*. Vol. 2. New York and London: Harper and Brothers, 1900.

Basler, Roy P., ed. *The Collected Works of Abraham Lincoln.* Vol. 6. New Brunswick, NJ: Rutgers University Press, 1953.

Beale, Howard K. *The Diary of Gideon Welles: Secretary of the Navy under Lincoln and Johnson.* Vol. 1. New York: W.W. Norton and Company, 1960.

Blackman, Ann. *Wild Rose: Rose O'Neale Greenhow, Civil War Spy.* New York: Random House, 2005.

Bode, Carl. *The Anatomy of American Popular Culture, 1840–1861.* Berkeley, University of California Press, 1959.

Boyden, Anna L. *Echoes from Hospital and White House: A Record of Mrs. Rebecca R. Pomroy's Experience in War-Times.* Boston: D. Lothrop, 1884.

Bradford, Sarah H. *Harriet, the Moses of Her People.* New York: J. J. Little, 1901.

Breault, Judith Colucci. *The World of Emily Howland: Odyssey of a Humanitarian.* Millbrae, CA: Les Femmes, 1976.

Brooks, Noah. *Washington, D.C., in Lincoln's Time.* Herbert Mitgang, ed. Chicago: Quadrangle Books, 1971.

Brooks, Noah. *Washington in Lincoln's Time.* New York: The Century Company, 1896.

Buckingham, J.E. *Reminiscences and Souvenirs of the Assassination of Abraham Lincoln.* Washington, DC: Press of Rufus H. Darby, 1894.

Burlingame, Michael, ed. *Abraham Lincoln: the Observations of John G. Nicolay and John Hay.* Carbondale: Southern Illinois University Press, 2007.

Burlingame, Michael, and John R. Turner Ettlinger, eds. *Inside Lincoln's White House: The Complete Civil War Diary of John Hay.* Carbondale: Southern Illinois University Press, 1997.

Burnap, George. *Sphere and Duties of Woman.* 5th ed. Baltimore, 1854.

Burr, Agnes Rush. *Russell H. Conwell: The Work and the Man.* Project Gutenberg, 2004. www.gutenberg.org/cache/epub/11421/pg11421.txt.

Burton, Orville Vernon. *The Age of Lincoln.* New York: Hill and Wang, 2007.

Bynum, W. F. *Science and the Practice of Medicine in the Nineteenth Century.* New York: Cambridge University Press, 1994.

Caldwell, Mark. *The Last Crusade: The War on Consumption, 1862–1954.* New York: Atheneum, 1988.

Carpenter, Frank B. "Abraham Lincoln: Personal Recollections and Incidents of a Six Months' Sojourn in the White House during the Lincoln Administration." *The Peterson Magazine*, April, 1896.

———. *Six Months at the White House with Abraham Lincoln: The Story of a Picture.* New York: Hurd and Houghton, 1867.

Cashin, Joan E. *First Lady of the Confederacy: Varina Davis's Civil War.* Cambridge: Harvard University Press, 2006.

———, ed. *The War Was You and Me: Civilians in the American Civil War.* Princeton: Princeton University Press, 2002.

Chaconas, Joan L. "Unpublished Atzerodt Confession." *Surratt Courier,* October 1988, III, 19–21.

Channing, Steven A., ed. *Confederate Ordeal: The Southern Home Front. The Civil War* series. Alexandria, Va.: Time-Life Books, 1984.

Cheney, Ednah D., ed. *Louisa May Alcott: Her Life, Letters, and Journals.* Boston: Little, Brown, 1898.

Chinoy, Helen Krich, and Linda Walsh Jenkins, eds. *Women in American Theatre.* 3rd ed. New York: Theatre Communications Group, 2006.

Clarke, Asia Booth. Terry Alford, ed. *John Wilkes Booth: A Sister's Memoir.* Jackson: University Press of Mississippi, 1999.

———. *The Unlocked Book: A Memoir of John Wilkes Booth by his sister Asia Booth Clarke.* New York: G. P. Putnam's, 1938.

Clinton, Catherine. *Harriet Tubman: The Road to Freedom.* New York: Little, Brown, 2004.

———. *Mrs. Lincoln: A Life.* New York: HarperCollins, 2009.

Clinton, Catherine, and Nina Silber, eds. *Battle Scars: Gender and Sexuality in the American Civil War.* New York: Oxford University Press, 2006.

———. *Divided Houses: Gender and the Civil War.* New York: Oxford University Press, 1992.

Cole, Donald B., and John J. McDonough, eds. *Benjamin Brown French: Witness to the Young Republic: A Yankee's Journal, 1828–1870.* Hanover, CT: University Press of New England, 1989.

Colfax, Schuyler. *Life and Principles of Abraham Lincoln.* Philadelphia: James B. Rogers, 1865.

Conrad, Earl. *The Governor and his Lady.* New York: Putnam, 1960.

Cooney, Charles F. "Seward's Savior: George F. Robinson." *Lincoln Herald,* Fall 1973: 93–96.

Cott, Nancy F. *The Bonds of Womanhood: "Woman's Sphere" in New England, 1780–1835.* New Haven: Yale University Press, 1977.

Crawford, Elizabeth. *Harriet Tubman Home Chronology 2003.* Crawford & Stearns Architects and Preservation Planners, Syracuse, New York. Part of the research and documentation work for the Harriet Tubman Home, Inc., 2003.

Culley, Margo, ed. *A Day at a Time: The Diary Literature of American Women from 1786 to the Present.* New York: The Feminist Press, 1985.

Davis, William C. *Lincoln's Men: How President Lincoln Became Father to an Army and a Nation.* New York: The Free Press, 1999.

Denney, Robert E. *The Civil War Years: A Day-by-Day Chronicle of the Life of a Nation.* New York: Sterling Publishing, 1992.

Donald, David Herbert. *Charles Sumner and the Coming of the Civil War.* New York: Alfred A. Knopf, 1965.

———, ed. *Inside Lincoln's Cabinet: The Civil War Diaries of Salmon P. Chase.* New York: Longmans, Green, 1954.

———. *Lincoln.* New York: Simon and Schuster, 1995.

———. *"We are Lincoln Men": Abraham Lincoln and his Friends.* New York: Simon and Schuster, 2003.

Doster, William E. *Lincoln and Episodes of the Civil War.* New York: G. P. Putnam's Sons, 1915.

Drew, Benjamin. *A North-Side View of Slavery. The Refugee: or the Narratives of Fugitive Slaves in Canada. Related by Themselves, with an Account of the History and Condition of the Colored Population of Upper Canada.* Boston: John P. Jewett and Company, 1856. Reprint, Tilden G. Edelstein, ed. Reading, Massachusetts: Addison-Wesley, 1969.

Dudden, Faye E. *Women in the American Theatre: Actresses and Audiences 1790–1870.* New Haven: Yale University Press, 1994.

Duffy, John. *The Sanitarians: A History of American Public Health.* Urbana and Chicago: University of Illinois Press, 1990.

Epstein, Daniel Mark. *Lincoln and Whitman: Parallel Lives in Civil War Washington.* New York: Ballantine Books, 2004.

Faust, Drew Gilpin. *This Republic of Suffering: Death and the American Civil War.* New York: Alfred A. Knopf, 2008.

Faust, Patricia L., ed. *Historical Times Illustrated: Encyclopedia of the Civil War.* New York: Harper and Row, 1986.

Fite, Emerson David. *Social and Industrial Conditions in the North during the Civil War.* New York: Frederick Ungar Publishing, 1968.

Fisher, Paul. *House of Wits: An Intimate Portrait of the James Family.* New York: Henry Holt, 2008.

Frank, Anne. *The Diary of a Young Girl.* New York: Doubleday, 1953.

Furgurson, Ernest B. *Chancellorsville 1863: The Souls of the Brave.* New York: Alfred A. Knopf, 1992.

———. *Freedom Rising: Washington in the Civil War.* New York: Alfred A. Knopf, 2004.

Gaff, Alan D., and Maureen Gaff, "The Dread Reality of War: Gibbon's Brigade, August 28–September 17, 1862." In *Giants in Their Tall Black Hats: Essays on the Iron Brigade.* Alan T. Nolan and Sharon Eggleston Vipond, eds. Bloomington: Indiana University Press, 1998.

Garrison Family Papers. Sophia Smith Collection. Smith College, Northampton, Massachusetts.

Giblin, James Cross. *Good Brother, Bad Brother: The Story of Edwin Booth and John Wilkes Booth.* New York: Clarion Books, 2005.

Gienapp, William E. *Abraham Lincoln and Civil War America: A Biography.* New York: Oxford University Press, 2002.

Glover, Edwin A. *Bucktailed Wildcats: A Regiment of Civil War Volunteers.* New York: Thomas Yoseloff, 1960.

Goodwin, Doris Kearns. *Team of Rivals.* New York: Simon and Schuster Paperbacks, 2005.

Gray, John A. "The Fate of the Lincoln Conspirators: The Account of the Hanging, Given by Lieutenant-Colonel Christian Rath, the Executioner." McClure's Magazine (October, 1911), 626–636.

Grier, Katherine C. *Culture and Comfort: People, Parlors, and Upholstery 1850–1930.* Rochester, New York: Strong Museum, 1988.

Hall, Henry. *The History of Auburn.* Auburn: Dennis Bros & Co., 1869.

Halpern, Daniel, ed. *Antaeus: Journals, Notebooks, and Diaries.* New York: Ecco Press, 1988.

Hamilton, Gail. "A Call to My Country-Women." *Atlantic Monthly* 11, no. 65 (March 1863).

Hanchett, William. *The Lincoln Murder Conspiracies.* Urbana and Chicago: University of Illinois Press, 1983.

Hatch, Frederick. "I'm Mad! I'm Mad!" *Journal of the Lincoln Assassination* 3, no. 2 (August 1989): 34–38.

———. "Lincoln's Doctors." *Journal of the Lincoln Assassination* 17, no. 3 (December 2003): 42–47.

Hendrick, Burton J. *Lincoln's War Cabinet.* Boston: Little, Brown, 1946.

Henry, Mary. "Eyewitness to the Civil War: First Battle of Manassas, July 1861." Smithsonian Institution Archives. http://siarchives.si.edu/history/exhibits/stories/mary-henry-eyewitness-civil-war. Accessed July 8, 2014.

Hoig, Stan. *A Capital for the Nation.* New York: Cobblehill Books, 1990.

Holliday, Laurel. *Heart Songs: The Intimate Diaries of Young Girls.* New York: Methuen, 1980.

Howland, Emily, Papers. Division of Rare and Manuscript Collections, Cornell University Library.

Humphreys, Margaret. "A Stranger to Our Camps: Typhus in American History." *Bulletin of the History of Medicine* 80, no. 2 (May 26, 2006): 269–90.

James, Edward T., ed. *Notable American Women, 1607–1950: A Biographical Dictionary.* Cambridge, MA: Belknap Press of Harvard University Press, 1971.

Johnson, Alexandra. *The Hidden Writer: Diaries and the Creative Life.* New York: Doubleday, 1997.

Johnson, Patricia Carley. "'I Could Not be Well or Happy at Home . . . When Called to the Councils of My Country': Politics and the Seward Family." *University of Rochester Library Bulletin* 31, no. 1, Autumn 1978.

———. "Sensitivity and Civil War: The Selected Diaries and Papers, 1858–1866, of Frances Adeline (Fanny) Seward." PhD diss., University of Rochester, 1964.

Johnson, Thomas H., ed. *The Complete Poems of Emily Dickinson.* Cambridge, MA: The Belknap Press of Harvard University Press, 1955.

Kasson, John F. *Rudeness and Civility: Manners in Nineteenth-Century Urban America.* New York: Hill and Wang / The Noonday Press, 1990.

Kauffman, Michael W. *American Brutus: John Wilkes Booth and the Lincoln Conspiracies.* New York: Random House, 2004.

Keckley, Elizabeth. *Behind the Scenes or, Thirty Years a Slave, and Four Years in the White House.* Reprint of the 1868 edition (New York: G. W. Carlton and Company). Project Gutenberg, 2008. www.gutenberg.org/cache/epub/24968/pg24968.txt

Kimmel, Stanley. *Mr. Lincoln's Washington.* New York: Coward-McCann, 1957.

Laas, Virginia Jeans, ed. *Wartime Washington: The Civil War Letters of Elizabeth Blair Lee.* Urbana and Chicago: University of Illinois Press, 1991.

Lamon, Ward Hill, and Dorothy Lamon, eds. *Recollections of Abraham Lincoln 1847–1865.* Chicago: A. C. McClurg, 1895.

Larson, Kate Clifford. *The Assassin's Accomplice: Mary Surratt and the Plot to Kill Abraham Lincoln.* New York: Basic Books, 2008.

———. *Bound for the Promised Land: Harriet Tubman, Portrait of an American Hero.* New York: Ballantine Books, 2004.

Lattimer, John K., M.D. *Kennedy and Lincoln: Medical and Ballistic Comparisons of their Assassinations.* New York: Harcourt Brace Jovanovich, 1980.

———. "The Stabbing of Lincoln's Secretary of State on the Night the President Was Shot." *Journal of the American Medical Association* 192, no. 2 (April 12, 1965): 107–14.

Laughlin, Clara E. *The Death of Lincoln: The Story of Booth's Plot, His Deed and the Penalty.* New York: Doubleday, Page, 1909.

Leach, Joseph. *Bright Particular Star: The Life and Times of Charlotte Cushman.* New Haven: Yale University Press, 1970.

Leale, Charles A., M.D. "Lincoln's Last Hours." Address, in observance of the one hundredth anniversary of the birth of President Abraham Lincoln. Delivered Before the Commandery of the State of New York Military Order of the Loyal Legion of the United States, New York, NY, February 1909.

Leech, Margaret. *Reveille in Washington.* New York: Carroll and Graf, 1941.

Leepson, Marc. *Desperate Engagement: How a Little-Known Civil War Battle Saved Washington, D.C., and Changed the Course of American History.* New York: Thomas Dunne / St. Martin's Press, 2007.

Leonard, Elizabeth D. *Lincoln's Avengers: Justice, Revenge, and Reunion after the Civil War.* New York: W.W. Norton, 2004.

Lewis, Betty. Memo. "Underground Railroad" file. Seward House, July 13, 1998.

Lewis, Lloyd. *Sherman: Fighting Prophet.* New York: Harcourt, Brace, 1958.

Lockwood, John, and Charles Lockwood. *The Siege of Washington: The Untold Story of the Twelve Days that Shook the Union.* New York: Oxford University Press, 2011.

Lutz, Alma. *Emma Willard: Daughter of Democracy.* Boston: Houghton Mifflin, 1929.

Maguder, Ted. "Typhus, Typhoid Fever Were Deadly to Soldiers." Fredericksburg, Va.: Free Lance-Star Publishing, September 30, 2006. http://fredericksburg.com/News/FLS/2006/092006/09302006/225093.

Mallon, Thomas. *A Book of One's Own: People and Their Diaries.* New York: Ticknor and Fields, 1984.

Marbut, F. B. *News from the Capital: The Story of Washington Reporting.* Carbondale and Edwardsville: Southern Illinois University Press, 1971.

Marcoccia, Joan. "Emanuel Leutze." Lecture at Seward House, Auburn, NY, October 24 and November 14, 2007.

Marks, Geoffrey, and William K. Beatty. *The Story of Medicine in America.* New York: Charles Scribner's Sons, 1973.

Markus, Julia. *Across an Untried Sea: Discovering Lives Hidden in the Shadow of Convention and Time.* New York: Alfred A. Knopf, 2000.

Marten, James. *The Children's Civil War.* Chapel Hill and London: The University of North Carolina Press, 1998.

———. *Civil War America: Voices from the Home Front.* Santa Barbara, CA: ABC-CLIO, 2003.

Marvel, William. *Lincoln's Darkest Year: The War in 1862.* Boston: Houghton Mifflin Company, 2008.

Massey, Mary Elizabeth. *Bonnet Brigades.* New York: Alfred A. Knopf, 1966.

Maxwell, Jerry H. "The Bizarre Case of Lewis Paine." *Lincoln Herald* 81 (1979): 223–233.

McCarthy, Molly. "A Pocketful of Days: Pocket Diaries and Daily Record Keeping among Nineteenth-Century New England Women." *New England Quarterly* 73, no. 2 (June 2000): 274–296.

McPherson, James M. *Battle Cry of Freedom: The Civil War Era.* New York: Oxford University Press, 1988.

Means, Howard. *The Avenger Takes His Place: Andrew Johnson and the 45 Days that Changed the Nation.* New York: Harcourt, 2006.

Mitgang, Herbert, ed. *Abraham Lincoln: A Press Portrait.* Athens: University of Georgia Press, 1989.

Moffat, Mary Jane, and Charlotte Painter, eds. *Revelations: Diaries of Women.* New York: Vintage Books, 1975.

Moore, John L. *Speaking of Washington: Facts, Firsts, and Folklore.* Washington, DC: Congressional Quarterly, Inc., 1993.

Myerson, Joel, and Daniel Shealy, eds. *The Journals of Louisa May Alcott.* Boston: Little, Brown, 1989.

Nelson, Scott Reynolds, and Carol Sheriff. *A People at War: Civilians and Soldiers in America's Civil War, 1854–1877.* New York: Oxford University Press, 2007.

Nevins, Allan. *The Emergence of Lincoln.* Vol. 2: *Prologue to Civil War, 1859–1861.* New York: Charles Scribner's Sons, 1950.

Nevins, Allan, and Milton Halsey Thomas, eds. *The Diary of George Templeton Strong.* Vol. 3: *The Civil War, 1860–1865.* New York: Macmillan, 1952.

*New York Times.* "The Attempt to Assassinate Seward." March 14, 1909.

Nicolay, Helen. *Lincoln's Secretary: A Biography of John G. Nicolay*. New York: Longmans, Green, 1949.

Nicolay, John G., and John Hay. *Abraham Lincoln: A History*, abridged edition. Chicago: University of Chicago Press, 1966.

Niven, John. *Gideon Welles: Lincoln's Secretary of the Navy*. New York: Oxford University Press, 1973.

Nye, Russel B. *Society and Culture in America 1830–1860*. New York: Harper and Row, 1974.

Ostendorf, Lloyd. *Lincoln's Photographs: A Complete Album*. Dayton, Ohio: Rockeywood Press, 1998.

Ownsbey, Betty J. *Alias "Paine": Lewis Thornton Powell, the Mystery Man of the Lincoln Conspiracy*. Jefferson, NC: McFarland and Company, 1993.

Panzer, Mary. *Mathew Brady and the Image of History*. Washington, DC: Smithsonian Institution Press for the National Portrait Gallery, 1997.

Pattee, Fred Lewis. *The Feminine Fifties*. New York: D. Appleton-Century, 1940.

Perrine, William. "The Dashing Kate Chase and her Great Ambition," *Ladies' Home Journal* 18, no. 7 (June 1901): 11–12, 30.

Pitman, Benn. *The Assassination of President Lincoln and the Trial of the Conspirators*. Cincinnati: Moore, Wilstach and Baldwin, 1865. Special edition privately printed for the Notable Trials Library, 1989.

Pool, Daniel. *What Jane Austen Ate and Charles Dickens Knew: Fascinating Facts of Daily Life in the Nineteenth Century*. London: Robinson, 1998.

Poore, Ben Perley, ed. *The Conspiracy Trial for the Murder of the President and the Attempt to Overthrow the Government by the Assassination of its Principal Officers*. 3 vols. New York: Arno Press, 1972.

Prior, Leon O. "Lewis Payne, Pawn of John Wilkes Booth." *The Florida Historical Quarterly* 43, no. 1 (1964): 1–20.

Randall, Ruth Painter. *Mary Lincoln: Biography of a Marriage*. Boston: Little, Brown, 1953.

*Record of the Trial of John H. Surratt in the Criminal Court for the District of Columbia*. 2 vols. Washington, DC: US Government Printing Office, 1867.

Reynolds, David S. *Mightier Than the Sword: Uncle Tom's Cabin and the Battle for America*. New York: W. W. Norton, 2011.

———. *Waking Giant: America in the Age of Jackson*. New York: HarperCollins, 2008.

Rhodehamel, John, and Louise Taper, eds. *"Right or Wrong, God Judge Me": The Writings of John Wilkes Booth.* Urbana and Chicago: University of Illinois Press, 1997.

Roe, Alfred Seelye. *The Ninth New York Heavy Artillery: A History of Its Organization, Services in the Defenses of Washington, Marches, Camps, Battles, and Muster-Out, with Accounts of Life in a Rebel Prison, Personal Experiences, Names and Addresses of Surviving Members, Personal Sketches, and a Complete Roster of the Regiment.* Published by the Author. Worcester, MA, 1899.

Rose, Anne C. *Victorian America and the Civil War.* Boston: Cambridge University Press, 1992.

———. *Voices of the Marketplace: American Thought and Culture, 1830– 1860.* Lanham, MD: Rowman and Littlefield, 1995.

Ruggles, Eleanor. *Prince of Players: Edwin Booth.* New York: W. W. Norton, 1953.

Seward, Fanny. Diaries. William Henry Seward Papers. Rare Books, Special Collections, and Preservation Department, Microfilm Reel 198. Boxes 134–135, Section IV F. University of Rochester, Rochester, New York.

Seward, Frederick W. Reminiscences of a War-Time Statesman and Diplomat, 1830–1915. New York: G. P. Putnam's Sons, 1916.

———. *Seward at Washington as Senator and Secretary of State: A Memoir of his Life, with Selections from his Letters, 1846–1861.* New York: Derby and Miller, 1891.

———. *Seward at Washington as Senator and Secretary of State: A Memoir of his Life, with Selections from his Letters, 1861–1872.* New York: Derby and Miller, 1891.

———. *William H. Seward: An Autobiography from 1801 to 1834 with a Memoir of his Life, and Selections from his Letters, 1831–1846.* New York: Derby and Miller, 1891.

Seward, Janet Watson. "Personal Experiences of the Civil War." Address prepared for "The Fortnightly," an Auburn women's club, January 20, 1898. William Henry Seward Papers. Rare Books, Special Collections, and Preservation Department, University of Rochester, Rochester, New York.

Seward, Olive Risley, ed. *W. H. Seward's Travels Around the World.* New York: D. Appleton, 1873.

Seward, William Henry. Papers. Department of Rare Books, Special Collections, and Preservation, University of Rochester, Rochester, New York.

Shapiro, Ann R. *Unlikely Heroines: Nineteenth-Century American Women Writers and the Woman Question.* New York: Greenwood Press, 1987.

Shutes, Milton H., M.D. *Lincoln and the Doctors: A Medical Narrative of the Life of Abraham Lincoln.* New York: Pioneer Press, 1933.

Simons, Judy. *Diaries and Journals of Literary Women from Fanny Burney to Virginia Woolf.* Iowa City: University of Iowa Press, 1990.

Smith-Rosenberg, Carroll. "The Female World of Love and Ritual: Relations between Women in Nineteenth-Century America." *Signs: Journal of Women in Culture and Society* 1, no. 1 (Autumn 1975): 1–29.

Stahr, Walter. *Seward: Lincoln's Indispensable Man.* New York: Simon & Schuster, 2012.

Stam, Deirdre C. "Growing up with Books: Fanny Seward's Book Collecting, Reading, and Writing in Mid-Nineteenth-Century New York State." *Libraries and Culture* 41, no. 2 (2006): 189–218.

Standage, Tom. *The Victorian Internet: The Remarkable Story of the Telegraph and the Nineteenth Century's On-line Pioneers.* New York: Walker, 1998.

Stanton, Elizabeth Cady. *Eighty Years and More: Reminiscences, 1815– 1897.* Amherst, NY: Humanity Books, 2002.

Stanton, Henry B. *Random Recollections.* New York: Harper & Brothers, 1887.

Staudenraus, P. J., ed. *Mr.Lincoln's Washington: Selections from the Writings of Noah Brooks, Civil War Correspondent.* New York: Thomas Yasaloff, 1967.

Steers, Edward, Jr. *Blood on the Moon: The Assassination of Abraham Lincoln.* Lexington: University Press of Kentucky, 2001.

Stoddard, William O. *Inside the White House in War Times.* New York: Charles L. Webster, 1890.

Strouse, Jean. *Alice James: A Biography.* Boston: Houghton Mifflin, 1980.

Sutherland, Daniel E. *The Expansion of Everyday Life: 1860– 1876.* New York: Harper and Row, 1989.

Swanson, James L. *Manhunt: The Twelve-Day Chase for Lincoln's Killer.* New York: William Morrow, 2006.

Swanson, James L., and Daniel R. Weinberg. *Lincoln's Assassins: Their Trial and Execution: An Illustrated History.* Santa Fe: Arena Editions, 2001.

Taylor, John. *William Henry Seward: Lincoln's Right Hand Man.* New York: HarperCollins, 1991.

Thomas, Benjamin P., and Harold M. Hyman. *Stanton: The Life and Times of Lincoln's Secretary of War.* New York: Alfred A. Knopf, 1962.

Ticknor, Caroline. *Hawthorne and His Publisher.* Boston: Houghton Mifflin, 1913.

Titone, Nora. *My Thoughts Be Bloody: The Bitter Rivalry between Edwin and John Wilkes Booth that Led to an American Tragedy.* New York: Free Press, 2010.

Townsend, George Alfred. *The Life, Crime, and Capture of John Wilkes Booth.* New York: Dick and Fitzgerald, 1865.

Toynton, Evelyn. *Growing Up in America: 1830–1860.* Brookfield, Connecticut: Millbrook Press, 1995.

Trefousse, Hans L. *Andrew Johnson: A Biography.* New York: W. W. Norton and Company, 1989.

Trudeau, Noah Andre. *Bloody Raids South: The Wilderness to Cold Harbor, May–June 1864.* Boston: Little, Brown, 1989.

Turner, Justin G., and Linda Levitt Turner, eds. *Mary Todd Lincoln: Her Life and Letters.* New York: Alfred A. Knopf, 1972.

Turner, Thomas Reed. *Beware the People Weeping: Public Opinion and the Assassination of Abraham Lincoln.* Baton Rouge: Louisiana State University Press, 1982.

Tyler, Alice Felt. *Freedom's Ferment: Phases of American Social History from the Colonial Period to the Outbreak of the Civil War.* New York: Harper and Row, 1944.

"Understanding *Uncle Tom's Cabin.*" *Seward House Diplomatic Pouch* 1, no. 2 (Spring 2003): 2.

Van Deusen, Glyndon. *Thurlow Weed: Wizard of the Lobby.* Boston: Little, Brown, 1947.

———. *William Henry Seward.* New York: Oxford University Press, 1967.

Verdi, T. S. "The Assassination of the Sewards." *Journal of the Lincoln Assassination* 16. no. 3 (December 2003): 46–50.

———. "Full Particulars of the Attempted Assassination of the Hon. Secretary Seward, his Family and Attendants." *The Western Homeopathic Observer* 2, no. 7 (May 15, 1865): 81–86.

Villard, Henry. *A Journalist's Story: Lincoln on the Eve of '61.* New York: Alfred A. Knopf, 1941.

Vinovskis, Maris A., ed. *Toward a Social History of the American Civil War: Exploratory Essays.* Cambridge: Cambridge University Press, 1990.

Volo, Dorothy Denneen, and James M. Volo. *Daily Life in Civil War America.* Westport, Connecticut: Greenwood Press, 1998.

Ward, Geoffrey C. *The Civil War: An Illustrated History.* New York: Alfred A. Knopf, 1990.

Warner, Ezra J. *Generals in Blue: Lives of the Union Commanders.* Baton Rouge: Louisiana State University Press, 1964.

Welter, Barbara. *Dimity Convictions: The American Woman in the Nineteenth Century.* Athens: Ohio University Press, 1976.

———. "The Cult of True Womanhood: 1820–1860." *American Quarterly* 18, no. 2 (Summer 1966): 151–174.

Werner, Emmy E. *Reluctant Witnesses: Children's Voices from the Civil War.* Boulder, Colorado: Westview Press, 1998.

Wert, Jeffry D. *Gettysburg: Day Three.* New York: Simon and Schuster, 2001.

———. *The Sword of Lincoln: The Army of the Potomac.* New York: Simon and Schuster, 2005.

*While Lincoln Lay Dying: A Facsimile Reproduction of the First Testimony Taken in Connection with the Assassination of Abraham Lincoln as Recorded by Corporal James Tanner.* Philadelphia: The Union League of Philadelphia, 1968.

Wiley, Bell Irvin. *The Life of Billy Yank: The Common Soldier of the Union.* Indianapolis: Bobbs-Merrill, 1951.

Williams, T. Harry. *Lincoln and His Generals.* New York: Alfred A. Knopf, 1952.

Wilmeth, Don B., and Christopher Bigsby, eds. *The Cambridge History of the American Theatre.* Vol. 1, *Beginnings to 1870.* Cambridge, England: Cambridge University Press, 1998.

Wilson, Francis. *John Wilkes Booth: Fact and Fiction of Lincoln's Assassination.* Boston: Houghton Mifflin Company, 1929.

Wilson, Rufus R., ed. *Intimate Memories of Lincoln.* Elmira, NY: Primavera Press, 1945.

Wineapple, Brenda. *White Heat: The Friendship of Emily Dickinson and Thomas Wentworth Higginson.* New York: Alfred A. Knopf, 2008.

Winik, Jay. *April, 1865: The Month That Saved America.* New York: HarperCollins, 2001.

Winthrop, Theodore. *Life in the Open Air and Other Papers.* New York: John W. Lovell, 1862.

Winther, Oscar O., ed. *With Sherman to the Sea: The Journal of Theodore F. Upson.* Baton Rouge: Louisiana State University Press, 1943.

Wisbey, Peter. "In the Emancipation Business: William and Frances Seward's Abolition Activism." February 2004. www.rootsweb.ancestry .com/~nycayuga/ugrr/seward.html

Woodward, C. Vann, ed. *Mary Chesnut's Civil War.* New Haven and London: Yale University Press, 1981.

Woolf, Eugene T. *Theodore Winthrop: Portrait of an American Author.* Washington, DC: University Press of America, 1981.

# Index

*Italic page number denotes illustration.*

Trudy Krisher has been a professional writer for almost forty years. She has been a book columnist, a feature writer, a freelance journalist, and an award-winning author of historical novels for young adults. She has been awarded the American Library Association's Best Book Award, the International Reading Association Award, The Parents' Choice Honor Book Award, and many others. The historical backgrounds of her novels include the civil rights lunch counter strikes of the 1960s (*Spite Fences*); the growth of suburbia in the 1950s (*Kinship*); the antebellum women's rights and abolitionist movements (*Uncommon Faith*); and the Cold War during the McCarthy period (*Fallout*).

Born in Macon, Georgia, and raised in South Florida, Trudy Krisher holds degrees from the College of William and Mary and the College of New Jersey. She has been a professor in the Liberal Arts, Communication, and Social Sciences Division at Sinclair Community College in Dayton, Ohio. She is the mother of three grown children. More information is available at www.trudykrisherauthor.com.